Robert.

19368

The · Master · Musicians

SIBELIUS

Series edited by Stanley Sadie

The Master Musicians Series

Titles Available from Schirmer Books

Brahms	*Malcolm MacDonald*
Liszt	*Derek Watson*
Mahler	*Michael Kennedy*
Sibelius	*Robert Layton*
Stravinsky	*Paul Griffiths*

In Preparation

Elgar	*Robert Anderson*
Handel	*Donald Burrows*
Vivaldi	*Michael Talbot*

The · Master · Musicians

SIBELIUS

Robert Layton

SCHIRMER BOOKS
An Imprint of Macmillan Publishing Company
New York

Maxwell Macmillan International
New York   Oxford   Singapore   Sydney

This American edition published in 1993 by Schirmer Books,
An Imprint of Macmillan Publishing Company

Schirmer Books
An Imprint of Macmillan Publishing Company
866 Third Avenue
New York, NY 10022

First published in Great Britain by
J. M. Dent
The Orion Publishing Group Ltd.
Orion House
5 Upper St. Martin's Lane
London WC2H 9EA

Macmillan Publishing Company is part of the Maxwell Communication Group of Companies.

Library of Congress Catalog Card Number: 92–46313

PRINTED IN GREAT BRITAIN

Printing number
1 2 3 4 5 6 7 8 9 10

Library of Congress Cataloging-in-Publication Data
Layton, Robert.
    Sibelius / Robert Layton. – [3rd ed.]
       p.   cm. — (The Master musicians)
    "First published in Great Britain by J. M. Dent, The Orion Publishing Group,
Ltd. ... London"—T.p. verso.
    Includes bibliographical references and index.
    ISBN 0–02–871322–2 (hard cover) $30.00
    1. Sibelius, Jean, 1865–1957.   2. Composers—Finland—Biography.
I. Title.   II. Series: Master musicians series.
ML410.S54L35   1993
780'.92—dc20
[B]
                                                    92–46313
                                                       CIP
                                                       MN

Preface

When in 1947 Gerald Abraham's symposium on Sibelius first appeared, the critical climate differed a good deal from the present time. The Sibelius' 'cult' which Gray's books and Constant Lambert's *Music Ho!* had helped to foster was still at its height, and it was only in the mid 1950s that signs of a reaction began to show. To a certain extent the reaction is that of a younger generation of critics against the critical Establishment of the day, and as much a protest against their sins of omission as anything else. Such a reaction was as inevitable as it will be temporary.

It was an encounter with some unfamiliar Sibelius that rekindled my childhood love of the composer, and in returning to him in the late 1950s I found my admiration for the familiar seven symphonies increasing, while the exploration of less familiar terrain proved no less exciting an experience. I have attempted in this short volume to represent the findings of other writers as well; Abraham, Parmet, Rosas and Wood are authorities whose writings have a different brief from those in the Master Musicians series but whose ideas cannot be ignored.

I owe a special debt of gratitude to Mr John Rosas of the Sibelius Museum, Turku, and to Mrs Alfhild Forslin. To Mrs Eva Paloheimo, the composer's eldest daughter, I am indebted for numerous kindnesses. Thanks are also due to Sir Jack Westrup, and to Peter Branscombe and David Palmer for their assistance in reading the book in proof.

The Music examples are reproduced by kind permission of Breitkopf & Härtel (London) Ltd on behalf of the copyright owners.

London, June, 1965   R. L.

Note on the fourth edition

When this volume first appeared in 1965, Sibelius's music had fallen from its former pre-eminence in the repertory, though the allegiance of the wider musical public remained relatively unshaken. The 1970s and 80s brought a completely different climate and enormous changes in perspective. Early works such as the *Kullervo* Symphony, the G minor Piano Quintet, the A minor and B flat string quartets, the opera *Jungfrun i tornet* (The Maiden in the Tower), as well as the first versions of the Violin Concerto and the Fifth Symphony, fleshed out the picture of his growth. We have a clearer picture, too, of the songs and the piano music, which were then less accessible. But above all, it has been the publication of Erik Tawaststjerna's definitive five-volume survey of the composer that has transformed and enriched our knowledge of Sibelius both as man and musician. His work is in the highest traditions of humanistic scholarship and this new edition of my book owes much to his insights and generosity of spirit. It also takes full account of the researches of Fabian Dahlström and Kari Kilpeläinen whose catalogues have rendered the list of works in earlier editions of this book out of date. This edition has also benefited enormously from the tireless and patient ministrations of Julia Kellerman to whom I am much indebted.

London, 1992   R. L.

Contents

Illustrations

Introduction

In the 1940s and 1950s, one could say of Sibelius that rarely had there been a case of a great composer who had gained during his lifetime so enormous a hold on the Anglo-Saxon public while scarcely impinging on the concert repertory in France and the Latin countries. But in the late 1950s the climate began to change: Harold Johnson's monograph[1] was one of the first signs of the reaction against the hagiography of the 1930s and 40s. Delius's prophecy from his retreat at Grez-sur-Loing – 'the English like vogues for this and that. Now, it's Sibelius and when they're tired of him they'll turn to Bruckner and Mahler' – was fulfilled.[2] Sibelius became a rarity in the London concert halls though he still retained a strong foothold in broadcast programmes. All the same, the English public – as opposed to the critical establishment – remained faithful, and we have the gramophone, an unfailing barometer of public taste, to thank for this. During the mid-1960s Bernstein and Maazel embarked on recording the symphonies, and since then there have been complete cycles of the symphonies from Sir John Barbirolli, Gennady Rozhdestvensky, Vladimir Ashkenazy, Colin Davis, Alexander Gibson, Simon Rattle, two from Paavo Berglund, two from Akeo Watanabe, Neeme Järvi, Jukka-Pekka Saraste and, on the horizon, Herbert Blomstedt – and, last but not least, the most faithful Sibelian of them all, Karajan, who recorded the last four symphonies three times and the Fifth Symphony no fewer than four times. In addition, the great classic performances of Koussevitzky, Beecham, Kajanus and Toscanini have returned to circulation. Not even the symphonies of Mahler or the tone-poems of Richard Strauss have been better served, though they enjoy commensurate representation. Admirers of, say, Vaughan Williams, Nielsen, Elgar, Roussel and Honegger would be happy with a tithe of that exposure – as indeed would those of Schoenberg, Berg and Webern.

The 1970s and 80s brought enormous changes in perspective and a

[1] Harold E. Johnson, *Sibelius* (New York, 1959).
[2] Eric Fenby, *Delius as I knew him* (London, 1936), p. 123.

completely different climate. Indeed one might speak of 'global warming' as far as Sibelius is concerned, for his music has enjoyed much greater acceptance and exposure, even in countries that traditionally did not respond to his art. Moreover, our own perspective has completely altered. In the 1930s and 40s, English admirers like Gray, Lambert and Newman spoke of Sibelius as 'a self-formed composer'. At that time the only early work of Sibelius we knew was the *Karelia* Suite of 1893. Both the op. 22 *Legends* that were then played – *The Swan of Tuonela* and *Lemmin-käinen's Homeward Journey* – and *En Saga* were known in their revisions, which were made *after* the First Symphony. They were the tip of the iceberg. True, the *Kullervo* Symphony had been performed but it scarcely registered until it was recorded in the early 1970s. But in the last two decades the early chamber music, the G minor Piano Quintet, the two string quartets from his student years, even such juvenilia as the 'Lovisa' Trio have come to wider currency, all the songs have been recorded, including the newly-discovered *Serenade* (1895) and so, too, has his opera, *Jungfrun i tornet* (The Maiden in the Tower). Furthermore, the publication of Erik Tawaststjerna's masterly five-volume survey, with which I have had the privilege of being associated in its English-language form, has immeasurably enriched and deepened our knowledge of Sibelius as man and musician. And he still remains larger than life.[1] The two-dimensional granite-like, carefully-groomed figure we knew suddenly came to life as real flesh-and-blood, with his weaknesses, vanities, problems, extraordinary self-knowledge and his compound of self-doubt and awareness of the quality of his gifts.

So intrigued were English writers of the 30s and 40s by Sibelius's early years and the influences on him that the notion put forward by Gerald Abraham that he had studied the E flat Symphony of Borodin died hard. As recently as 1985, Edward Garden[2] in a short chapter on Sibelius and Balakirev firmly states, 'That he [Sibelius] had studied Borodin's First Symphony in E flat is certain, since as Abraham points out, in the first movement of his Second Symphony of 1902, "Sibelius adapts to his own ends the structural principle" of the initial movement in the Borodin work, which proved to be of seminal importance for the Finnish composer.' A footnote tells us that Sibelius averred that he did not know this Borodin symphony when he was writing his First Symphony. For my

[1]We owe this in a round-about way to Harold Johnson. His book, 'cutting Sibelius down to size', full of all sorts of innuendos, caused great offence to the family, who decided to open the archives to Erik Tawaststjerna.
[2]Brown and Wiley, *Slavonic and Western Music: Essays for Gerald Abraham* (Oxford, 1985), p. 215.

2

part I should not be surprised to hear that he did not know it at all at this time. The resemblances to which I alluded in 1965 between *Lemminkäinen and the Maidens of the Island* and the First Symphony of Balakirev, and the slow movement of Sibelius's First Symphony and Tchaikovsky's *Souvenir de Florence* were intended to show a common cultural language. Sibelius obviously could not have known the Balakirev and probably did not know the *Souvenir de Florence* either.

Taking stock, how does Sibelius look to us in 1990 as opposed to a quarter-of-a-century ago when this volume first appeared? Do we still see him as self-formed, springing fully armed on to the musical arena? It was always granted that Sibelius is able to establish within a few seconds a sound world that is entirely his own. Like Berlioz, his thematic inspiration and its harmonic clothing were conceived directly in terms of orchestral sound: the substance and the sonority were indivisible one from the other. Many of the fingerprints of his orchestral style are instantly recognizable: the 'cross-hatch' string writing (i.e. moving tremolando strings such as at the storm section in *Tapiola* or the development of the first movement of the Fifth Symphony), woodwind instruments in thirds, long sustained brass chords that open *sforzato subito pianissimo* and then make a slow crescendo, the long-held pedal notes and the openness of the textures, show a thorough assimilation of Wagner and Berlioz and its transmutation into a wholly individual expressive technique.

Twenty five years ago, I wrote of his 'acutely developed sense of identification with nature and a preoccupation with myth that at one and the same time define his unique strength and his basic limitation', and went on to say that 'as a symphonist he imposes a greater degree of order on the materials of the symphony and exercises a greater discipline in the selection of those very materials', than his major contemporaries. Few works have greater tautness and concentration than the Fourth Symphony: it surpasses anything that came before. The distance Sibelius traversed between *Kullervo* and the Fourth Symphony (i.e. between 1892 and 1911), is greater than that between the Second and Ninth Symphonies of Mahler – during much the same period. Ill-health and the proximity of death turned the thoughts of both masters inwards. In the Ninth Symphony Mahler, too, had reached the point at which he was prepared to dispense with the trappings of flamboyant rhetoric in favour of harsh, monosyllabic truth. Both reach the threshold of atonality or at least indeterminate tonality. But their concentration is of a different kind: to revert to an astronomical analogy, a white-dwarf in the case of the Sibelius, a massive red-giant in the case of the Mahler.

One could say that Sibelius belonged to the last generation before what one might call the urbanization of music, for which Nature was a central source of inspiration: Delius, Bartók, Debussy and Janáček. The role of mythology in his musical make-up was no less crucial. Mythology is a vehicle for universal truths about the human psyche, and the very fascination it holds for mankind is an acknowledgment of its power. It was certainly of consuming importance to Wagner, and, with the exception of *The Bard*, all the symphonic poems of Sibelius inhabit its world. Eero Tarasti speaks of myth and music constituting 'two forms of discourse which are closely related, and in following the history of Western culture we discover how, during some periods, these two areas approach, touch or intersect each other, while in other periods they diverge.[1] In Sibelius they certainly converge. Finnish mythology as enshrined in the *Kalevala* struck more than a responsive chord in his sensibility: it was of crucial importance to the growth of his artistic personality. And though it is obvious that the atmosphere of the *Kalevala* was a central source of inspiration, what is less obvious was the effect of its verbal music on Sibelius's melodic style. There's no doubt that when you hear *Kullervo*, his first major work inspired by a *Kalevala* theme, you are immediately aware of a new voice in music: something totally unlike anything that's come before. That doesn't mean to say there are not resonances of other composers (Bruckner in the development of the first movement and Tchaikovsky in the second). But how was it possible for the composer of some two-dozen relatively conventional chamber works such as the A minor String Quartet (1889) or its successor in B flat, op. 4, and the G minor Piano Quintet (1890) to emerge almost overnight as a composer of such ambition, breadth and originality, as he did in the *Kullervo* Symphony? Its language is suddenly much more distinctive, and this Erik Tawaststjerna[2] attributes possibly to Sibelius's re-reading of the *Kalevala* during his year in Vienna and the subsequent encounters with Larin Paraske (see p.147). He even goes so far as to compare Sibelius's study of the runes of the *Kalevala* with Bartók's first encounter with Hungarian peasant tunes. Influenced he undoubtedly was, and at a profound level, not only by the world evoked by the *Kalevala* but by its verbal music. Now, while I can think of plenty of twentieth-century composers who have been inspired by the universal truths of myth – Bartók in *Bluebeard's Castle*, Enescu in *Oedipe*, Szymanowski in *King Roger*, – and one of the most powerful of all, Martinů's *The Epic of*

[1] Eero Tarasti, *Myth and Music. A Semiotic Approach to the Aesthetics of Myth in Music, especially that of Wagner, Sibelius and Stravinsky*. Finnish Musicological Society (Helsinki, 1978).
[2] Erik Tawaststjerna, *Sibelius*, vol. 1 (1865–1905) (London, 1976), p. 121.

4

Gilgamesh – I can think of no twentieth-century composer consumed and affected by it in quite the same way. Indeed, it is tempting to argue that it was the melodic inflections of the *Kalevala* (and the Finnish language) every bit as much as the substance of the epic that was the driving force in Sibelius's inspiration – which is why it is that his language is so distinctive. The genesis of *Pohjola's Daughter* rather supports this view (see p.105).

But if this formative element in his musical language was not fully grasped in the 1950s and 60s, his genius for form was another matter and did not go unremarked in the writings on music with which I grew up – Cecil Gray, Constant Lambert and Ernest Newman. The reason for this is that in Sibelius, form and substance are indivisible. And it is that unity of matter and manner, of content and form that make the last symphonies so remarkable. Sibelius himself made a telling analogy. 'I let the musical thought and its development in my mind determine matters of form. I'd compare a symphony to a river: the river is made up of countless streams all looking for an outlet: the innumerable tributaries, streams and brooks that form the river before it broadens majestically and flows into the sea. The movement of the water determines the shape of the river bed: the movement of the river-water is the flow of the musical ideas and the river-bed that they form is the symphonic structure. Nowadays', he went on, 'people *fashion* [his italics] wide and majestic river beds – in other words they construct a river artificially but then where does the water come from? In the same way they do not let musical inspiration find its true form, instead they specify a large-scale majestic form and then try to fill it.' It is the hallmark of a great work of art that we can conceive of it in no other form: we cannot perceive the current taking any other course. Schoenberg put it differently but no less trenchantly: 'form means that a piece of music is organized: i.e. that it consists of elements functioning like those of a living organism'. Yet how does that square with his claim that 'the composer conceives an entire composition as a spontaneous vision? In a sense the two are not incompatible, for conception and realization are different processes and the impression left on the listener is certainly of a spontaneous vision. That the composer has caught a glimpse of something that has been going on all the time and that he has stretched out and captured. A letter Sibelius wrote to Carpelan in the autumn of 1914 puts it perfectly: 'God opens his door for a moment, and his orchestra is playing Sym. 5.'

All sorts of sketches and manuscripts from the Sibelius Estate have gone to the Helsinki University Library. It is clear from the sketches that the Seventh Symphony had a much longer period of gestation than was generally thought. It was first performed in 1924 and mentioned in a letter to Carpelan in 1918 – Sibelius first spoke of it in a diary entry the previous year, but the earliest ideas go back even further to the period 1914–15 and are mixed up with sketches to the Fifth and Sixth symphonies, the projected second violin concerto and a tone-poem, *Kuutar* (The Moon Goddess), which never came to anything. But to return to the different perspectives of the mid-1960s and the early 1990s, we know now that Sibelius's relationship with Wagner is a more complex one than the composer admitted to. The ghosts of his visit to Bayreuth in 1894 surely hover over his inspired and wonderful song, *Höstkväll*. But it is more than this or that melodic line or detail of texture. Tovey put it like this, way back in the 1930s: 'The symphonies and other larger orchestral works of Sibelius would, if they had no other merits, command the attention of every lover of music who is interested in the problem which baffled Bruckner and eluded Liszt: the problem of achieving the vast movement of Wagnerian music-drama in purely instrumental music.[1] And this is what Sibelius achieves. And more than that, he has a remarkable ability to sustain simultaneous tempos, which is one of the most extraordinary characteristics of the Seventh Symphony. The slow motion of Sibelius's pedal-points is as huge and as inexorable as that of the earth itself; and upon them there is teeming muscular activity. And what an extraordinary feat of virtuosity is *Tapiola*: mono-tonal (it never really leaves B minor) and monothematic (everything is distilled from its opening bars). And as Gray, and practically everybody else, has said, if no other work survived from his pen, we would still have a pretty comprehensive picture of his stature. His handling of the orchestra is totally original and its organic cohesion has tempted some to speak of it as a symphony. But there are important differences, as the composer Robert Simpson pointed out, between *Tapiola* and its neighbour, the Seventh Symphony. 'The symphony', he says, 'is like a great planet in orbit, its movement vast and inexorable, seemingly imperceptible to its inhabitants. But you say, the Finnish forests are on the surface of such a planet, revolving. And so they are, but we never leave them, we are filled with expectation and nothing but a great wind arises. The symphony has both the cosmic motion of the earth and the teeming activity that is upon it; we are made to observe one or the other at the composer's will. Indeed "observe" isn't the right word – we experience these extremes, and when one is operative, the other doesn't exist for us.'[2] It is difficult for us to imagine a composer of this level of mastery plagued by self-doubt. Yet so

[1]Sir Donald Tovey, 'Sibelius's Symphony No. 3', in *Essays in Musical Analysis*, vol. II (Oxford, 1935), p. 121.
[2]Robert Simpson, *Sibelius and Nielsen. A centenary essay* (BBC, 1965), p. 34.

strong did these forces become towards the end of his life that not only the Eighth Symphony, and probably much else, succumbed but even *Tapiola* itself was threatened. Fortunately the score was at too advanced a stage of production to be withdrawn.

A word concerning the work of cataloguing Sibelius's output may be in order. It is far more complicated than the general reader might think, and it is not always easy to establish the kind of order that scholars like. Nielsen's opus numbers do not give an accurate picture of the chronology of his output, but they are not so totally arbitrary or as misleading as those of Sibelius. In 1987 Professor Fabian Dahlström published a provisional list of works. Some of his conclusions have already been modified in Kari Kilpeläinen's recent catalogue,[1] but it will take many years before every detail is in place. There are some thirty or so songs – mostly in fragmentary form – that are in the process of coming to light, and Sibelius himself is to blame for the confusion surrounding the chronology of his works. Take, for example, the case of his op. 6, the *Cassazione*. The beginning almost recalls the 'Les trois sœurs aveugles' movement in *Pelléas et Mélisande* – which is hardly surprising since it was written at roughly the same period. Thus it ought to be somewhere in the early opus 40s – and originally it was. Sibelius put it in the same concert in which he conducted the first version of the Violin Concerto in 1904. So how could it be op. 6? That would place it before the *Kullervo* Symphony, which was way back in 1892. Up to 1905 Sibelius simply did not give his works proper opus numbers at all, whether they were published or just in manuscript. The question only cropped up that year, when he signed a contract with the publisher Robert Lienau. He made up a list from this year in which there were gaps – there was an opus number all right but no music attached to it. Of course he could always fill these in from his reserves of unpublished music, but those were limited. Or he could put in new pieces to fill the gaps even at the risk of causing chronological confusion. But more often than not, he would also move a piece from its existing opus number and then place that further back until he came across a piece he was ashamed of and could push out altogether.

The longer Sibelius thought about it, the more unhappy he became with his first list. He made three later lists – in 1909, 1911 and then in 1915, at the time of his fiftieth birthday when the first version of the Fifth Symphony was given. Incidentally, all three lists have different op. 1s. He regretted that he had included some of his youthful indiscretions like the String Quartet in A minor – originally op. 2 – and so that was omitted.

[1] Kari Kilpeläinen, *The Jean Sibelius Musical Manuscripts at Helsinki University Library. A complete catalogue* (Wiesbaden, 1991).

Both the 1911 catalogue and his diaries paint a pretty chaotic picture. He put blue crayon marks in the margin beside some twenty works that he intended to remove or revise. There are countless changes, underlinings and crossings-out, additions, rings made with pencil or pen, red, green or blue crayon, and so on. Sibelius did not think highly of the *Cassazione* and decided to revise it, but even when he had done so, he was unsatisfied. The work remains in manuscript even now. He was also unhappy with a piece called *Ödlan* (The Lizard), incidental music he had written in 1910 at the time of the Fourth Symphony. This started off as op. 59 but was then moved in his next list to op. 40. But op. 40 was already occupied by the *Cassazione* so this was in its turn pushed back to op. 34. In the next purge he knocked *The Lizard* from op. 40 down to 29a, and the *Cassazione* down four numbers to op. 30. In the 1915 list there were more agonizing realignments. At this point he decided that he didn't want the *Kullervo* Symphony, now op. 7, flanked by the E major Overture from his year in Vienna and banished the latter from the opus list altogether. And so the *Cassazione* was moved from op. 30 into the place of the Overture, at op. 6, and *The Lizard* moved from op. 29a down to op. 8. This is just one example of the disorder he created by regarding an opus number as a symbol of quality rather than chronology. There are other instances in the choral music where he absent-mindedly gave two opus numbers to the same piece. Of course, in some cases his criticism was well-founded, but in others not. The early A minor String Quartet of 1889 certainly deserves a place in his opus list, for it is every bit as good as the B flat Quartet, op. 4, to which he assigned a number though he did not publish it or permit its performance. But the *Serenade* for baritone and orchestra dating from 1895, two years after *The Swan of Tuonela*, certainly deserved better than its fate. He put this piece on one side after its first performance, perhaps intending to revise it – he certainly didn't think it good enough to have an opus number or to publish it. When it came to light, the Sibelius family, so Erik Tawaststjerna told me, were unsure whether they should let it be performed. Here we have a case of a beautiful and subtle piece that suffered from Sibelius's excessive self-criticism.

Each of the symphonies shows a continuing search for new formal means and in none is the search more thorough or prolonged than in the Fifth. The Fifth Symphony, like its two successors has the universality of great art. Like Debussy's *La Mer* or Fauré's late chamber music, it is music that steps outside its immediate time. Nothing Sibelius composed in the 1920s was in the least related to the kind of music being produced anywhere else in the world. He was 'out of step' with the main currents of his time. And in the 1960s or 1970s nothing could seem more out of step than his prediction that 'classicism is the way of the future'. Some years ago I heard an ingeniously-argued paper by Harry Halbreich on Martinů (who, incidentally, shared Sibelius's birthday twenty-five years apart), in which he argued that far from being out of touch with the spirit of his times (or *unzeitgemäss*), as he seemed to his more radical contemporaries, Martinů was paradoxically both not of his time and ahead of it. The great currents that appear to fashion musical history soon lose their impetus and leave those who drift with them stranded and forgotten. It is those composers who are true to their inner vision, who are concerned with what only they can do, that survive. The French critic Marc Vignal has spoken of Sibelius as 'the aristocrat of symphonists': he was referring to the sophistication of his symphonic means. The late Sibelius symphonies are aristocratic in another way – in their complete unconcern for the gallery and their total concentration on truth as he saw it. And, of course, the public has found its way to him (and stayed with him) because of this.

1

The early years

Few great composers have equalled Sibelius in terms of longevity, and few have witnessed so great a change in the language of music during their lifetimes. When Sibelius was born, Berlioz was still alive and Liszt in his fifties; the deaths of Chopin, Mendelssohn and Schumann were as recent as are those of Shostakovich and Britten to the 1990s, while the late works of Beethoven and Schubert were no more distant in time than are Bartók's last quartets now. Much music that has since passed into the standard repertory, including that of Tchaikovsky, Dvořák and Brahms, was 'contemporary music', and while Sibelius was a young man, Richard Strauss was the young revolutionary. At his death in 1957 the language of music was transformed out of all recognition: Strauss was thought of as a tired Establishment figure and Sibelius himself was witnessing the inevitable wane of his fortunes. New composers were now at the centre of the stage, though Stravinsky was still at the forefront. A reaction against serialism was under way, and the avant garde were moving in the direction of electronic music and random composition.

Such far-reaching changes are not confined to music. No period has ever seen such an enormously accelerated rate of technological progress as the present century; and the political structure of Europe has changed in ways that few could have imagined in 1865. In the year of Sibelius's birth Finland was a smallish province on the north-western perimeter of Tsarist Russia, a country that had itself abolished serfdom only four years earlier.

The Treaty of Tilsit between Napoleon and Tsar Alexander in the summer of 1807 was to have far reaching effects for Finland. In February 1808, Russian troops crossed the border, so ending the six hundred years of union between Finland and Sweden. From that time until the Russian revolution, Finland was an autonomous Duchy of the Tsarist empire.

For the greater part of the century Russian hegemony entailed no special encroachments on the country's autonomy. Within certain limits the Finns were masters in their own house, though towards the end of the century as Finnish national self-consciousness gathered strength, so the

Tsarist regime became more repressive, the one undoubtedly feeding the other. Successive Tsarist regimes exploited the tension between the Swedish-speaking élite and the Finnish-speaking majority. The day-to-day administration of the country's affairs remained in the hands of the Swedish-speaking civil service. Swedish was the language of the educated classes, for most were descendants of Swedes who had emigrated to Finland during the *Storhetstiden*, while Finnish, spoken by the large majority of the people, enjoyed a subservient status. Many Finns never mastered both tongues; formal education, as well as the business of government, was conducted in Swedish, but as the movement for self-determination gathered impetus during the course of the nineteenth century, so Finnish began to assert itself as a cultural force.

It was into a Swedish-speaking home that the young Sibelius was born on 8th December 1865. He was the second of three children, all of whom showed some musical aptitude. The eldest was a girl, Linda, born two years earlier, and the youngest a boy called Christian. Their father was a doctor attached to the military garrison at Hämeenlinna (Tavastehus),[1] a small town in south-central Finland; and his wife, Maria, also came from a Swedish-speaking family in whose veins the blood of clergymen, government officials, landowners and other members of the professional classes freely mingled. The surname itself seems to have come into being during the eighteenth century, when Johan Martinpoika, a farmer from Artjävi (Artsjö) in central Finland (and the composer's great-grandfather on the paternal side), had moved south to Lapinjärvi (Lappträsk), where he took the name 'Sibbe' from the plot of land that he farmed. It is clear that the Latinized form of the name soon came to be adopted. His son, Johan (Sibelius's grandfather), moved to Lovisa, a coastal town to the east of Helsinki: here he was active as a business man and town councillor. He subsequently married Catharina Fredrika, the daughter of a Swedish doctor, Mathias Åkerberg, who had emigrated from Skåne. Both she and her son, Christian Gustaf (Sibelius's father) were musical.[2] Christian studied in Porvoo (Borgå), where his Latin master was none other than the poet Runeberg. He had already become a heavy drinker

---

[1]Tavastehus is the Swedish name of the town and Hämeenlinna the Finnish, which serves to show how totally unrelated the languages are. Throughout the text, place-names are given in Finnish with the Swedish equivalent in brackets.

[2]In his biography of Sibelius published in 1931 Cecil Gray declared that 'of the thirty-two direct ancestors of Sibelius living about 1700, eighteen were Finnish Swedes – i.e. persons of Swedish origin living in Finland – nine were pure Swedes, and one was German, leaving only four pure Finns'. He then went on to conclude that 'Sibelius is predominantly, even overwhelmingly, Swedish, not Finnish'. This is a highly misleading statement, since the Swedish-speaking Finns possess a distinctive and highly developed culture which is purely Finnish. To describe Sibelius as Swedish is as inaccurate as calling a French-speaking Canadian a Frenchman.

before he settled in Hämeenlinna, where he married Maria Charlotta Borg, a local beauty in her early twenties and the daughter of a priest.

Christian Gustaf and his young wife gave their first son the names Johan Julius Christian, the first presumably to honour the memory of his grandfather or that of his uncle, Christian's eldest brother, who had died in Havana two years before Janne's birth. The boy was always called Janne by his relatives and friends rather than Johan or Jan. He acquired the Christian name by which he is universally known from his widely travelled uncle Johan, who was a sea captain: his uncle used the French form of his name when abroad (a not uncommon practice at that time), and the discovery some twenty years later of a bunch of visiting-cards bearing the name Jean Sibelius prompted Janne to follow his uncle's example.

Janne's father died during the typhus epidemic which swept Finland during 1867–8. No doubt his propensity for alcohol served to lower his resistance, and his extravagance over the years reduced the family to something approaching penury. As Sibelius himself once wrote, 'My father loved his pleasures too much and played cards and so on; we Sibeliuses, once rich are now poor'. Poor they certainly were, but rich they had never been. His mother who was twenty-seven and expecting a third child at the time she was widowed, brought up her young family to the best of her ability but it was not easy for her to make ends meet on a small widow's pension. Christian Gustaf had left his affairs in disarray with arrears of rent and a mountain of unpaid bills, as well as loans to insolvent friends – in all some 4,500 Finnish marks, a tidy sum in those days. Maria Charlotta bore the consequences of her husband's extravagances and begged to be allowed to keep 'necessary clothes and linen together with two white quilts' from the bankrupt estate. The family returned to her mother's home in Hämeenlinna where Janne spent most of his childhood winters. His summers, which he spent with his paternal grandmother at Lovisa, gave rise to an early and enduring love of nature. Since both his grandmothers were widows, Janne was deprived of masculine influence during these formative years, though he was deeply attached to his uncle Pehr, amateur musician and astronomer, who had a successful business as a seed-merchant in Turku (Åbo), Finland's leading seaport on the south-west coast.

Maria Charlotta was a caring and devoted mother, though Janne had perhaps an even closer bond to his aunt Evelina, who had a keen love of music and was an enthusiastic though not greatly accomplished pianist. His summers with Evelina and his paternal grandmother were spent playing with the children of Lovisa friends, the Sucksdorfs, for whom he would later write a quartet, the Gyllings and other families.

As he approached his seventh birthday, he was enrolled in Mlle Eva Savonius's Swedish-language preparatory school but was soon removed in preparation for enrolment in the first Finnish-language grammar school. In 1873 the *Hämeenlinna Suomalainen Normaalilyseo*, the first grammar school to use Finnish rather than Swedish and Latin as the medium of teaching, opened its doors. It was both far-sighted and enlightened on the part of the family to send him to this particular school, for the Finnish language opened up to him the whole repertory of national mythology embodied in the *Kalevala*. His imagination was to be fired by this, as it was by the great Swedish-language lyric poets Runeberg and Rydberg and, above all, by the Finnish countryside with its abundance of forests and lakes. But he still moved almost entirely among Swedish-speaking circles, and was not to become entirely proficient in Finnish until his twenties. Swedish remained his mother tongue and he spoke it with greater facility even in his maturity. He had no great language problems at the new school as many of the pupils there were of Swedish background and one of them, Walter von Konow, was with him at the preparatory school. Even as late as 1891, in writing to his fiancée-to-be from Vienna, he would revert to Swedish in the middle of a sentence.

Janne did not excel academically; he was for the most part bored with the usual academic drill, though he was an avid reader even at that age, devouring among other things a good deal of classical literature and Swedish poetry. His school friend Walter von Konow has given a charming portrait of Janne as a child: he described him as something of a dreamer, and testified to his passionate love of nature, his extraordinarily vivid fantasy, and his sudden changes of mood from a playful exuberance to the deepest melancholy. He seems to have been a spontaneous child, easily moved and with an affectionate nature.

At first sight, a provincial garrison town in south central Finland might seem an unpromising milieu for the childhood of a great composer. True, Hämeenlinna was no musical or cultural centre of importance, but then neither was Helsinki itself. After all, the Finnish capital did not have a permanent symphony orchestra until the 1880s, when Robert Kajanus, later to be one of Sibelius's staunchest champions, founded the Helsinki City Orchestra (variously known as the Finnish National Orchestra and, more recently, the Helsinki Philharmonic). Nor was the Finnish Opera put on a solid basis until as late as 1912 when the soprano Aino Ackté, for whom Sibelius composed *Luonnotar*, founded it and the publishing firm of Fazer. However, a number of artists did make guest appearances in the town, among them Emmy Achté who took part in the first performance of *Kullervo*, the virtuoso violinist, August Wilhelmji and Liszt's pupil, Sophie Menter.

Although Janne showed early musical ability, it was not as a pianist. His first lessons with his aunt Julie were not particularly happy and he never developed a strong feeling for the instrument. He had a highly developed sense of pitch, and Tawaststjerna thinks it possible that the square piano they possessed at home which was almost a tone flat, coloured his later feeling for the instrument. Having built up a tone-world based on an out-of-tune instrument, the encounter with reality came as a shock. He had a very good ear, too. When Janne was nine, the Swedish harpist Adolf Sjödén visited Hämeenlinna and played Handel's Harp Concerto (the Organ Concerto, op. 4, no. 6). Janne went home and played much of it, together with other pieces he had heard that evening. But the violin was his real love, and his first attempt at composition, a simple piece for violin and cello *pizzicato* called *Vattendroppar* (Water drops), comes from his tenth year. However, it was not until he was fourteen that he began studying the violin in earnest with Gustav Levander, the local bandmaster. From Levander he acquired his basic technical training, but in theoretical matters he turned to Adolf Marx's *Die Lehre von der musikalischen Komponisten*. Hämeenlinna's isolation may have entailed few opportunities to attend concerts, but it gave an even stronger inducement to the family to make their own music. Linda, the eldest, was a pianist, Christian, the youngest of the three became a good amateur cellist and inherited the father's medical gifts, while Janne's developing powers on the violin even encouraged him to think in terms of a soloist's career. They formed a family trio, and Janne acquired a thorough knowledge of the Viennese classics, in particular Haydn and Beethoven. He wrote extensively not only for the family trio but for whatever combination happened to be to hand. So absorbed was he in music-making and composition that he neglected his schoolwork during the years before the *studentexam*, the advanced examination that qualified for entrance to the university. However, after some months of assiduous application to the school curriculum, he finally gained his 'studenten' in May 1885, when he was nineteen.

In the autumn, Maria Charlotta moved home to Helsinki and settled in a small villa in Brunnsparken where they were joined by Evelina. But life was not easy and they eked out a frugal existence. The rent consumed a half of Maria's pension, and although Evelina earned a little by dressmaking and needlework, and an uncle paid for Linda's studies, Maria had to manage on a pittance. The family, and in particular his grandmother Catharina Juliana Borg, thought music far too precarious a career, and so, like other composers before him, Janne was enrolled in the Faculty of Law. The act of enrolment appears to have been his only serious connection with the discipline, for at the same time he also became a pupil of Mitrofan Vasiliev at the Music Institute. Under his guidance he rapidly developed in 'power, attack and taste' (Aunt Evelina writing to her brother Pehr).

His musical studies tended to absorb most of his energies, and Sibelius himself told his biographer, Karl Ekman, how when one of his uncles who taught at a provincial school paid a surprise visit to him in Helsinki, he discovered Janne's textbooks untouched, while musical activity, on the other hand, was greatly in evidence. The family wisely bowed to the inevitable, and when the next academic year began Janne was allowed to devote his whole time to music.

Thanks to Vasiliev's encouragement he played a Viotti concerto, and in the following term he played the E minor concerto of Félicien David in public and took part in the Mozart D major Quartet, K499. Wegelius, the Director of the Institute, reported to Evelina: 'his teacher Vasiliev says that he has genius, and for my part I cannot think of a future for him except as a great musician', praise that finally assuaged family anxieties. From the autumn of 1887 a change of teacher, Herman Csillag, brought even greater strides, and Richard Faltin, who had spoken with some reserve of his playing the previous year, noted that (in a violin concerto by Pierre Rode), 'his tone is much fuller, he seems more secure and composed and the technical demands posed by the concerto were overcome in a way that did him honour'. His solo repertory extended to Bériot's Seventh Violin Concerto and Vieuxtemps' *Fantaisie-Caprice*, and at one time his technique was even equal to the demands of the Mendelssohn concerto. He became a member of the string quartet that the Music School boasted, taking part in performances of the Mozart G minor Quintet as well as quartets by Haydn and Schumann. For all his solo ambitions, however, he never proceeded to the last part of the conservatory course, which would have entailed mastery of the Bach solo sonatas and the Paganini caprices. As a player he was handicapped, it would seem, both by nerves and a childhood accident that affected his bowing arm. The nerves took the form of a metallic taste in the mouth, accompanied by a tremor, a phenomenon that recurred in later life when making crucial visits to his bank manager!

Even though the violin continued to exercise a considerable hold on him, composition was claiming more of his time. The dominant force in his life during these years was Martin Wegelius, a pupil of Reinecke, Svendsen and Hans Richter. He was a figure of unusual versatility and wide experience, and was not slow to recognize Sibelius's musical gifts. Janne was a frequent guest at his summer house, studying counterpoint with him in the mornings, playing violin sonatas during the afternoon and relaxing over a bottle of wine in the evening. Wegelius's enthusiasms infected most of his pupils: he was an ardent Wagnerite, and consequently works of Brahms seldom appeared in any of the conservatoire's concerts. He also had relatively little sympathy for Tchaikovsky, whose influence on Sibelius was strong at this period – and, indeed, right up to the Second Symphony.

Janne continued to compose profusely. Three of his student works from this period find their inspiration in literary sources: *Trånaden* (Longing) for piano, to accompany verses by Stagnelius, *Svartsjukans nåtter* (Nights of jealousy) to accompany the declamation of a poem of Runeberg, and thirdly, two songs for Gunnar Wennerberg's fairy-tale drama *Näcken* (The water-sprite). These were written for a production of the play in the spring of 1888 for which Wegelius wrote the bulk of the music. It is a measure of the esteem in which he held his young pupil that Wegelius asked Janne to provide two of the vocal numbers of the play. Later in the same spring, on 31st May, his Theme and Variations in C sharp minor for string quartet were first given at a concert at the conservatoire: these received the blessing of no less a person than Karl Flodin, the most influential Finnish critic of the day.

If Faltin had reservations about Sibelius the violinist, neither he nor Wegelius, two of the high priests of Finnish musical life, were ashamed to accompany him. But composition continued to make further inroads on his time and energy and in his last term as a student, in the spring of 1889, he produced two new works of quality, the Suite in A major for string trio, and the String Quartet in A minor. Flodin hailed the quartet with enthusiasm and prophetic insight: 'Mr Sibelius has with one stroke placed himself foremost among those who have been entrusted with bearing the banner of Finnish music.'

One of Wegelius's greatest gifts was the ability to attract talent to his thriving conservatoire. The twenty-two-year-old Busoni was on the staff in 1888, and Sibelius, though still a pupil, became a lifelong friend of the great pianist and composer. They both spent a good deal of time together at various Helsinki cafés and restaurants, their conversation ranging over a wide field of topics. Busoni was to show in practical form his admiration of Sibelius's art when he later introduced some of his work to continental audiences. He dedicated the first movement of his *Geharnischte* Suite to Sibelius, the last two movements being inscribed to the Järnefelt brothers.

17

Sibelius was seeing a good deal of the Järnefelts at this time, and Elisabeth, their mother confided to her diary that spring, 'Armas has had his Sibeliuses here: one of them plays the violin rather well and it was a real pleasure to hear him and Armas improvise together.' But it was Aino on whom his main attention was soon to focus, although he briefly succumbed to the charms of Betzy Lerché, the daughter of a Finnish senator. The family was artistic and influential; the eldest brother, Arvid was a writer, much under the sway of Tolstoyan ideas as was his mother, Eero (Erik) was an accomplished painter, while General Järnefelt himself was a provincial Governor. For a while, Sibelius was not completely at ease with them, sensing their assumption, albeit unspoken save for one occasion, of social superiority. Another companion of these years was the writer Adolf Paul, also a member of the 'Leskovites', the group of friends that gathered round Busoni and named after his dog, Lesko. No doubt contact with Busoni, seeing his transcendental technique and prodigious pianistic command at close quarters, brought home to Sibelius the unreality of his own ambitions as an executant. Already before the performances of his suite and quartet, Wegelius had recommended him for a state scholarship to study abroad, and when the autumn came, it was to Berlin that Sibelius went for further study, his scholarship supplemented by a grant of fifteen hundred Finnish marks from the Nyland Student Corporation.

2

1889–1899

As usual Sibelius spent the summer in Lovisa where he started work on a new string quartet, the B flat, op. 4. He gave some concerts at the casino, playing a newly-composed violin sonata and then with his brother, Christian, another new composition, a Fantasia for cello written specially for him. But the time soon came for his first year of study abroad, and on 7th September 1889 he set off on the first leg of his journey to the Continent. His travelling companions included Eero Järnefelt, who was on his way to Paris, and the future Sibelius scholar, Ilmari Krohn. Wegelius was among the party waving them off, so was Aino Järnefelt, but the flirtation with Betzy Lerché had cast a temporary cloud over their relationship and Sibelius affected not to see her. At first when the question of further studies had arisen, his thought had turned to St Petersburg and Rimsky-Korsakov. At this time there was little of the hostility that was to develop in the late 1890s towards Russia and things Russian. Eero Järnefelt had studied painting there, naturally enough since there were family connections on his mother's side. Her brother and cousin both taught at the St Petersburg Academy and her uncle was the sculptor Peter Clodt whose horse statues adorn the Anitchkov Bridge. But Wegelius set his mind against this move: a strict contrapuntist of the old school was what Sibelius needed and his choice fell on Albert Becker. The experience was undoubtedly chastening. Sibelius was soon sending plaintive accounts of his new professor's pedantry, and no doubt the severe regime of strict counterpoint and fugue that he underwent was an unwelcome diet. 'Becker won't hear about anything other than his fugues. It is deadly boring to concern oneself exclusively with that. I know the German Psalmbook inside out.' He wrote little of his own during this period, though there are numerous choral settings and other exercises, as well as a fugue and a Sonata in F minor. Sibelius's impatience with his new master met with little sympathy from Wegelius who replied somewhat pompously, 'the composer of the B flat minor Mass and *Die Wallfahrt nach Keevlaer* is no stuffshirt from top-to-toe — you can put such ideas out of your mind'.

But if Sibelius found Becker's teaching uncongenial, Berlin, though by no means the greatest of the European musical centres at this period, offered an enormous range of music and must have been a salutary corrective to the provincial musical horizon of Helsinki. True, he found the Prussian atmosphere of the capital unsympathetic, but he was able to hear for the first time *Don Giovanni*, on his night of arrival, *Tannhäuser* and *Die Meistersinger*. Nor did he forget Hans von Bülow conducting the first Berlin performance of Strauss's *Don Juan*. The sight of the young composer, only one year his senior yet already a master who could write for the orchestra with real virtuosity, must have been a sobering reminder of his technical limitations and orchestral inexperience, just as his encounter with Busoni's virtuosity must have put his own aspirations as an executant into perspective. He recalled other great musical experiences: Hans von Bülow conducting Beethoven symphonies, as well as his legendary recitals of the Beethoven sonatas, the Joachim Quartet playing the late quartets, and Joachim's own sonata recitals. Interestingly enough, he heard two 'wonderful pieces' by Berlioz from *Lélio* and the Dvořák D minor Symphony. But the overall climate of Wilhelmine Berlin was predominantly conservative in feeling, and though the roster of visiting artists included such distinguished pianists as Eugen d'Albert and Teresa Carreño, and violinists like Sauret and Wilhelmji, Berlin's dominant composer was the now-forgotten August Bungert. As Sibelius put it a year later when he was living in Vienna, 'as far as art is concerned the Germans are finished. They could not produce an Ibsen, a Zola or a Tchaikovsky; they see everything through blinkers!'

If this was a period of creative abstinence, abstinence is not a word that one would use to describe his life otherwise; his circle of friends in Berlin was hard-drinking and Sibelius got through his allowance all too quickly. Already at the beginning of November he wrote home asking for funds; other appeals followed with startling regularity until by the beginning of March, all sources of help were exhausted. No sooner had he received money than he spent it and borrowed more. Sibelius is not, of course, alone among composers in his inability to handle money, but among those composers with an incapacity for managing their financial affairs, he holds a place of honour: he was beset by financial worries for the greater part of his creative life, but never permitted limited means to inhibit his extravagant life-style. He outraged Wegelius by insisting on buying the best seats at the opera. He spent some time carousing with other Scandinavians, Christian Sinding, the Danish violinist Fini Henriques, the Norwegian pianist Alf Klingenberg and the writer Adolf Paul; they would drunkenly dance with chairs in their arms to Sinding's playing and then provocatively goose-step down to their local hostelry, the *Augerstinerbräu*. As Tawaststjerna elegantly puts it, 'the circle was completed by some young ladies who studied musicians rather more closely than music'. The medical attention to which he alludes in letters home, might possibly be related to their ministrations. In the spring Busoni came to see him and insisted that he accompanied him to Leipzig where he was to play Sinding's Piano Quintet in E minor with the Brodsky Quartet. Sibelius spent his last pfennigs on a top hat in Sinding's honour. It was Busoni who saw that Berlin was not the right place for him and who was the driving force in encouraging the young composer to go to Vienna.

Perhaps in terms of the future, his most important visitor was Robert Kajanus, who came to Berlin to conduct his *Aino* Symphony at one of the Philharmonic concerts. Because of the schism between Kajanus and Wegelius, Sibelius had relatively little contact with his countryman during his student years. Wegelius generally discouraged his students from attending Kajanus's concerts except on special occasions, such as when Svendsen made a guest appearance, and though Sibelius must have disregarded him from time to time, his privileged position in Wegelius's circle would have made regular attendance difficult. However, it was not so much the *Aino* Symphony itself that made so strong an impression but the sudden realization that the *Kalevala* possessed so much musical potential. During the 1890s, as he grew closer to Kajanus, so his relationship with Wegelius was gradually to cool. In the autumn of 1890 Wegelius had included two movements of the A minor Quartet in an Institute concert, and repeated his music from *The water-sprite*. The following spring he suggested to Sibelius that he should offer a new work for performance, and the visit to Leipzig doubtless spurred him on to complete the Piano Quintet which he had been turning over in his mind. The piece is on quite a large scale, lasting some forty minutes, and the finished score did not arrive early enough to give the players adequate time to prepare all five movements. Perhaps it was not purely a matter of time, as Busoni did not particularly like the *Intermezzo* and, according to Wegelius, none of them cared for the fourth movement. Indeed Wegelius's long critique was distinctly negative both in tone and substance. Sibelius was undoubtedly hurt by the former while acknowledging the latter: he dismissed the piece as 'absolute rubbish' in a letter to one of his friends.

On his return to Finland for the summer, Sibelius spent some time in Lovisa before going on to stay with Wegelius and, later, with the Järnefelts. After some initial awkwardness (as the Betzy Lerché affair left painful memories), the ice between Aino and him began to melt. She was a passable pianist and accompanied him in chamber music evenings, and by the end of the summer they had both declared their feelings. The depression he had felt after the Piano Quintet had lifted and the summer saw the completion of a new work, the Quartet in B flat, op. 4. Its première that October by the Music Institute's Quartet led by the Norwegian composer, Johan Halvorsen, was a great success and prompted an appreciative notice from Flodin. A few days later he repaired to Vienna where he was to feel far more at home. On the way he stopped off for a few days in Berlin where his old circle of cronies was reinforced by the addition of Armas Järnefelt and Carl Nielsen; but after the Prussian capital, Vienna captivated him and he adored its heady atmosphere. Busoni had furnished him with a letter of introduction to Brahms, albeit to no purpose. Brahms had long given up teaching, though a few years later one of Sibelius's Runeberg settings was to make a great impression on him. However, thanks to another introduction from Wegelius, Sibelius was accepted as a pupil of Goldmark, then a highly respected and successful operatic composer. His tuition comprised the tactful word of advice and guidance rather than the more thorough contrapuntal drilling he had received from Becker in Berlin. To counter-balance the more relaxed approach of Goldmark, he sought another tutor and on the advice of Hans Richter went to Robert Fuchs. Though he is relatively little played these days, Fuchs was a highly prolific and accomplished composer with a good command of the orchestra but a less-than-outsize musical personality; since his pupils had included Wolf and Mahler, there could have been no doubt of his credentials.

As had been the case in Berlin, Sibelius lived wildly beyond his means, enjoying the best seats at the opera and generally indulging in wine, women and song. It was here that he measured himself for the first time against an orchestral canvas. He took along an overture to Goldmark for criticism and later on composed another, in E major, on which Goldmark pronounced favourably. During the early part of his stay he composed two songs to words of Runeberg, *Hjärtats morgon* (The heart's morning) and *Likhet* (Resemblance) and also the slow movement of a symphony. A third Runeberg setting *Drömmen* (The dream) followed in January. He took up the violin again and played in the conservatoire orchestra under Fuchs, and mixed with musicians other than string players so as to broaden his practical knowledge. Tawaststjerna records a letter to Wegelius in January saying that he had been with the oboist Heber who 'played to me for three hours on his cor anglais so that I now feel I know the instrument's potentialities inside out', a reminder that *The Swan of Tuonela* lies only two or three years ahead. The same month, perhaps to supplement his scholarship, he sought an audition for the Vienna Philharmonic but fortunately was turned down on account of his nerves, and advised to concentrate on the piano as he was a composer. His musical experiences at this time included *Tristan* and *Siegfried*, which prompted him to join the Wagner Society, and a performance of Bruckner's Third Symphony (obviously the 1888–9 revision) which fired his enthusiasm. His letters home do not speak well of the Brahms F major String Quintet or, for that matter, his friend Busoni's first violin sonata (I do not understand how they manage to get these and works like them published'). Alas, although the First Sonata is neither characteristic nor mature, he never came to appreciate Busoni's stature as a composer. He never encountered his greatest work, *Doktor Faust*, in the flesh and his knowledge even of his other work must, one suspects, have been confined to his lesser music. His reading, on the other hand, included Tolstoy and Pushkin: he loathed the *Kreutzer Sonata* every bit as much as he adored *Eugene Onegin*; he devoured Zola and, above all, the *Kalevala*, and as he said in a letter to Aino, was 'beginning to understand much more Finnish'. (For ease of expression Sibelius wrote to Aino in Swedish and she in Finnish.) His months in Vienna saw him acquiring a taste for high society or, as he put it, the company of 'the high and mighty'. In the early months of 1891 he was frequently to be found in the salons of the Viennese aristocracy, and in particular of Pauline Lucca (who was married to a Baron) and of the Count Amadei. In this unaccustomed luxury, Sibelius blossomed and flourished, and enjoyed life to the full.

In February the first ideas of what was to have been a symphony in three movements began forming in his mind; from his letters home to Aino it is clear that the first was the overture, the second 'an idealized Ball scene' and the third a set of variations on a Finnish theme. Goldmark was very much preoccupied with his own creative work and could give Sibelius little time, but some of his advice took root. When the young Finn pressed him for criticism, he replied that the ideas in the overture needed greater character, and urged him at this stage to model himself on Haydn, Mozart and Beethoven rather than Berlioz and Wagner: 'Work over your ideas so that they have greater inner character. Beethoven recast his some fifty times'. This was an admonition Sibelius took to heart. In early April he wrote to Kajanus, sending him the first two movements of his intended symphony, the Overture and *Scène de ballet*, asking him to perform them, adding that he had not much longer to live. He subsequently apologized for this absurd bit of melodrama by saying that he was recovering from a party! Kajanus performed them both that same month despite a subsequent telegram asking him not to, though neither piece occasioned

Sibelius

much enthusiasm. Something of Goldmark's advice had, however, taken root in *Kullervo*, the first ideas of which were now surfacing in his mind. But it was the general atmosphere rather than the thematic material itself that was clearest. He told Aino that he had 'already torn up at least fifty ideas so far', though when it finally took shape, he was pleased enough to show it to Fuchs and even more pleased by his response. His return home to Finland was delayed by another spell in hospital, which he was not allowed to leave before the bills were settled. This resulted in a plea for further loans, and money had to be sent him. More was needed a little later, when during a stopover in Berlin he caroused so copiously with his friends that money again ran out.

Back in Finland, he had to face the realities of earning a living and paying off his debts. It took a little time for him to readjust to life after the wider horizions of Europe; he spent the summer with the Järnefelts and was encouraged by Aino's continuing enthusiasm for what he had written of *Kullervo*. This now dominated his life though there are smaller pieces, the song *Jägargossen* (The young huntsman) and a letter mentions an *Andantino* for horn septet. In the early autumn he advertised lessons in the violin and music theory and soon acquired a few pupils, but composing still occupied most of his time. To deepen his insights into the *Kalevala*, he made an expedition to Porvoo (Borgå) to hear Larin Paraske, a runic singer of some celebrity, intoning episodes from the epic, and carefully studied her inflections and rhythms. But suddenly during the same month he was disturbed by a tinnitus which naturally filled him with alarm and prompted a visit to a specialist in Helsinki. What he heard from him was not reassuring: his ears were defective and his hearing would eventually decline. In the meantime he must give up drinking and smoking – and bathing in cold water. Perhaps the specialist was trying to shock him into abstinence: Tawaststjerna treats the whole episode with some caution, for although Sibelius periodically had some trouble with his ears, he could still conduct effectively into his sixties and never lost his hearing. Somewhat shaken, he threw himself into his symphony with renewed vigour and through his correspondence with Aino one can follow its development in some detail (see *Tawaststjerna* vol. I, pp. 99–106).

The winter brought him closer to Kajanus, and saw the first real strains appearing in his relationship with Wegelius. Kajanus belonged to the circle of liberal and nationalist artists and writers represented by the paper *Päivälehti*: he was, like the Järnefelts, a 'Fennoman', who sought the advancement of the Finnish language. Wegelius did not. He belonged to the Swedish faction and viewed with profound misgiving the growing bonds that Janne was developing with the Järnefelts and Kajanus. Sibelius reports that when he told him of his plans for the *Kullervo* Symphony, he went red in the face and snorted! After this period they grew apart; Wegelius transferred his affections to a younger pupil, Erkki Melartin, on whom his hopes rested, and Sibelius's visits to him became rarer. But only when he published the expanded Finnish edition of his *History of Western Music* in 1902 did any rancour surface; Mahler, who had reached his Fifth Symphony, was hailed as music's saviour and Sibelius was dismissed in a few lines!

As we have seen, Sibelius's encounter with Kajanus's *Aino* in Berlin had already opened his eyes to the musical possibilities of the epic and his lifelong passion for it first finds eloquent expression in the symphony. He immersed himself in it during the spring and conducted its first performance in April 1892. He had appeared only once before on the podium, at one of Kajanus's concerts the previous autumn when he conducted his Overture and *Scène de ballet*, and so had neither technique nor experience behind him. However, by sheer force of personality he imposed himself on the sceptical orchestra, largely German in composition, the mostly Swedish-speaking male chorus and the Finnish-speaking boys. Basically Sibelius's musical values were classical: he worshipped Mozart, Haydn and Beethoven, and this no doubt explains why he called *Kullervo* 'a symphonic poem for soloists, chorus and orchestra', rather than a symphony, on the title-page of the score. However, it is as much a symphony as, say, Mahler's *Resurrection* Symphony, which was yet to be composed. The first movement, Introduction, is generally descriptive of Kullervo's character and sets the scene in broad brushstrokes without dwelling on narrative detail. It is cast in sonata form and the striking thing about it is not so much the faltering proportions or inexpert scoring but its astonishing assurance and immediate sense of identity. In ambition, scale and originality, *Kullervo* had no precedent in the then provincial world of Finnish music even if the *Kalevala* had been the source of inspiration for earlier composers (Filip von Schantz had written a tone-poem called *Kullervo* some thirty years earlier). But if it was his first major work to draw on the *Kalevala* for its inspiration, Sibelius's feeling for it is of earlier provenance. *Drömmen* (The dream), to words of Runeberg, op. 13, written in 1891 in Vienna, bears witness to his growing awareness of the *Kalevala* and the kind of speech rhythms and colours it has. (It even makes oblique reference to a progression we later encounter in *Lemminkäinen and the Maidens of the Island* and has a wonderfully compelling and dark quality.)

Kullervo was an enormous success and put Sibelius firmly on the musical map. It shows the emerging nationalist as well as the incipient symphonist, and its triumph was so resounding as to still, if not dispel, any doubts that the Järnefelt family may have entertained about marrying their daughter to a musician. The couple were married two months later on 10th June 1892 in the Järnefelt's home and spent their honeymoon in Karelia in the vicinity of the village of Lieksa on the eastern shores of Lake Pielisjärvi. In all, their marriage was to last no fewer than sixty-five years. With it Sibelius entered one of the most prominent and aristocratic Finnish-speaking families. Alexander Järnefelt was an untiring advocate of the Finnish-language though he was born into the higher echelons of the Swedish-speaking upper-classes and after service in the Russo-Turkish war became a provincial Governor of Mikkeli and the Kuopio. Despite his espousal of the Finnish cause, he was not popular with the Finnish community on account of his somewhat aloof bearing and conservative views, and he certainly felt uneasy with the liberal views of his sons. Perhaps it was a sign of Sibelius's uncertainty in Finnish or, as Tawaststjerna suggests, a gesture of independence that when he asked for Aino's hand, he wrote in Swedish. His mother-in-law, Elizabeth, who came from the other side of the Baltic and was born Clodt von Jürgensburg, was even more fanatical than her husband. She never learnt Swedish and did not mix in the Swedish-speaking community.

Both Maria Charlotta and the Järnefelts entertained some anxiety as to how Sibelius would be able to support a family. Certainly after *Kullervo*, his prospects looked bright. His Seven Runeberg Songs were due to appear under the imprint of Breitkopf & Härtel later in the year and Kajanus had commissioned an orchestral work, a repertory piece to generate income as well as further his reputation: the outcome was *En Saga*. But his main problem was to secure a regular income. He decided against joining Kajanus's orchestra or becoming a choral conductor but took what teaching was on offer, both from Wegelius's Music Institute and Kajanus's Orchestra School. He also returned to his old desk in the Institute's Quartet for the 1892–3 season. Sibelius and Aino settled in a small house in Helsinki where they were joined by Christian, then still studying medicine at the university, as a lodger. Aino was with child; their first daughter was born in the spring of 1893, and named Eva after Sibelius's ailing aunt Evelina, who died, alas, not long afterwards. Despite his income from teaching, Janne was beset by financial worries. At the turn of the year he returned to Lovisa to raise money, though its absence somehow never seemed to inhibit him from spending it; his days went in teaching, composing, conducting and playing, while, as he put it, the evenings were spent 'dining, holding forth and playing the dilettante'. During the 1890s Aino would sometimes see little of him and periodically returned to her parents' home in Vasa. She was by no means unaware of Sibelius's peccadillos (of which, to do him justice, he warned her even before they married and which she viewed with a blend of aloofness and resignation). The 1890s was the period of the famous 'Symposium' evenings, which scandalized Finnish society at the time, and so called because of the then celebrated painting by Axel Gallén-Kallela which shows Sibelius, Kajanus and other Bacchic companions at the dinner table in their cups. The author Adolf Paul was among them, and Sibelius was not best pleased when his autobiographical novel, *En bok om en människa* (A Book about a Man) appeared on the bookstalls in the autumn of 1891. It portrayed the thinly-disguised composer, the 'boy-genius Sillén', living it up in Berlin, lying in bed until well past noon, going on drinking bouts and freely indulging himself: Aino read it with displeasure and Sibelius himself later complained to Paul that it quite spoilt his credit-rating.

Sibelius conducted the première of *En Saga* in February 1893, and with some success: it received four further performances that year, though it was not perhaps quite the showpiece that Kajanus had expected after the *Kullervo* Symphony. It puzzled Faltin on first acquaintance though he subsequently hailed its 'incomparable beauty'. It paved the way for the succession of orchestral works, strongly national in feeling, that he was to write in the immediate wake of his marriage. The *Karelia* music, written for a pageant in Viipuri (Viborg), has obvious patriotic overtones, so much so that Sibelius complained to his brother that not much of the music could be heard at the performance he conducted in November 1893, as everyone was either shouting or applauding. A few days later he conducted a concert version of the score in eight movements together with *En Saga* and other new pieces. But his main preoccupation was a projected opera, *Veenen luominen* (The Building of the Boat), for which he returned to the *Kalevala*. Tawaststjerna quotes a long letter to the poet Erkko giving a synopsis and describing its layout, and dismisses Sibelius's theorising as 'Wagner *réchauffé*'. He had spent the bulk of the summer engrossed in it and had already composed some of the music, including the prelude that was to become *The Swan of Tuonela*. Not that it consumed him to the exclusion of all else. When Faltin visited him during the summer he showed him a new Piano Sonata in F major over which shades of Grieg hover.

The following season saw the *Academic Cantata*, a commission for the university encaenia, for which he had Faltin to thank, and another for the Vasa Festival. For this he composed his *Improvisation* for orchestra, better known under the title it later assumed at its Helsinki première, *Spring Song*

27

or *La Tristesse du printemps*). But the most memorable work of these months was the first, choral version of *Rakastava*, more familiar in its much later transcription for strings, triangle and timpani. Earlier, in 1893, Sibelius had composed his first piece for male voices, *Venematka* (The Boat Journey), to words from the *Kalevala* which showed a quite distinctive feel for the medium, and *Rakastava* was even further removed from the conventional repertory piece. Perhaps this was why, when it was submitted for a competition sponsored by a student choir, it was not given first prize. In the summer of 1894 Sibelius's thoughts returned to his opera, which he had laid on one side the previous autumn. In July he planned a visit to Bayreuth, making a detour to visit Paavo Cajander, the translator of Shakespeare, to discuss his operatic plans. He went armed with scores of *Lohengrin, Tannhäuser* and *Walküre*, but it was *Parsifal*, which he saw on the day of his arrival, that made the most overwhelming impact on him. Gradually doubts about his own opera began to surface; the first act he thought 'flawed by Luonnotar's motif, which is in the minor and rhythmically weak'. Although in later life he professed an indifference to Wagner, the performances he saw made an enormous impression on him at the time. He told Ekman in the 1930s that he was 'unable to feel any fervour for Wagner's art' and that he would 'not be persuaded to hear the other operas' (p. 125). But at the time, in a letter to Aino he writes, 'I can't begin to tell you how *Parsifal* has transported me. Everything I do seems cold and feeble by its side. *That* is really something!' And he wrote with even greater enthusiasm of *Tristan* which he saw after meeting Armas Järnefelt in Munich. An ardent Wagnerite, Järnefelt dragged Sibelius back to Bayreuth for another *Parsifal*. He also heard *Walküre, Siegfried*, and *Götterdämmerung*, and was 'bowled over' by *Die Meistersinger*.

By this time it had become obvious to him that the kind of operatic enterprise on which he had ventured simply would not do. He abandoned the opera altogether, though some of the thematic material was absorbed in the *Four Legends*, op. 22. Otherwise it would have fallen to Sibelius to have composed the first opera on a theme from the *Kalevala*. This particular honour must go to Oskar Merikanto whose *Pohjan metti* (The Maid of Pohja) followed a few years later in 1898. But there is no mistaking that *The Swan of Tuonela* is the first sign of genius, as opposed to talent, in Sibelius's output: its opening bars instantly proclaim a new voice in music and establish a strongly Finnish atmosphere and identity. Nowhere is the *Kalevala* more powerfully evoked and the Finnish landscape brought more vividly before one's eyes. Sibelius himself must have known this, as even at the height of his depression about his own operatic sketches he speaks of the opening idea as 'superb, one of my best'. From Munich he made his first trip to Italy, a country for which he had a life-long affection. All the same, his stay in Venice was brief and by the end of August he was back in Berlin where he spent some time with Busoni, to whom he showed *En Saga* and the *Karelia* music. At his insistence he went to see *Falstaff*, then very much 'contemporary music' – it was only a year old – as well as *Carmen* and *The Bartered Bride*. But for the best part of his stay he steeped himself in the tone-poems of Liszt and in the *Faust Symphony*, 'a marvellous piece – I am learning a lot from it', he wrote.

Doubtless his Lisztian studies were in preparation for the *Four Legends* and more immediately *Skogsrået* (The Wood-Nymph). This was a melodrama for speaker, strings, horn and piano to words of Runeberg, written for a concert in aid of the Finnish Theatre, which he immediately refashioned into a purely orchestral tone-poem. Meanwhile, Aino was expecting their second child and had the support of her parents who had moved to Helsinki; her father had become Secretary for Defence. Sibelius rented a room not far away where he could work undisturbed, though the period was relatively unproductive. He was still widely played: *En Saga*, the *Karelia* music and *Spring Song* were frequently given, and at the all-Sibelius concert at which the first performance of the orchestral version of *The Wood-Nymph*, was heard, the great Finnish baritone Abraham Ojanperä sang another novelty: a *Serenade* to words of Stagnelius. A glorious song of great subtlety and haunting atmosphere, the *Serenade* succumbed to the attacks of self-doubt that periodically assailed its composer. After two performances he withdrew it and (according to Tawaststjerna) it was only after some persuasion that the family agreed to it being recorded in 1983. The following month Busoni came to Helsinki to give three recitals, and afterwards suggested interesting Belaiev in becoming his publisher. But 1895 was for the most part the year of the *Four Legends*, which were ready by the following spring.

The *Lemminkäinen Legends* can legitimately be regarded as another symphony, at least in the matter of scale and vision, and it would seem that in his last years Sibelius spoke of it in these terms. In any event they consolidated his position in the Finnish musical world: they enjoyed as great a public success as *Kullervo* and hardly less critical acclaim. Flodin particularly admired *Lemminkäinen and the Maidens of the Island* for building on 'modern, cosmopolitan groundwork . . . thematic structures are more closely related to the Lisztian style while the influence both of Wagner and Tchaikovsky can be discerned', but sounded a note of caution about its companions which he thought relied too greatly on atmosphere and an undoubted hypnotic power. The day after its première Aino's father died and the small legacy she received was sufficient to pay for her and Sibelius to visit Busoni in Berlin. A sketchblock from this period records one of those swings of creative fortune that afflict all artists at some time or another: 'Tried to compose but it has not been with *schwung*. Why does it come so rarely these days? Perhaps my excesses *in Venere* or *in Baccho* have produced a spiritual paralysis?' The very next day saw an upsurge of spirits, 'Life is so rich. *Nox sine excessu.* What vitality, vitality, *cum excessu.*' In September several new commissions loomed: a cantata to honour the coronation of Tsar Nicholas II and, despite *The Building of the Boat*, opera again tempted him. He promised to deliver a one-acter, *Jungfrun i tornet* (The Maiden in the Tower) later that autumn, and apart from that assumed a heavier teaching burden. Faltin had retired and he was groomed to succeed him. He had to present a paper of considerable substance in November which was to give an idea of his purely academic achievements. The opera, to a dreadfully banal libretto by Rafael Hertzberg, was performed to some acclaim in November, though the Swedish-language *Nya Pressen* thought it a pity that the composer had squandered so much good music on 'so simple a yarn'. The *Coronation Cantata*, however, did not advance his cause. The music was at best routine and the performance disastrous: the university archive records that some of the orchestral material was missing at rehearsal but Sibelius himself blamed a drunken tuba player who improvised freely during the fugal section to somewhat alarming effect. His paper ('Some reflections on folk music and its influence on the development of Art music') later that month must have been an ordeal, for while its beginning was a relatively well-ordered exposition, the development soon assumed the improvisatory character of a cadenza. The examining report noted drily that it was 'full of original ideas of which some appeared to occur to him on the spur of the moment'!

To his consternation Sibelius discovered that his was not the only name to be advanced for Faltin's post: there were two other candidates, Ilmari Krohn and Robert Kajanus. The selection committee ruminated for some time before the decision was finally reached in the spring of 1897 recommending him ('a composer of Sibelius's standing would be an adornment to any university') in preference to either rival by twenty-five votes to three. His consternation turned to alarm when Kajanus appealed against the verdict, and he was even more astonished when the appeal was upheld. Kajanus was doubtless peeved that his own achievements had been brushed aside so lightly, and argued (not unreasonably) that one was tempted to question whether the committee were not offering Sibelius a composition scholarship rather than a university teaching post. Kajanus's appeal may have outraged Finnish musical circles and certainly carried little weight with the University Consistory, but the final decision was made in St Petersburg by the Secretary of State for Finnish Affairs who also happened to be the Chancellor of the University. Despite Sibelius's growing celebrity and greater prestige, he ruled in Kajanus's favour and overturned the election. It goes without saying that all this had put their friendship under great strain; Sibelius felt a sense of betrayal and although fences were mended and bridges rebuilt, the old relationship was never fully restored. All this is worth mentioning because the State Pension that the Finnish Senate voted Sibelius some months later was only partly an acknowledgment of his creative achievements to date, and very much a gesture to meet the body of opinion that felt Sibelius had been badly treated. 'More than usual with artists', wrote Senator Yrjö Koskinen in his letter to the Secretary of State, 'he seems to lack completely any feeling for practical affairs'. The pension was intended to relieve him of some of his teaching burdens and followed a precedent established when the poet Runeberg had been similarly passed over for a university chair. Norway had of course set an example in honouring both Grieg and Svendsen in this way. Some years later this was turned into a Life Pension, but even so, Sibelius's finances remained precarious and as he became a more important national figure, private patronage had to be mobilized on his behalf.

In the autumn of 1897 Sibelius conducted the revised version of the *Four Legends* that he had made earlier in the year. They were presented together with another new work, *The Rapids-shooter's* (or more accurately but cumbersomely titled *Rapids-Rider's) Brides*, long known in the English-speaking world as *The Ferryman's Brides*. This time round the *Legends* prompted a very diffferent response from Flodin. In a review of a symphony by the youthful Ernst Mielck he had deplored the weakening sense of form among the younger generation ('they can all turn out rhapsodies, symphonic poems, suites galore but few dare test their strength against the magisterial symphonic edifice') but Sibelius's newly-revised score prompted a quite extraordinary outburst, almost reminiscent of *Pravda's* denunciation of Shostakovich's *Lady Macbeth*: 'pathological . . . the *Lemminkäinen* portraits depress me, make me miserable, exhausted, apathetic'. Both Flodin and Wegelius were keen to see Sibelius measure himself against the 'magisterial symphonic edifice'. No doubt the successful performance of a symphony by the prodigy Ernst Mielck acted as a spur: Finland had no history to speak of in this area, and Mielck's was the first essay in the genre since the 1863

Symphony of Ingelius. Sibelius returned to *The Swan of Tuonela* and *Lemminkäinen's Homeward Journey* after finishing the First Symphony but withheld the remaining two for many years, discouraged not so much by Flodin but (according to Aino's testimony) Kajanus's lack of enthusiasm for them.

But before he embarked on the composition of the First Symphony Sibelius enjoyed some success early in the year with his incidental music to Adolf Paul's play *King Christian II*, after which he and Aino left for Berlin. Adolf Paul had greater success in finding a major publisher for Sibelius than had Busoni the previous year. They went together to Leipzig where Breitkopf & Härtel agreed to take *King Christian II*. Indeed, although the 1914–18 war prompted a breach in their relationship, and there were a few years during which he went to Robert Lienau, Breitkopf & Härtel remained his main publisher right up to *Tapiola* and beyond. In the 1950s they published revised versions of the two *Legends* Sibelius had withheld up to that point, and after his death added the *Kullervo* Symphony to their list. During his time in Berlin, Sibelius heard the *Symphonie fantastique*, which fired him with enthusiasm, but after Aino returned to Finland he threw himself into his own First Symphony. However, he did not maintain the initial impetus and succumbed to many of the temptations a big city had to offer. In mid-May he announced that he had become a teetotaller, but the return to Berlin of Axel Gallén-Kallela, his old friend from the 'Symposium' days, saw Sibelius fall from grace. At one stage in their carousing they came to blows with some Polish street workers and, as Tawaststjerna puts it, 'it is difficult to know whether burgundy or blood flowed more freely'.

After his return to Finland he stayed longer in the country than usual, and did not even return to Helsinki for Busoni's recitals at the end of September, contenting himself with a note of apology. By now he was engrossed in work on the First Symphony, finishing it early in 1899 and conducting its first performance in April. It must have been evident right from the very first bars that he had made enormous strides since *Kullervo*, not only as a master of the orchestra but in terms of the concentration of his material and mastery of form. The organic cohesion that informs the first movement is of a much higher order than anything he had done before. True, the slow movement proclaims a clear debt to Tchaikovsky, though even here the distinctive colouring and personality of Sibelius is still strongly in evidence. Its success was immediate, but it was not the new symphony that created the greatest stir that year.

1899 was a period of considerable political unrest in Finland, and Sibelius was caught up in a mounting fever of nationalism. The so-called

February manifesto had deprived Finland of her autonomy and drastic-ally curtailed the freedom of speech and assembly that the Finns had hitherto enjoyed. Sibelius had responded to the general mood with a number of patriotic works, including a setting of Rydberg's *Atenarnas Sång* (Son of the Atheians) but it was the music to a seemingly innocuous celebration that was to make the greatest waves. This was a Pagaent, a series of tableaux mounted in aid of the Press Pension Fund, which proved the most highly charged in patriotic fervour. Kajanus conducted four of these tableaux, three of which we know as the first set of *Scènes historiques*, the last being *Finland Awakes*. It was this, to which Sibelius gave the title *Finlandia* when he revised it the following year, that blazed his name abroad in the early years of the century. Its importance in terms of Finnish national self-awareness was to be immeasurable.

3

1900–1914

If the 1890s had seen the consolidation of Sibelius's position as Finland's leading composer, the next decade was to see the growth of his international reputation. In 1900 Kajanus took the Helsinki Orchestra on its first European tour, and Sibelius went with them. Their itinerary included Stockholm, Christiania (as Oslo was then called), Copenhagen, Berlin, Hamburg and Amsterdam, and culminated in their appearance at the Paris World Exhibition. Their programmes included *The Swan of Tuonela, Lemminkäinen's Homeward Journey* and *Finlandia*, as well as the newly-composed First Symphony. It was in Stockholm that Sibelius made his first foreign appearance as a conductor: he was fêted by the Swedish musical establishment – and records that he drank too much absinthe with Alfvén, Sjögren and Stenhammar. The First Symphony was a great success although Sjögren preferred *Lemminkäinen*: the symphony he thought too indebted to Tchaikovsky. 'I know that there is much in that man I also have', Sibelius told Aino, 'but there isn't much one can do about that! *Das muss man sich gefallen lassen.*' He spoke of Stenhammar as being stiff and formal on this their first encounter, but two years later, when the Swedish composer visited Helsinki to give a recital, he heard the Second Symphony, which swept him off his feet. He became one of his staunchest and most loyal champions, and in the 1930s Sibelius was to describe him to Ekman as 'a rare friend – an uncommonly noble personality . . . a gentleman from top to toe'. By the time the tour finally reached Paris, however, it was late July and most of the influential people in French musical life had already left the capital.

Not long after the composition of the First Symphony, a highly important person surfaced in Sibelius's life: Baron Axel Carpelan. They met on the eve of the departure of the Helsinki Orchestra for Paris, though Carpelan had written to Sibelius as an anonymous admirer before this. Even in the early days of their relationship he was forward in tendering advice. The 'Concert Overture' *Finlandia* should be followed by a *Wald-Symphonie* and a Violin Concerto. It was thanks to Carpelan's energy that Sibelius was encouraged and, more to the point, enabled to make the celebrated trip to Italy during which he began to plan the Second Symphony. His title, together with the fact that he acted as the composer's patron, has prompted the belief that he was a man of means. In fact Carpelan was endowed neither with affluence nor robust health, and the funds for Sibelius's Italian trip came through rather than from him: he raised some 5,000 Finnmarks from a number of patriots, including Axel Tamm, who had for a time been Carpelan's own benefactor. (They felt that after the success of the First Symphony, the appearance of a successor was in the national interest. *Finlandia* had carried awareness of the Finnish cause all over the globe so that one could say without much exaggeration that Sibelius was Finland's voice in the world.)

An enigmatic and somewhat neurasthenic figure, Carpelan eked out a frugal existence as something of a recluse in Tampere. He had nourished youthful ambitions to take up the violin but met with strong parental opposition, which seems to have had a traumatic effect on him, prompting him to withdraw from the competitive world. He was to play a vital role in Sibelius's life, not only in organizing financial support from a variety of sources, among them wealthy industrialists, but also in providing a sounding-board for ideas. (Sibelius was not his only idol: he maintained a long correspondence with the great Swedish poet, Viktor Rydberg.) It may seem an exaggeration to claim that he was the greatest single catalyst in Sibelius's career, for there were other important figures: Aino, the Järnefelts, Busoni, Kajanus and Koussevitzky, but without Carpelan, Sibelius would have ploughed slightly different furrows. Tawaststjerna takes the view that he 'lived for Sibelius and his moods were undoubtedly affected by him', and one suspects that the absence of a strong motivation in his own life either in professional achievement or strong personal attachments took its toll. 'Look here, Herr Sibelius', he once wrote, 'should you not turn your mind to Shakespeare's dramas and in particular to *Cymbeline, A Winter's Tale* and *The Tempest*? Tchaikovsky has written an Overture to the last but without altogether succeeding in bringing it off, but *The Tempest* is made for you – Prospero, Miranda, the spirits of Earth and Air.'

Sibelius came to set ever greater store by his musical judgment and practical advice even if their correspondence was sporadic on the composer's side. For him Carpelan was an important sounding-board for his creative plans and an invaluable source of help. Time and again during the first decade of the century he mounted rescue operations to see Sibelius through his recurrent financial crises: time and again he would offer reassurance when Sibelius felt his standing threatened. Not that their friendship was without its moments of strain: Carpelan must have grown tired of the one-way dialogue, for Sibelius, engrossed in a creative problem, could often be remiss in responding to his letters and his silence could last for months on end. Yet he showed an intuitive understanding of Sibelius's mind and considerable musical perception in, for example, his comments on the second version of the Fifth Symphony, and was prodigal with advice and concern. He did not live to see either his *Wald-Symphonie* or *The Tempest*. When news of his death came on 24th March 1919, Sibelius wrote: 'Axel dead. How empty life seems. No sun, no music, no affection. How alone I am with my music.'

The success of the First Symphony had been surpassed only by *Finlandia*, which focused, from the Russian point of view, unwelcome attention on the plight of the Finns. So as not to seem unduly provocative, it was thought wiser not to bill it as *Finlandia*; indeed Kajanus was even doubtful about doing so in Paris, and when Sibelius himself conducted it in Estonia in 1903, (another part of the Tsarist Empire) it went under the title 'Impromptu for orchestra'. But interest in Sibelius's music continued to grow. His increasing fame was not confined to Germany: Henry Wood included the *King Christian II* Suite at a Promenade concert as early as 1901, and Granville Bantock conducted the First Symphony two years later. Sibelius was riding on the crest of a wave, and during the first years of the century his works were conducted by such figures as Hans Richter, Felix Weingartner and Arturo Toscanini.

Carpelan urged him to spend the autumn of 1900 in Italy, away from the day-to-day pressures of life in Helsinki and devote himself to composition. At the end of October, Sibelius and his family set out for Berlin, where they remained until the end of January with a view to consolidating the ground he had won earlier during the year. He went to Leipzig and saw Nikisch, who promised to include *The Swan of Tuonela* in future programmes, and met Weingartner, whose String Quartet he heard. In February the family arrived in Rapallo and were installed in the Pension Suisse while he rented a room in a small mountain villa. His plans were slow to take firm shape: his sketchbooks at the time include ideas for an orchestral piece to be called *The Stone Guest*, among the jottings for which is to be found the main theme of the *Andante* of the Second Symphony. After two months in Rapallo he suddenly made off to Florence, leaving a note together with a few hundred lire for Aino (not without subsequent pangs of conscience). Here his plans for a work on the Don Juan theme took a different turn. He speaks of 'Festivals: four tone poems for orchestra', and among the sketches for it the second theme of the Andante is to be found, with the superscription 'Christus'. To Carpelan he wrote of plans for a setting of part of *The Divine Comedy*.

36

What he did, however, set, albeit the following year, was Rydberg's poem, *Höstkväll* (Autumn evening) to which his thoughts often turned in Rapallo as he watched the winter storms in the Mediterranean. A few days later he went on to Rome and immersed himself in its treasures, not least in Verdi and Palestrina, before making his way back a little sheepishly to Rapallo and reconciliation. On his way home to Finland, he stopped off in Vienna to learn that he had been invited to Heidelberg to conduct *The Swan of Tuonela* and *Lemminkäinen's Homeward Journey*. Earlier, on his way south, he had heard the Bohemian Quartet, of whom Suk was a member, playing a Weingartner Quartet, and so made a detour to Prague to renew his acquaintance with him. Naturally, he also met Suk's father-in-law, Dvořák, whom he found as warm and spontaneous as his music, but alas, the long account of their conversation that he gave Carpelan does not survive. In the autumn, back in Finland, he received an invitation from Busoni to conduct *En Saga* at one of his New Music concerts, and set about revising it.

If the genesis of the Second Symphony shows that the pull of the tone-poem was still a powerful one, all his ideas were to forge a symphonic course. By the turn of the year it was almost complete, though not sufficiently ready for the projected date in January: Sibelius conducted its first performance in Helsinki in March 1902. He prefaced it with a hastily composed Overture in A minor and the rather pale *Impromptu*, op. 19., for female voices and orchestra to words of Rydberg. The concert was repeated four times to capacity houses. The symphony in particular possesses a combination of Italianate warmth and Nordic intensity that has ensured its wide popular appeal. Some of its success was extra-musical in that, coming immediately after *Finlandia*, the work struck a responsive patriotic nerve. If it inhabits much the same spiritual world as the First, it views it through more subtle and refined lenses. As in the First Symphony, it is the opening movement that makes the most profound impression. Its very air of relaxation and effortlessness serves to mask its inner strength. Each motif seems to evolve naturally from its immediate predecessor. His Italian visit may account for the sunnier, more relaxed atmosphere and the softer, warmer light, though it is only fair to note that *Tapiola*, the coldest and bleakest of his works, was written in the same country. The success of the symphony was soon to be repeated abroad: Busoni invited him to conduct it in Berlin, and performances followed from Hans Richter and, later, Toscanini and Weingartner.

With the Symphony behind him, Sibelius's thoughts turned to the Violin Concerto which he had promised Willy Burmester. Burmester was one of the most respected soloists of the day, who also made occasional 'guest appearances' at their convivial 'Symposium' gatherings when he was briefly leader of Kajanus's orchestra, and he had long pressed Sibelius to write a concerto. The period of the Violin Concerto was turbulent, with mounting debts and bouts of heavy drinking which imposed a considerable measure of domestic strain. But he was enjoying great success with the incidental music he had composed for a play by his brother-in-law, Arvid Järnefelt, *Kuolema* (Death), one of whose numbers was *Valse triste*. In its original form (1903), it was scored for strings alone, though the following year Sibelius scored it for small orchestra. Like *Finlandia*, it soon took the world by storm: Sibelius was to sell it to Fazer (and through them Breitkopf) on derisory terms, a decision he never ceased to lament until his dying day. In 1903 he had bought a plot of land at Järvenpää, not far from Helsinki in what was at the time the depths of the countryside, where he built the villa in which he spent the remainder of his life. It was called Ainola after his wife, but although he enjoyed its seclusion, he made frequent and sometimes long visits to Helsinki 'to go to the bank'! Before they moved in to their new home in the autumn of 1904 he had suffered something of a reverse: in March the première of the Violin Concerto had been a fiasco, when Viktor Nováček endeavoured to surmount its difficulties. (Although Sibelius had promised the concerto to Burmester, he needed a concert in order to raise money, so asked him to waive his rights and offered him its continental première.) The expense of the new villa, his financial problems, periodic Bacchic excesses, worries about his hearing and so on, were compounded by anxieties about his health: the Helsinki doctors suspected diabetes. But when he eventually consulted a specialist in January 1905, while he was in Berlin to conduct the Second Symphony, he was told of his 'fine physical condition and outstanding hypochondria', and advised that 'his wine should be lemonade'.

Success was bringing in its train a variety of commissions which distracted him from the Third Symphony, ideas for which had begun to form in his mind as early as 1904. First, there was incidental music to write for Bertel Gripenberg's translation of Maeterlinck's *Pelléas et Mélisande*. Still in Berlin, Sibelius broke off from his labours on the revision of the Violin Concerto and made good progress with his new score. He had intended to go on to England, where Granville Bantock had engaged him to conduct the First Symphony in Liverpool, but pulled out at the last minute because of *Pelléas*. But in 1905 came some unwelcome news: Carpelan wrote to tell him that the sources of support on which he had been relying were drying up, and this naturally intensified Sibelius's concern to generate more income from his works. The period of his contract with Fazer and Breitkopf & Härtel was running out and he decided to move to Robert Lienau of Berlin, even though the terms of his new contract were onerous. They bound him to deliver four works per annum for a minimum of 8,000 Reichsmarks (Busoni had advised him not to settle for less than 5,000 for the Violin Concerto alone). Somewhat piqued, his Finnish publisher, Fazer, sold all the rights he owned in Sibelius's works to Breitkopf for three times the amount he had paid for them. In the meantime Breitkopf had offered to renew their contract and were, to say the least, displeased to read in the press that the Violin Concerto and *Pelléas et Mélisande* were to be published by a rival house. The concerto was played by Karl (or Karel) Halir – yet again Sibelius had disappointed Burmester to whom he had promised the première – and the conductor was Richard Strauss. Sibelius was much impressed by the trouble Strauss took in preparing the score and by the fact that he had three full orchestral rehearsals. Despite the travails, the Violin Concerto was very much a labour of love, as one would expect from a violinist *manqué*. Commentators often speak of Richard Strauss's 'love affair with the soprano voice'; Sibelius's affair with the violin, on the other hand, was not quite so intense, even if he long nursed a nostalgia for his youthful love. To some extent his subsequent career as a conductor fulfilled his needs as an executant, and it is not without significance that his creative and conducting careers ended pretty well simultaneously.

In November 1905 Sibelius at last made the trip to England, postponed from the early part of the year. If England made a strong impression on him, it was largely due to the liberality of Granville Bantock, thanks to which, as Sibelius told Ekman, he never 'made the acquaintance of English coinage'. Carpelan's admonitions ('don't forget that their etiquette is rigorous') were soon forgotten as Bantock worked hard to put him at his ease. After conducting the First Symphony and *Finlandia* in Birmingham, to the acclaim of press and public alike, he went with Bantock to London. On the train he was introduced to Rosa Newmarch, whose pen was to be one of the most active on his behalf during the first decades of the century, and in the capital itself he was well taken care of by Henry Wood. London quite bowled him over: 'what Järvenpää is to Berlin, so Berlin is to London', he told Aino after a later visit. But he contented himself with a relatively short stay, and only a day or two after his concert, he made his farewells and took the overnight train to Paris. Here he installed himself in the Pavillon Henri IV at Saint Germain, longed for Aino to join him, an impossibility given their precarious finances, and spent his time wrestling with his new tone-poem, *Luonnotar*.

On his return to Finland, Sibelius was plunged into various social duties; he conducted his *Elegy* when his old teacher, Martin Wegelius died, though their friendship had long since fallen into disrepair, and was obliged to meet a new commission. This was the cantata *The Captive Queen*, written for the Snellman centenary celebrations in May and not a particularly good work. (Sibelius himself dismissed it in a letter to Lienau as an occasional piece.) He was still enmeshed in his continuing struggles with *Luonnotar*, but in the event no such work materialized; when the new orchestral work emerged from its chrysalis, it was *Pohjola's Daughter* (see p.105). Though it was dedicated to Kajanus, Sibelius himself conducted its first performance later the same year, albeit not in Helsinki. The pianist-conductor Alexander Siloti was one of Sibelius's admirers, and when Sibelius was offered the opportunity of conducting it with Prince Scheremetyev's Grand Symphony Orchestra – with its sixteen first violins, fourteen seconds and so on – at the Marinsky Theatre, he leapt at the chance. Siloti's concerts were among the more adventurous in St Petersburg, and so in December he conducted both the new work and *Lemminkäinen's Homeward Journey*, sharing the programme with no less a star than Ysaÿe. Busoni conducted its first Berlin performance shortly afterwards, and Armas Järnefelt introduced it to Stockholm in February. Unusually, for England was by now quick to take up new Sibelius scores, *Pohjola's Daughter* had to wait until 1932 before it was heard in London under its dedicatee who subsequently recorded it with the London Symphony Orchestra. England had been promised the first performance of the Third Symphony for early March 1907 but it was not ready in time, and he wired his apologies. He had put the symphony on one side the previous autumn so as to write the incidental music for his friend Hjalmar Procopé's play, *Belshazzar's Feast*, and the set of op. 50 Songs to German texts. He now had to remember that Lienau's quota had to be met. In the end he conducted its première in Helsinki that September in a concert which also included the two novelties of the previous year, *Pohjola's Daughter* and *Belshazzar's Feast*. Not long after the Third Symphony first saw the light of day, Mahler came to Helsinki where he conducted a Beethoven-Wagner programme. Sibelius called on him at his hotel to pay his respects, where their oft-quoted conversation concerning the nature of the symphony took place. Mahler did not form a particularly positive impression of Sibelius's music (not surprisingly, since *Spring Song* and *Valse triste* was all he heard) though they obviously established a good personal rapport. But when at one point Mahler asked him which of his works he wanted him to conduct, Sibelius's response was distinctly maladroit. With a mixture of awkwardness and shyness, which Mahler must have interpreted as ungracious, he replied, 'Nichts'. ('I did not want him to think that I had come to see him merely to interest him in my compositions', he told Ekman.)

Up to this time, although there had been minor setbacks, his star had been steadily in the ascendant. But with the change of direction in his musical path that took place at the time of the Third Symphony, a change in his fortunes can be discerned. With the Violin Concerto and the Second Symphony, Sibelius reached the peak of what one might for the sake of convenience call his first period. But the Third Symphony showed him to be out of step with the times. Alongside the more lavish orchestral canvas and vivid colourings of such contemporary works as Skryabin's *Le Poème de l'extase*, Debussy's *La mer*, Ravel's *Rapsodie espagnole*, Dukas's *La Péri* or even the young Stravinsky's *Feu d'artifice*, his palette was almost monochrome. In Finland, Flodin hailed its classicism thus: 'It can – and indeed, will – be understood in every part of the globe where people have a feeling for music in its newest and most sublime form.' But in fact the Third Symphony did nothing of the kind. It puzzled audiences both in Russia, where it was included in a Siloti concert, and Germany while Paris remained coldly indifferent: it was not given there until 1920. Even London received it with respect rather than the enthusiasm that had greeted its predecessor.

In 1908 the shadows started to lengthen, and the new year did not find him in good shape; he was drinking as heavily as ever, often felt unwell and was plagued with money worries. Moreover, as England was opening its doors, his stock in Germany was beginning to show signs of decline though he did not lack advocacy, for Weingartner and Nikisch both programmed the First Symphony. But even in England his appearance at the exclusive London Music Club a few months later hardly advanced his cause. The event must have been sheer torment: the guest of honour sat on a platform while he was eulogized and then some of his works were played. But whereas Debussy (who declared that he would rather compose a symphony than repeat such an ordeal) had at least been represented in the series by the String Quartet, Sibelius's programme consisted of piano music and songs that scarcely did justice to his depth and range. Arnold Bax attributed the relatively slow growth of his reputation in England after 1909 to this single event, though it must be admitted that the Fourth Symphony, *The Bard* and *Luonnotar* were all performed there before the First World War.

After conducting the new symphony in St Petersburg the previous November, Sibelius had complained of a hoarseness which gradually became more severe; eventually a tumour was diagnosed. He was operated on in Helsinki with some success but anxiety was not dispelled. His brother Christian referred him to a Berlin specialist for further treatment, adding that 'it would appear not to be malignant, even though it cannot be denied that there is a marked possibility of recidivity'. He had cancelled his concerts in Rome, Berlin and Warsaw but had recovered sufficiently to travel to London for the British première of his long-promised symphony which he dedicated to Bantock. This period saw him consumed with the music for Strindberg's *Swanwhite*, two of his greatest songs, *Jubal*, to words of Josephson, and the almost expressionist *Teodora*, to a poem of Bertel Gripenberg, and perhaps his most underrated and misunderstood tone-poem, *Night Ride and Sunrise*, which he finished in November. The première was in St Petersburg early in the New Year and Alexander Siloti, its conductor, was among those who, it would seem, misunderstood it for he made cuts and changed a tempo marking.

During the heatwave in Berlin that July Sibelius eventually underwent successful treatment for his tumour, but for many years he lived in fear that the growth might recur and was forced to abjure alcohol and cigars. The bleak possibilities that the illness opened up, served to contribute to the austerity, depth and concentration of the works that follow in its wake: the Fourth Symphony, *The Bard* and *Luonnotar*. Nothing concentrates the mind on essentials more than the thought that one's days may be numbered, and it is in these works that one senses the closeness of death and an overwhelming feeling of isolation. In London, to which he repaired in February 1909 to conduct performances of *En Saga* and *Finlandia*, he worked with increased urgency on the String Quartet, *Voces intimae*, the first – and only – occasion on which he was to return to quartet writing. (Some of the Fourth Symphony had originally been sketched out as a quartet – and there were rumours of another essay in this medium.) Debussy was in London to conduct the *Nocturnes* and *Prélude à l'après-midi d'un faune*, and Sibelius later told Aino that when he went to pay his respects in the green room, he felt an immediate rapport with him. He also heard the First Symphony of Elgar and Bantock's *Omar Khayyam*, though a less congenial musical experience was also in store for him from his London neighbour, a daily onslaught on the 'Moonlight' Sonata, which finally forced him to move. He worked intently on *Voces intimae*, but made slow progress, and decamped to Paris. Recurrent throat pains filled him with such alarm that he went to Berlin for further treatment, to be soothed by reassuring news.

His contract with Lienau was by now due for renewal. By April *Voces intimae* was finished but this was only the second work of the year, *Night Ride and Sunrise* being the first. Lienau agreed not to hold him to the letter of their agreement but to settle for the op. *57* Josephson Songs. However, Sibelius had had enough, and when he received flattering overtures from Breitkopf – and Lienau declined to pay 5,000 marks for the op. *58* Piano Pieces – he decided to return to the fold. With Aino under siege from creditors at home, it was time to leave Berlin for Finland. It is hardly surprising that given the anxiety at the back of his mind concerning his health and ever increasing alarm at his mountainous debts, now in the region of 100,000 marks, 1909 should prompt dark thoughts. His next piece was the Funeral March *In memoriam*, which he told his daughter Eva was composed as a tribute to Eugen Schauman who had assassinated the Tsarist Governor-General in 1904 and then committed suicide, but it is not unlikely that he had himself in mind. Despite its echoes of Mahler's Fifth Symphony, which he had studied in Berlin in 1905, it is a powerful piece though his struggles with the score plunged him into the blackest depressions. But it was in October 1909 that Sibelius began the first sketches for his most desolate work, the Fourth Symphony. Its painful gestation is minutely detailed in the diaries he had begun keeping earlier that year, and it is extensively cited in Tawaststjerna (vol. II, pp. 139–69). During the next eighteen months, beset by other commissions and financial anxieties, he was forced to lay it aside several times. First in order to work on a new tone-poem, *The Dryad*, and to revise the *Impromptu* op. 19 and *The Origin of Fire* – largely to generate income, possibly in fear that were his health to fail, he might not live to put them into their final shape – then in May to look after Rosa Newmarch, who was visiting Finland on her way back from St Petersburg, and to finish the op. 61 Songs. Later in the year there were conducting engagements in Christiania where the Second Symphony and *Night Ride and Sunrise* had been programmed as well as the first performances of two new pieces, *The Dryad* and *In memoriam*. On leaving Norway he proceeded to Berlin, where he finished work on the revision of *The Origin of Fire*. All these interruptions were frustrating, though his spirits were doubtless lifted in Berlin by his encounters with Busoni. Perhaps with *Voces intimae* or some of his piano pieces in mind, Busoni urged him to concentrate on the orchestra, and 'not stray into other media'. His spirits must also have been raised by hearing a performance of his Violin Concerto with the seventeen-year-old Ferenc Vecsay to whom he dedicated it. But if his symphony was ever to be finished, it was increasingly clear that it must have his undivided attention. However, uninterrupted concentration would not feed the family and so, when he received an invitation to tour Germany in 1911 with Aino Ackté, the leading Finnish soprano of her day, and to compose a new work for her, he decided to accept. He saw

Ackté in November, and for a text his choice alighted on Edgar Allan Poe's *The Raven*. Ackté had hoped for a concert work that she could use as a pendant to the closing scene from *Salome*, a role which she had sung with such success under Beecham at Covent Garden. But, as Tawaststjerna has shown, the longer Sibelius worked on it, the stronger his conviction became that its thematic substance belonged to the Fourth Symphony. The chorale-like figure that occurs during the second group in the finale originally formed part of the song. Moreover the realization soon grew that with earlier commitments looming on the horizon more speedily than he had bargained for, he might have to cancel. He had promised to go to Gothenburg, where at Stenhammar's invitation he was to conduct the Third Symphony and *Pohjola's Daughter* before proceeding on a tour of the Baltic countries. Hence, despite all the advance publicity (or perhaps because of its tone), Ackté had to be disappointed. Sibelius's telegram to Covent Garden, where she was then appearing, produced what one can only call a spirited response! It was a further three years before Sibelius set matters to right with *Luonnotar*. But for all the depression and despondency, and the corresponding periods of elation, the symphony was finally ready two days before its première on 3rd April 1911. Whatever difficulties it may have given Sibelius, it certainly posed them in abundance for its first night audience. Sibelius prefaced the symphony with less taxing fare: *The Dryad*, the *Canzonetta* for strings (drawn from the incidental music to *Kuolema*) and *Night Ride and Sunrise*, which was cheered to the echo. But the new symphony in the second half simply baffled the audience and the mood of the Sibeliuses after the concert was distinctly subdued. It was not only in Helsinki that it bewildered the public; it was denounced as 'ultra modern' in Sweden which was receptive to his art, while in Gothenburg when Stenhammar conducted it in January 1913, it was actually hissed. When it crossed the Atlantic, it scandalized America: Toscanini's response when the work was greeted with derision was to announce an immediate repeat! England was another matter. At its first performance at the Birmingham Festival, where it shared the programme with Elgar's *The Music Makers*, it received a far more sympathetic hearing. Indeed on the strength of the new symphony, a new choral work was commissioned for the following year for the Gloucester Festival. *The Times* wrote that 'it stands apart from the common expression of the time. Yet it is not a self-conscious apartness, and the composer could not have used such a motto, because he lives so much in his own world, thinks his own thoughts, and translates them into sound so spontaneously that he is under no temptation to measure himself against his hearers.' As Sibelius himself said on one occasion, 'there is absolutely nothing of the circus about it'. No work, except perhaps its immediate successor, over which he laboured so long, better illustrates the telling analogy he drew in a diary entry of 1st August 1912 where he compares the course of a symphony to a river. 'It is composed of innumerable tributaries, brooks and streams, and eventually broadens majestically into the sea. It is the movement of the water that determines the shape of the river bed', in short the flow of the musical ideas (the water) shapes the river bed (the formal structure); the ideas are not poured into any preconceived formal mould.

The period immediately after the Fourth Symphony saw him turning to other creative tasks, including the transcription of his early choral suite *Rakastava*, for strings, timpani and triangle, and the revision of the first set of *Scènes historiques* and, later, the composition of a second. From the *Scènes historiques* or the Sonatinas for piano, op. 67, he would earn 3,000 Reischmarks; for the symphony which consumed him from 1909–11, a mere 4,000. The financial worries and other domestic strains made life in Järvenpää increasingly difficult, and he even toyed briefly with the idea of moving house to Paris. In spite of his love for London, Paris was for Sibelius 'the city of cities', and the autumn of 1911 found him making his way there. En route he heard the legendary Emmy Destinn in Berlin. To Carpelan he wrote, 'Must get out of it. Everything is lacking in charm. This evening I am going to Paris. How terribly alone we all are! Alone and misunderstood. And then afterwards, who knows what happens to us?' In the French capital he heard among other things, the Dukas Symphony in C ('a marvellous piece'), and Boieldieu's *La dame blanche*. But he did not make as many contacts as he would have wanted. When he met M. D. Calvocoressi, a close friend of Ravel, it was at Sjögren's flat where he had to endure some of his own songs and lashings of Sjögren ('is it to suffer this sort of thing that one comes to Paris?').

Back at Ainola for Christmas and the New Year, he found a flattering offer of the Chair of Composition at the Imperial Academy of Music in Vienna, which he decided against accepting. The Fourth Symphony continued to make its way outside Finland: Busoni conducted it in Amsterdam with success; Walter Damrosch introduced it to New York and Boston, but even after eight rehearsals confessed his bewilderment, scribbling a note when he returned the score, 'Bless me, if I know what he means'. One critic called it 'cubist', but at least it was performed and overall the press was far from negative. In Vienna Weingartner was forced to abandon it after the Philharmonic Orchestra simply refused to play, and when Sibelius conducted it in Copenhagen in early December, even in the sectional rehearsals he took some of the violins would stop in the middle of a passage (surely in the development section of the first movement) thinking they were lost or had made a mistake. The reviews came in time to spoil his birthday. ('The demons are out in the Copenhagen papers. Am abused in a scurrilous fashion.') However, the year was productive: *The Bard*, a dark, inward-looking tone-poem, whose first performance Sibelius conducted the following year, and *Luonnotar*, the tone-poem for soprano and orchestra he composed for Aino Ackté. This she sang at the Gloucester Festival instead of the new choral work for which they had asked him. Even Ackté who was thrilled by the work found it daunting ('I am frightened that I will not be equal to its demands for it is madly difficult and my otherwise sure sense of pitch may fail me'). But another project was troubling him. He had agreed to meet a commission from the Danish publisher Hansen to write music for *Scaramouche*, a pantomime by Poul Knudsen, thinking that it would not involve the composition of more than a few dance numbers. It soon emerged however that a full-length ballet was involved and that he had bound himself contractually. He felt he had made a terrible blunder and cursed his own stupidity ('Was in such a temper about it today that I smashed the telephone. My nerves are in a terrible state'). In the event the work was not staged for the best part of the decade.

Travel was an important stimulus for Sibelius, and apart from his trip to Copenhagen, he had remained in Finland throughout the year. Much though he loved Ainola, the atmosphere could be claustrophobic, and despite visits from Nielsen, to conduct the Third Symphony, and recitals from Busoni, playing late Beethoven, he missed contacts with the mainstream of music-making and longed to stretch his wings. So far, however, he had not crossed the Atlantic and was at first ill-disposed to do so. When the invitation to make a concert tour in America first came in August 1913, he declined though he accepted a commission for a thousand dollars from Carl Stoeckel for a new orchestral work. In the end an offer from the American composer Horatio Parker of 1,200 dollars to conduct the new work settled matters. 1913 had not been a happy year; apart from his own worries, his brother Christian had been seriously ill.

Early in the new year, Sibelius decided to spend some time in Berlin to listen to new music and to get on with his American commission. In spite of his creative concerns he threw himself into concertgoing with some energy. His reputation was obviously high at this time and he noted that a number of composers were influenced by him. He heard Paul Juon's Violin Concerto, which paid him the highest form of flattery, and a piano concerto by Julius Weissman, which he thought plagiarized him. He heard a fair amount of Mahler, including the Fifth Symphony and

Kindertotenlieder and thought *Das klagende Lied* 'a wonderful piece'; and would seem at this time to have responded positively to Schoenberg's Second Quartet and the *Kammersymphonie* ('a legitimate and valid way of looking at things but painful to listen to it . . . but there is something important there all the same'). He heard the then sixteen-year-old Korngold's *Sinfonietta* ('a young eagle'). On his return home in mid-February he had difficulty in settling down; there were domestic strains, too, but his spirits were raised by academic honours, the Alexander University of Helsinki was to give him an honorary doctorate of philosophy and Parker wrote to say Yale University was to confer on him an honorary doctorate of music while he was in America. Progress on the new commission was slow and it was not until the end of March that he was in a position to entrust the score to the post. At this stage the *Rondo der Wellen*, as *The Oceanides* was at first called, was in three movements and in D flat. The whole score ran to seventy pages but with the perspective of an Atlantic crossing to enrich him, he revised it. With *The Oceanides* the darkness that had consumed his spirits begins to lift. Its orchestral layout, with the liquid sounds from the harp and its delicate string writing, produces an effect which differs from almost any other Sibelius work up to that time but despite its impressionist appearances, it remains deeply Sibelian in its organic evolution.

The American visit was one of the highlights of his career. Never before had he feasted so deeply on the fruits of success and been made so consistently aware of his own celebrity and popularity. (In the 1930s when his fame was at its height in both England and America, he experienced it only at second hand.) In America he was a pampered guest, adoring the luxury with which he was surrounded and exhilarated by the attention lavished upon him. A chance remark dropped by the composer even prompted his host to indulge him to the extent of giving him the attentions of a private barber to carry out his morning shave. The quality of the ad-hoc orchestra Stoeckel had assembled for him at his Festival in Norfolk, Connecticut, drawn from the New York Philharmonic, Metropolitan and Boston Orchestras, surpassed his highest expectations; he thought it superior to anything in Europe. His morale was boosted to such an extent that he planned a return visit. He wrote to his brother, Christian, 'I think that a planned tour of forty or fifty concerts would succeed. Then I could pay off both your debts and my own.' But war clouds were already gathering when he made the crossing home in late July. He was not pleased to discover on his arrival in Malmö that the concert he was to have conducted at the so-called Baltic Festival had been cancelled (and with it his fee of 1,000 Swedish kronor).

4

1914–57

With the outbreak of the war Finland, as a Grand Duchy of the Tsarist Empire, found herself automatically aligned with Britain, France and Russia against Germany. Apart from the obvious privations common to all, there were two other important factors for Sibelius. He was cut off from his source of income, the publisher Breitkopf & Härtel in Leipzig, and secondly, his concert tours and travels outside the Scandinavian countries came to an abrupt end. The stream of piano music and other trivia that poured from his pen during these years was determined by economic necessity rather than inspiration.

The war had presented him with some alarming prospects. The conflict between *real* composing and composing to make a living, always acute in his career, sharpened still further. His natural bent was for the larger symphonic forms but the day-to-day realities of life forced him towards lighter trifles that would make money. There were various plans afoot, none of which he found particularly congenial: a ballet that the dancer Maggie Gripenberg had suggested for London, an operatic venture on *Juha*,[1] in which Aino Ackté was trying to interest him, as well as numerous commissions from choral groups. His financial burdens were again mounting: a diary entry from August 1914 records that he was nearly 90,000 Finnish marks in debt, so that the necessity for him to generate income was more pressing than ever.

The most important work during this period was the Fifth Symphony which was first performed on his fiftieth birthday. From the time of *Finlandia* onwards, Sibelius was probably the best-known living Finn, and many people who would never have become aware of Finland's existence and her national aspirations, did so because of his music. Hence he was a national figure to a much greater extent than Elgar in England or Falla in Spain, and as a result his fiftieth birthday was a national event, as indeed were subsequent major birthdays. The first ideas for the symphony had begun to take shape in his mind in 1912 and in its original form it was

[1]This project was eventually undertaken with conspicuous success by Aarre Merikanto.

in four movements. But it is clear from a study of the sketches[1] that Sibelius was at work on not one but two symphonies, for the basic thematic substance of the Sixth was already beginning to take shape. The stormy D minor theme in the finale as well as the opening flute theme (originally destined for the Second Violin Concerto) are to be found in a sketchblock dating from 1915.[2] Of course, he had constantly to turn aside to the smaller pieces that brought in some income if he was to fight off his creditors. For all his fears, it emerged that he was not completely cut off from his earnings. Late in 1914, *Det Skandinaviska Musikførlaget* in Copenhagen established contact with Breitkopf's Head Office in Leipzig and through their good offices Sibelius continued to receive some royalty payments even though they were much delayed. The route through Copenhagen took time and Sibelius's need of money was always acute, and so he turned to two of the Helsinki publishers – Lindgren and Westerlund – and later on to Wilhelm Hansen in Copenhagen. However, while publishers accepted piano miniatures, a large-scale symphonic work was less practical in wartime circumstances.

The war years proved to be a singularly fallow period. While the years in the wake of his throat operation, say from 1909 to 1914, were creatively rich, when, as Tawaststjerna puts it, 'one key work seemed to unleash the next', from *Voces intimae* to the Fourth Symphony through to *The Bard*, *Luonnotar* and *The Oceanides*, the next period was consumed by only one major piece, the Fifth Symphony. Otherwise there are the Six *Humoresques* for violin and orchestra, opp. 87 and 89, and a quantity of trifles. Not until 1922 do the creative fires burn with their old intensity. The continued isolation of the war and his concern at the inevitable approach of old age brought depression in their wake, and the unremitting struggle between the symphony and 'bread-and-butter' music took its toll. He was conscious of fewer performances of his music, particularly in America. The diary entries record moments of exaltation and elation alongside increasingly darker thoughts. 'Nature is pervaded by a sense of farewell. My heart sings full of melancholy – the shadows lengthen.'

Of course he did not altogether live the life of a recluse or a melancholic; nor did the war bring total isolation. Glazunov paid a visit to Helsinki; Sibelius stumbled across him and Kajanus in the *Kämp* 'huddled over a bottle of champagne', and felt twinges of conscience at missing the performance of his oratorio, *The King of Judea*. Rosa

[1]These are fully discussed by Erik Tawaststjerna in the fourth volume of the Finnish edition of his *Sibelius*, pp. 50 ff.
[2]Reproduced in Tawaststjerna vol. IV between pp. 176-7.

Newmarch and her daughter came unexpectedly to Helsinki *en route* to Petrograd, and after much persuasion from Stenhammar (he had previously declined because he had no new symphony ready), Sibelius went to Gothenburg to conduct the orchestra, relishing the journey and enjoying dinner with Armas Järnefelt at his favourite restaurant in Stockholm, *Operakällaren* (The Opera Cellar). He had also written to Busoni on Stenhammar's behalf testifying to the excellence of the orchestra in the hope of luring the great pianist to Sweden for a guest appearance. His birthday celebrations later in the year were extensive, with concerts from Kajanus and Schnéevoigt, and the publication of a book by Erik Furuhjelm. Two issues of the *Tidning för Musik* were devoted to him, and the Fifth Symphony in its four-movement form was given its première under his baton. Listening to the 1915 version of the symphony is rather like experiencing *Hamlet* in a dream. There are some familiar signposts and fragments of the familiar lines, but in the wrong places and spoken by strange voices: the image is somehow blurred and confused.

Not long after the first performance of the Fifth Symphony in 1915, Armas Järnefelt, then conductor of the *Hovkapellet* wrote inviting Sibelius to Stockholm to conduct the new work. Having been the victim of the scurrilous pen of the puffed-up Petersson-Berger, Sibelius demurred. 'This Stockholm philistinism in musical matters!! Their Swedish insularity – their blinkered view of everything that is not homegrown. It amazes me that Armas can put up with them. All the same there is Stenhammar – a golden apple in that Sodom.' Well might he hail Stenhammar, who had been his most loyal and faithful lancebearer and one of the first to grasp his real stature. Indeed, apart from the dedication of the Fourth Quartet, Stenhammer had earlier paid him the ultimate compliment of withdrawing his own First Symphony, ('idyllic Bruckner', he once called it) not long after its Stockholm première, as he had been so bowled over by Sibelius's Second Symphony. Sibelius was always full of admiration for his nobility, vision and artistry – and rightly so! And Stenhammar spoke of the Finnish master with awe. 'Of all living composers there is none that in my view can equal Sibelius' (*Dagens Nyheter*, 28.2.1909).[1] But his impatience with and distaste for Petersson-Berger was at least a factor in his decision not to go to Stockholm though, more seriously, he was troubled at the time by problems with his hearing. Much of 1916 was spent on composing smaller pieces; he had managed to reduce his debts slightly but his finances still worried him. He attended

[1]Bo Wallner, *Wilhelm Stenhammar och han tid*, vol II (Stockholm, 1991), p. 583.

fewer concerts though he did go to the première of his former pupil, Leevi Madetoja's First Symphony; his own music was being widely played at this period both home and abroad. He spent the autumn reworking the Fifth Symphony, completed in time for his fifty-first birthday which he celebrated by attending a performance of the new work in Åbo. He conducted it himself a few days later in Helsinki with the Third Symphony and the suite from *Pelléas et Mélisande*.

Naturally, the Finns were watching the declining fortunes of Imperial Russia with some measure of relief. Sibelius would follow with displeasure setbacks on the part of the Central Powers. He and his circle had welcomed opponents of the Tsarist régime, Gorky among others, to their circle before the war and naturally embraced the enemies of their enemy. In a move to win friends in the Allied camp, Kajanus came to see him at the end of January 1917 with a plan to take the orchestra to Paris and London with a programme of new works by Madetoja, Palmgren and the new Sibelius symphony – as well as his own newly-composed *Sinfonietta*. Sibelius was not wholly enamoured of the idea, which in the event came to nothing, but his low spirits were lifted by news that he had been given honorary membership of the *Accademia di Santa Cecilia* in Rome. (Toscanini had played *En Saga, Finlandia* and *The Swan of Tuonela* there the previous year.) His bouts of depression prompted him to forego his long abstinence and resume drinking. This together with his financial worries, fears of neglect and the approach of old age, imposed domestic strains and the atmosphere at Ainola was often dark. Aino left him to go to Petrograd early in 1917 where their daughter Eva was now living with her husband. Not long after her return came the news of the February Revolution and the return of political prisoners, among them P. E. Svinhufvud who was soon to become Head of State. It was a time of upheaval and unrest; the Russian soldiers and sailors stationed in Helsinki mutinied and murdered their officers. Kerensky offered the Finns a degree of autonomy that fell short of self-government but on a visit to Helsinki in May urged caution and restraint both on his own forces there and the Finns themselves. Only a few weeks later, Sibelius returned from a visit to Helsinki shocked by the lawless atmosphere; Russian soldiers and Finnish socialists were demonstrating and the prospect of increasing unemployment, inflation and even civil war loomed. After the October Revolution of 1917, the Finns were quick to proclaim their independence (on 6 December), which Lenin's Government recognized at the turn of the year. Recognition came from Germany and France, though England and America held their hand. The long-feared civil war broke out between the new bourgeois-dominated government and the forces of the Left, who at the end of January attempted a *coup d'état*. The four largest cities in the south, Helsinki, Åbo, Tampere and Viipuri, were controlled by the Reds; the Whites under the command of General Mannerheim launched a counter offensive to disarm the Russian garrisons in Ostrobothnia. Sibelius himself was in some personal danger since his sympathies were known to be with the White forces. He had only a few days earlier completed a patriotic march for the *Jägar* Batallion, a corps that had been trained in Germany against the day when they could raise their banner against the Russian forces in Finland. While the Red Guards obtained weapons and support from Petrograd, the Whites were supplied by the Germans. There was widespread unrest and random shootings and even Järvenpää, which was in rebel hands, was unsafe. At one point the Red Guards, albeit not from the locality, searched Ainola 'for arms', and behaved threateningly. The area was under curfew and Sibelius and the neighbouring Järnefelts were cut off, not only from the outside world but each other. Fearing for their safety, Kajanus went to the Red Minister of Defence in Helsinki who, given the fact that the situation was getting out of control, gave him an authorization to the local commander to arrange a special guard for Ainola, or better still, bring Sibelius and his family into Helsinki. After some persuasion, they left with Kajanus on five horse-drawn sleighs for the capital. Here Sibelius and his family lived in the relative safety of the Lapinlahti Hospital where his brother worked. Food was short and during the three months he lived in Helsinki, first with Christian and then in a hotel, Sibelius lost some 20 kilos. One of the provisions of the treaty of Brest-Litovsk was Russian withdrawal from Finland, and German forces were deployed during the spring to that end. By May, the civil war was over and Mannerheim led his forces back into Helsinki, though he was soon to resign in protest at the German domination of the Finnish forces.

In all the war cost some 10,000 lives and brought hunger and disease in its train. The rebel leaders fled to the Soviet Union and a new government was formed with Paasikivi, a younger school friend of Sibelius as its Prime Minister. Throughout these terrible months Sibelius continued to work, insofar as he could, and the conflict between the bread-and-butter output and his real work did not abate: he wrote to Carpelan at the end of June (prematurely, as it turned out) that he had finished the Fifth Symphony and earlier in the year a diary entry records that he was engrossed by his work on the first movement of the Sixth Symphony. Naturally he was grieved by what was going on around him, and also by the death of friends and acquaintances: the composer Toivo Kuula, who with Madetoja and Bengt de Törne had been one of his few pupils, died still in his mid-thirties and, above all, Axel Carpelan. It had been obvious throughout the year that Carpelan's condition was deteriorating but his death in the spring of 1919 came as a terrible blow. Sibelius's sister, Linda, had been committed to an asylum; he was drinking immoderately, with the inevitable domestic strain.

In the immediate post-war years, lighter miniatures continued to pour from his pen: he had always longed to write another *Valse triste* and, more to the point, reap its full commercial harvest. German post-war hyperinflation naturally wrought havoc with his royalties and it was not until the performing rights agreement came into force internationally in the 1920s that his financial security was assured. The Fifth Symphony with which he wrestled so long was at last complete, and the Sixth and Seventh forming in his mind. Breitkopf & Härtel had been fearful that he would abandon them for Hansen, but when he told them he would have to ask 25,000 Finnish marks for the new symphony, they declined it without making a counter offer. Hansen eventually published all three pieces.

In the summer of 1920 came an overture from America that attracted him. This was an invitation to be the Director of the newly-founded and handsomely endowed Eastman School of Music at Rochester, New York. Alf Klingenberg, an old friend from his student days in Berlin, visited Ainola to make soundings and Armas Järnefelt urged him not to dismiss the idea out-of-hand but to ask for $20,000. Indeed George Eastman offered him that sum for the first academic year. Among his duties would be to conduct five concerts, though the terms of his contract would preclude him conducting anywhere else during that period. Sibelius did, at first, accept and asked for an immediate advance of $10,000 so as to compose new works for the projected concerts and time to improve his English. Even this was agreed though the money was deposited in an American account. One of the factors that decided him to decline was his natural reluctance, late in his working life, to uproot himself to a country which, however stimulating, was alien to his culture and whose language he did not command. Moreover, the family would have had misgivings about the problems his propensity for drink would have posed both in the exercise of his administrative and, above all, social obligations. Of course these fears may have been exaggerated: all sorts of things are acceptable from great men that would be inadmissable in others. Moreover such embarrassments would have been more than outweighed by the possibility of a new and probably long career in the New World as a conductor. Though it lies in the realm of speculation, contact with the great American orchestras may well have proved the very stimulus he needed.

Apart from an invitation to the Nordic Music Festival in Copenhagen, he had not left Finland since the civil war, and so he eagerly grasped the opportunity to visit England in 1921 to conduct the Fifth Symphony. Sibelius's reluctance to talk about his music posed problems for Mrs Newmarch, who was busily preparing programme notes ('Even Henry Wood [who was to take the preliminary rehearsals before Sibelius's arrival] has asked me to write to you for the score, for, as you know, one can't learn your music at the last minute as if it was a Haydn symphony'). He set out for Stockholm and then Berlin at the end of January, arriving in London in February. (He was delighted that the immigration officer knew who he was!) Some seven years had elapsed since the Fourth Symphony's première in Birmingham and a younger generation had yet to make its acquaintance. Henry Wood's performance at the Queen's Hall in March 1920 had not been a success but the new symphony was received with enthusiasm. Wood had done the preparatory work with the Queen's Hall Orchestra well and Sibelius was delighted. He was recalled to the podium five times. After the concert he spent a couple of days at Oxford, whose beauty delighted him, and dined at New College with Sir Hugh Allen. Then came what was to be his last encounter with Busoni, already showing signs of the illness that was to claim him three years later (he played a Mozart concerto and his own *Indian Fantasy*, while Sibelius conducted the Fourth Symphony). In his memoirs Sir Henry Wood describes the headache their joint visit gave him:

I could generally manage Busoni when I had him to myself, but my heart was always in my mouth if he met Sibelius. I never knew where they would get to. They would forget the time of the concert at which they were to appear; they hardly knew the day of the week. One year I was directing the Birmingham Festival and had to commission a friend never to let these two out of his sight. He had quite an exciting time for two or three days following them about from restaurant to restaurant. He told me he never knew what time they went to bed or got up in the morning. They were like a couple of irresponsible schoolboys.[1]

One eyewitness of a concert Sibelius gave in Birmingham in 1921, Arthur Rankin, wrote:

His features were not at all forbidding; but I had the perhaps mistaken impression that he was rather tall. More reliable is my recollection of a certain youthful alertness and grace of movement . . . In conducting

[1]My Life of Music (London, 1938), pp. 141-2.

Sibelius's movements were restrained but incisive; and it was my impression, for what it was worth, that he readily obtained from the players the effects he wanted.[1]

Already on his arrival in England, Mrs Newmarch had advised Sibelius against accepting the invitation to the Eastman; his *métier* was not teaching, however light the duties, but composing – 'Au diable les dollars!' And to be frank, the thought of teaching in a foreign tongue rather terrified him. The post eventually went to a very young composer, Howard Hanson, who remained there until the 1960s. Back in London Sir Henry entertained him to dinner at Pagiani's where on a neighbouring table sat the critic Edward Evans with his protégé the pianist Harriet Cohen, then still in her mid-twenties and of striking appearance. It was for her that Arnold Bax had abandoned his family. She and Sibelius were to spend some time together, both on this visit and during a subsequent liaison that raised Mrs Newmarch's eyebrows and occasioned displeasure at Ainola, where she was never received.

When in the autumn of 1922 Stenhammar visited Helsinki to play his Second Concerto with Kajanus, Sibelius took him on one side and asked if he might dedicate his Sixth Symphony to him, which he had completed earlier in the year.[2] The following March he presented both the new work and his Fifth Symphony in Gothenburg. He arrived five days before the concert but for all that there was insufficient time to prepare them and *Pohjola's Daughter*. Not long before the concert was due to begin, he alarmed his hosts for he was nowhere to be found. A search of the local hostelries was mounted: he was discovered eating oysters and drinking champagne and, according to Aino's recollections,[3] seemed uncertain whether it was a rehearsal or concert. After the concert, surrounded by his Swedish friends, he appeared withdrawn and confused, and fumbling in his pocket, smashed on to the steps the bottle of cognac he had been carrying. When the time came in March 1924 for him to revisit Sweden to conduct the first performance of the Seventh Symphony in Stockholm, Aino refused to accompany him. Not only had his behaviour at the concert itself disturbed her but she also recalled that he had to be woken up to hear the speech given in his honour by Stenhammar's successor, the Swedish composer, Ture Rangström.

Oddly enough the new symphony which Sibelius took with him to

---

[1]From a long and thought-provoking critique he sent me on the first publication of this volume.
[2]When the score was published, the dedicatory page was mislaid, so that this fact is not widely known (Wallner, op. cit., vol II, p. 568).
[3]Tawaststjerna, *Sibelius*, vol. V (Helsinki, 1988).

Stockholm in 1924 was not so called at its first performance when it was billed as *Fantasia sinfonica*. Yet no work could be more symphonic or organic. In its control of contrasting tempos, the Seventh Symphony is as breathtaking as is the imaginative resource on which he draws in *Tapiola* the following year. We know now that 'the Hellenic rondo' to which Sibelius referred in his oft-quoted letter to Carpelan in 1918 was of even earlier provenance. Ideas for it are to be found as far back as 1914–15 among the sketches for the Fifth and Sixth symphonies. At the beginning of the 1920s he had sketched out a work clearly divided into four movements, but only during the summer of 1923 did it begin to take shape in the form we now know it. Apart from his travels and his work on the symphonies, Sibelius still composed prolifically in smaller forms. A vast quantity of miniatures flowed from his pen; the *Valse lyrique*, *Valse chevaleresque*, the *Suite mignonne*, the *Suite champêtre*, and the sets of piano miniatures, opp. 94, 97 and 99, all date from the immediate post-war years. Some of these orchestral pieces were included in the concert he gave on 19th February 1923 when his Sixth Symphony was presented to the Helsinki public for the first time. Immediately after this he proceeded to Italy, where he conducted his Second Symphony in Rome. (A little later in the decade there was some mild ill-feeling in Finland that the Seventh Symphony and *Tapiola* were widely heard in America and took so long to reach the Finnish musical public.)

His last two major works were both the product of commissions: in 1925 the Royal Theatre, Copenhagen, wrote to him announcing their plans for a lavish production of *The Tempest* to be mounted on 26th March 1926. Work on this occupied him for much of the year. In December he celebrated his sixtieth birthday, and tributes, gifts and telegrams were showered on him in even greater profusion than before. The government increased his pension; his Danish publisher Wilhelm Hansen gave him a substantial sum of money; and he received the proceeds of a nation-wide fund launched to pay him tribute and totalling 150,000 Finnish marks. Early in the new year came a letter from the conductor Walter Damrosch asking whether Sibelius would be willing to write a tone poem for the New York Philharmonic Society for $400, to be ready by November. It is an irony that so cold and terrifying a score as *Tapiola* was conceived in the warmth of a Roman spring. Yet in fact we are fortunate that it did not follow the Eighth Symphony into oblivion. The acute self-criticism that was so positive a force in the development of the Fifth Symphony was now becoming an inhibiting factor. His diary records, 'Have suffered because of *Tapiola* . . . it was unfortunate that I accepted this "commission", *The Tempest* and *Väinön virsi* [the cantata,

1 Sibelius's birthplace in Hämeenlinna

3 Sibelius at thirty

2 (*left*) Sibelius as a boy of eleven

5 Sibelius at the time of the Fourth Symphony

4 (*left*) 'Ainola', Sibelius's villa at Järvenpää

6 Sibelius in 1954 (*photo: Bertil Dahlgren*)

7 (*right*) Sibelius walking near his home

8 Autograph page from the first movement of the *Kullervo* Symphony
(courtesy of Helsinki University Library)

Väinämöinen's Song]. Was I really cut out for this sort of thing? Going downhill. Can't be alone. Drinking whisky. Physically not strong enough for all this.' He had delivered the score in late August but was immediately panic-stricken, and in mid-September demanded that Breitkopf return the manuscript for 'extensive deletions'. Fortunately the score and most of the orchestral material were already engraved and by the time the manuscript and proofs were returned, Sibelius had to leave for Copenhagen to conduct a performance of the Fifth Symphony. And on his return and in a more positive frame of mind he confined himself to minor changes.

For more than thirty years after the completion of his four last great works, the Sixth and Seventh symphonies, *The Tempest* music and *Tapiola*, Sibelius lived in retirement at Järvenpää where he maintained a virtually unbroken silence. Although rumours of another symphony persisted for many years, and its publication was promised after his death, nothing survives apart from the sketch of the first three bars. In 1924, the year in which the Seventh was first performed, Sibelius spoke to Schnéevoigt about an Eighth, and from Schnéevoigt's letter of May 1924, one can conclude that he offered him the dedication and was thinking in terms of a large-scale multi-movement work. Sibelius himself first mentioned it in a letter to Stenhammar's sister-in-law Olga Bratt in 1926 and the following year he told the American critic, Olin Downes whom he had met in Norfolk, Connecticut, in 1914 that two movements were already written down and that he had the ending in his head. His stay in Paris, to which he repaired early in 1927 to hear new music, did not lift his spirits, and he later went on to Berlin where he had worked so well before the war, but now to little effect. On the authority of the manager of the Boston orchestra Downes asked whether he would be interested in an American tour in the 1927–28 season but Sibelius declined, 'Completely occupied with new works'. The next approach came from Koussevitzky himself.

Like Kajanus and Beecham, Koussevitzky was to become closely identified in the public mind with Sibelius. Yet he was a relatively late convert to his cause. In the first decade of the century, he had been a frequent visitor to the Ushkov Estate at Villa Syväranta (near Halosenniemi) in Finland. Ushkov was his father-in-law and Syväranta the home of Chaliapin's sister-in-law. Apart from the great singer, Rakhmaninov was also a frequent guest there. Koussevitzky even made an abortive attempt to visit Sibelius at Ainola, nearby, though it was not until the late 1920s that he took to Sibelius's music. He did not actually conduct any Sibelius until 1916 (probably the First Symphony), though he would surely have heard quite a lot. (His friend Alexander Siloti conducted the Third Symphony and *Night Ride and Sunrise* in St Petersburg in the first decade of the century.) But it was not until 1926, two years after he had come to Boston in succession to Karl Muck and Pierre Monteux, that he returned to Sibelius. That same year Stokowski had conducted the Seventh Symphony in Philadelphia, Frederick Stock had given it in Chicago and Koussevitzky introduced it to Boston. It seems to have kindled his enthusiasm for the composer, for in 1928 he gave the Third Symphony to great acclaim ('Music far in advance of its time in 1907'). It was then that he wrote to the composer to ask if there was a new symphony, and for the next few months they corresponded frequently.[1] Sibelius promised him the Eighth (as indeed he did Beecham) to crown the complete cycles of the symphonies he gave. In 1931 Sibelius went to Berlin to bury himself in the isolation of a big city and to continue work on the new symphony. He remained there for some weeks, writing to Aino in May, 'Here I am living in my music. Am so caught up in my work – but anxiety about everything makes me so miserable just now ... The symphony is making great progress. And I must get it finished while I still have all my mental strength.' He refers later in the same letter to the fact that his hand is shaking less now. 'But anxiety makes it difficult for me to write again.'[2] Later that summer in responding to a letter from Koussevitzky concerning some interpretative queries about the Fourth Symphony, Sibelius went so far as to add, 'If you wish to perform my new symphony next spring, this will, I hope, be possible.' But, alas, this was not to be. In January 1932 Sibelius cabled a postponement and suggested October, though yet again it was not ready. Koussevitzky was not the only conductor to express an interest in the symphony and, encouraged by Cecil Gray who had visited Sibelius in 1929 in connection with his book,[3] Basil Cameron wrote asking him if he could schedule the new work in a Royal Philharmonic Society concert at the end of 1932. Further evidence that work on the Eighth Symphony was continuing and that it was nearing completion comes in the form of a note, written in September 1933, to his regular copyist to whom he had sent the first fascicle of 23 pages of the orchestral score. From this it is possible to conclude that these pages constituted the first movement and were to be succeeded by a

[1] Their letters are reproduced in Erik Tawaststjerna's articles, 'The Mystery of Sibelius's Eighth Symphony', *Finnish Musical Quarterly*, (1985), pp. 61–71 and 92–102.
[2] In earlier editions of this monograph, I suggested that this nervous tremor may have been an inhibiting factor during his later years, making the act of writing a laborious process. However Jussi Jalas has put on record the fact that he was able to wield a pen into his advanced old age providing that he was not in too great a state of agitation.
[3] Cecil Gray, *Sibelius* (Oxford, 1931).

Largo. In all, Sibelius calculated that in its finished form the binding should allow for eight such fascicles, so that the work would be roughly of the same dimensions as the Second Symphony. Both Aino and Margareta Jalas visited the copyist to collect or deliver manuscripts during this period, so that it would seem that the symphony, if not complete, was at an advanced stage. Some years after his death, the composer Joonas Kokkonen asked Aino whether some of the material of the symphony could have been used in the *Surusoitto* (Funeral Music) for organ, op. 111, that Sibelius had provided at very short notice for Axel Gallén-Kallela, which she thought highly plausible.[1]

Sibelius was enjoying enormous exposure in America. During a single week in November, New York heard Stokowski conduct the Fourth Symphony, Koussevitzky and Rodzinski conduct the First, Toscanini conduct *En Saga* while Klemperer conducted the Second and Seventh symphonies and Bruno Walter the Seventh and *The Swan of Tuonela*. But by the 1930s, the gramophone was becoming the crucial medium in the dissemination of his music. In 1930 the Finnish Government subsidized the first commercial recordings of the symphonies: Kajanus recorded nos. 1 and 2 in London together with two movements from *Karelia*, and went on to record nos. 3 and 5, *Pohjola's Daughter* and *Tapiola* two years later for Walter Legge's HMV Sibelius Society. Their prospectus also promised an early recording of the Eighth Symphony though they first took advantage of Koussevitzky's visit to London in May 1933 to record the Seventh Symphony, then barely a decade old. This was made during his guest appearances with the then newly-formed BBC Symphony Orchestra and it remains arguably the most highly charged and electrifying performance ever committed to disc. It has extraordinary intensity and concentration, though he was not wholly satisfied: 'some of it is good but some details and phrasings are not as clear as they should be'. He had, incidentally added a trumpet at the very end to strengthen the strings. Sibelius himself was overjoyed by the records: 'everything was so full of life and natural and I cannot thank you sufficiently'. (Koussevitzky went on to record a number of Sibelius works in the 1930s. First, the Second Symphony in 1935 – he recorded it a second time in 1950 – and in the following year, *Pohjola's Daughter*, the Fifth Symphony, which appeared with a movement *Tärnorna med rosor* (The maidens with roses) from *Swanwhite*, and finally, a breathtaking *Tapiola*.) In addition to Koussevitzky's Sibelius cycles in Boston, there was a Beecham cycle in

---

[1]Although it sounds unsymphonic, the fact remains that were one to transcribe say, the string threnody (10 bars after letter A) in the Seventh Symphony for the organ, it would give scant notion of the original.

London. An inquiry among listeners to the New York Philharmonic Society's broadcasts in 1935 revealed that he outstripped any other composer in popularity.

The image of the Nordic titan with the skull of granite, fostered during the last years of his life, does less than justice to the truth. His was a complex and many faceted personality: on the one side was the artist who subjected his work to the most searching self-criticism and was plagued with self-doubts, even though he was aware of his own genius. He was a compound of arrogance, vanity and pride one moment, yet totally vulnerable to slights, imagined or otherwise. He readily plummeted into bouts of deep depression and self-questioning. In these dark moments he entertained fears for his own equilibrium, and with the war years and his increasing alienation from the music of his contemporaries, his depression only gathered force.

What lies behind the failure of his creative nerve in this instance, and the drying-up of his inspiration is naturally a matter for speculation. It is probably due to a complex of factors: a growing sense of isolation in a world that was becoming increasingly alien; the cult of Sibelius in the Anglo-Saxon world where he was hailed as a symphonist of the order of Brahms and second only to Beethoven, while in Germany he was grossly neglected; all these must have been inhibiting factors. Given the achievement of the Seventh Symphony and *Tapiola*, it is obvious that his standards and artistic sights were higher than ever, and to reach them or surpass them would be more difficult. Just as he had striven not to write one note too many, and not to continue when there was no more to be said, he may well now have felt that this precept by which he had lived, must apply to his lifework: that what he had composed in the Eighth Symphony did not materially extend the vision of the Seventh and *Tapiola*.

Sibelius's life during these last years was uneventful. Despite press rumours that he was accompanying the Finnish Orchestra on their visit to London in 1934, and subsequently that he would attend the six concerts of his music also given there in January 1938, he remained at home. He conducted a broadcast of his *Andante festivo* for a short-wave programme beamed to the New York Fair in January 1939, but that again was a special exception to his retirement. In 1939 Europe was again plunged into war, though Finland was not at first involved. In November, however, the Soviet Union, having seized the Baltic states, launched an attack on Finland. Sibelius received more than a hundred offers of refuge abroad, but declined them all; wild rumours circulated, one of them claiming that he had been killed in an air raid. He made a radio appeal for

American help on 30th November, and a stamp with his head and the words 'I need your help' was released in America to raise funds for the Finnish cause. The cruel war ground on to its bitter and inevitable end, and the Finns signed the instrument of peace early the following year, ceding the Karelian Isthmus and other territory in the north. With the Nazi attack on Russia in 1941, Finland took the opportunity of retrieving her losses in territory, but instead of stopping at the 1939 frontier foolishly involved herself in a full-scale punitive attack on Russia proper. When the German invaders were thrown back in 1944 and a separate peace was sought, their German allies exacted a bitter and ruthless vengeance on the Finnish populace.

Even so he continued to compose. The American Paul Sjöblom, a retired Associated Press representative in Helsinki whose father had met Sibelius during his visit to Connecticut in 1914, recalled a conversation with Armas Järnefelt in the 1940s. Apart from his villa in Järvenpää, Sibelius kept an apartment in Helsinki in which there was a cupboard containing a large choral and orchestral work – a bulky score – which Järnefelt had seen, and many other works too. So Sibelius continued to work long after *Tapiola* and the Eighth Symphony. Like the Eighth, this choral piece based on a biblical text was presumably put to the flames in the early 1950s.

The privations of the war years left their mark on Finland. In early April 1945 *The Times* carried reports that Sibelius was in need, and the question of help was mooted. Though the reports were denied, public reaction both in England and America gave an idea of the firm hold he enjoyed on public affection. Few great composers have received such recognition and inspired such devotion in their own lifetime. On the occasion of his eighty-fifth birthday the President of Finland even motored out to Järvenpää to pay the nation's respects; while on his ninetieth in 1955 he received no fewer than 1,200 telegrams, presents from all the Scandinavian monarchs, specially recorded tapes from Toscanini, cigars from Sir Winston Churchill, and, as usual on his birthday, special arrangements had to be made to cope with the volume of parcels and mail. President Passikivi broadcast a birthday message, special radio programmes were arranged all over Scandinavia, while the ninetieth birthday concert given in London by Sir Thomas Beecham was relayed to Finland on an especially powerful signal so that the composer could hear it at Ainola. Even before this, the conservatoire he had attended had been renamed after him, a Sibelius Museum was set up at Turku (Åbo), an annual Sibelius Festival was instituted, as well as a Sibelius Prize whose recipients included Stravinsky, Shostakovich and

Hindemith. More than fifty streets have been named after him (including one in so improbable a place as Jamaica), and there are several parks also bearing his name.

In spite of this Sibelius's last years were for the most part quiet. Constant disturbance by tourists caused him to retire more firmly into his shell. His correspondence had for many years become so voluminous that he had to engage a secretary, but visitors were rarely permitted. The family itself was a large one – five daughters, fifteen grandchildren and twenty-one great-grandchildren – so that even they had to exercise restraint if Sibelius and his wife were to have any peace. The very necessary measures he took in self-protection against troublesome visitors earned him the reputation of aloofness and pride, though all who met him have testified to the contrary. There was a complete absence of haughty reserve; his personality was spontaneous, warm and immediate.

Though Sibelius had not always enjoyed perfect health (indeed at the time of his marriage he was so delicate that Aino was often warned that she would be nursing an invalid for the rest of her life), he was for the most part untroubled by serious physical ailments, and certainly enjoyed a robust constitution. He was well right up to the very end of his life. Death came on 20th September 1957. He had been normal and active earlier in the day, and read the morning papers as usual. However, after lunch he collapsed with cerebral haemorrhage: he was fully conscious until about four in the afternoon and recognized members of the family who gathered round him. He died during the evening while in Helsinki the orchestra under Sir Malcolm Sargent was playing his Fifth Symphony. The State funeral took place ten days later in the *Storkyrkan*; the slow movement of the Fourth Symphony, *In Memoriam* and *The Swan* were among the music played. Wreaths were laid by the President, and Aino and other close relatives, and the funeral oration was given by Kilpinen. He was laid to rest in the grounds of his villa at Järvenpää, where he had lived for more than fifty years.

Sibelius's personality was obviously far from uncomplex. There is no doubt that he possessed a warm and impulsive nature; he was instinctive in feeling and generous in spirit. Greatness attracts the malice of the mediocre, and since his death there have been the inevitable attempts 'to cut him down to size' both as man and artist. Many things about Sibelius were larger than life but he was far from physically outsize. The unsmiling Nordic giant with features of granite that we imagine from some of the formal photographic studies is a myth. A glance at a photograph taken in 1919 at the Nordic Music Festival in Copenhagen[1] shows him to be both

---

[1] *See* Harold Johnson, *Jean Sibelius* (New York, 1959), facing page 145.

smaller in stature and build than either Stenhammar or Halvorsen, and not much taller than Nielsen. There is no denying the enormous power of his features, which are often firm-set and forbidding, but Sibelius rarely felt at ease before the photographer's lens and rarely relaxed his guard. Yet for all his shyness and reserve, there was a considerable streak of vanity and pride in his physical appearance. Even when he was very young, this did not escape the attention of his elders, and throughout his life he was highly conscious of his image, both as a person and a composer. Despite his innate reticence, he was not unhappy to be the centre of attention; indeed in later life he would not like Aino to occupy the stage for too long. Sibelius's life-style imposed some strains on their relationship during the sixty-five years of their marriage. Acute self-doubt was offset by a sense of his own genius: this is already evident at the time of the *Kullervo* Symphony, when he had begun to sense the extent of his powers. His upbringing had been in relatively modest circumstances, and perhaps the grand style in which he lived from his university days onwards was a reaction to this. To have lived as he did in sybaritic fashion while heavily in debt for a period of almost three decades calls for strong nerves and great confidence. His appetite for drink, his extravagance and his generosity were all characteristic of his father. Yet such was Sibelius's national significance by the turn of the century that Carpelan had no difficulty in raising funds to keep him afloat. But money no sooner raised, ran through his fingers, for it never occured to him to buy inexpensive tickets at the opera, or order any but the best food and wine. These habits were no doubt acquired in his university years and the early 1890s, when the famous 'Symposium' evenings took place. Sibelius, Kajanus, the painter Gallén-Kallela, and one or two friends used to meet for long discussions stimulated by quantities of wine. A portrait of Sibelius looking rather the worse for wear won these evenings some notoriety at the time. But for all his extravagance and his heavy borrowing, it is worth noting that every loan was repaid.

His love of the classics and his insatiable appetite for reading were childhood passions that never left him. The extent and variety of his literary interests are evident from the large and impressive library at Ainola. The poetry of his native Swedish remained an enduring love, but he was more fortunate than many Swedish-speaking Finns of his class in receiving instruction in a Finnish-speaking school. This gave him access to the world of the *Kalevala* in its original form, which was a source of inspiration throughout his creative life. Naturally for many years he spoke Swedish better than Finnish, though he was remarkably sensitive to the musical inflexions of the Finnish tongue. With his children he spoke

Swedish for the most part, though in later life seems to have preferred Finnish.[1]

Although it was rarely touched upon, his neglect in Germany where the foundations of his international career had been laid early in the century, cast its shadow. For him Germany had been the centre of the musical world; but, whereas in England and America his cause enjoyed the advocacy of great conductors such as Koussevitzky (a late convert, incidentally) and Beecham as well as influential figures like Newman, Gray, Lambert and Olin Downes, he lacked champions in Germany. Furtwängler and Klemperer occasionally conducted his work but the German musical climate was by no means outgoing, and even in the post-war era his music inspired the venom of such figures as Adorno. Though he might well have interpreted the latter as a tribute, his neglect in Germany must have been a sensitive matter.

Whatever his sympathies, Sibelius maintained a lively interest in contemporary music. He always seemed to find something kindly to say to younger composers in need of encouragement, and his patience in this matter emerges in Bengt de Törne's portrait of him.[2] Among younger contemporaries, Bartók greatly excited his admiration and he spoke highly of many English composers of the older generation including Bax, who, like Vaughan Williams, dedicated his fifth symphony to him. He also spoke appreciatively of Britten's *Peter Grimes* and seems to have maintained a healthy curiosity about new developments in new music until his last years. The reason for the long 'silence from Järvenpää' lies in a complex of reasons: first and foremost, a heightened sense of self-criticism which eventually resulted in the destruction of the Eighth Symphony, and a growing sense of alienation from the musical world of his day. Moreover, the claims made by Cecil Gray, Constant Lambert and Olin Downes cannot have made his task easier. It is, of course, difficult to foresee the path he would have taken after *Tapiola*, though it would be no less difficult to imagine the Fifth Symphony after the Fourth, or the Seventh after the Sixth. Sibelius's creative evolution is as mysterious and unpredictable as it is individual.

---

[1]According to Mrs Lauri Kirves, the composer's grand-daughter, Sibelius mostly spoke Finnish with the grandchildren, though in moments of excitement he would revert to Swedish.
[2]Bengt de Törne, *Sibelius – A Close-up* (London, 1937).

5

The symphonies – 1

Sibelius's earliest compositions were all instrumental, and it was not until the early nineties that he turned to the orchestra. His first orchestral piece was an overture produced during his student days in Vienna, and once launched on the medium he rapidly developed an unfailing ear for idiomatic and individual orchestral sonorities. But with each successive step – the *Kullervo* symphony, *En Saga*, the *Karelia* music and the *Four Legends* – came a heightened awareness of colour and a growing mastery of orchestral resource. Even in the *Kullervo* symphony, his first large-scale work, written only a year or so after the overture, we find a vivid orchestral imagination; and only a few years were to pass before the assurance he showed in handling the medium ripened into genius.

But it is not merely the astonishing growth of his orchestral instincts that marks his development during the nineties. Comparison of the first movement of *Kullervo* with that of the First Symphony will show what enormous strides Sibelius had made as a symphonic thinker during the seven years that separate the two works. He was thirty-three by the time he came to write the First Symphony and spoke as a mature, creative personality with an impressive list of works behind him. While he does not satisfy all the demands made by a symphony, the first movement comes nearer to perfection than any of his other works up to that time with the exception of *The Swan*. It is in fact a *tour de force* of organic symphonic thinking. The thematic material is more carefully tailored for symphonic treatment than the magnificent but essentially lyrical idea which throbs and surges through the corresponding movement of *Kullervo*. It is true that the earlier work shows an amazingly secure handling of a large-scale design,[1] but it appears sprawling if put alongside the masterly economy of the First Symphony.

In a first-class analysis Gerald Abraham shows how organic this music is[2] and has traced the derivation of the opening motive of the second group, which sparkles away icily to the accompaniment of *tremolando*

[1]The *Kullervo* symphony is more fully discussed in chapter 12.
[2]*Sibelius, a Symposium* (London, 1946), p. 15ff.

strings and harp, back to the dark, sombre clarinet theme which opens the work:

Ex. 1a

Ex. 1b

This is only one of the many examples of the underlying unity of the thematic material. It is an organic process of which Sibelius was almost certainly not conscious. Nils-Eric Ringbom[1] relates a far more obvious similarity between two passages in two different movements of the Fifth Symphony which Sibelius himself declared to be 'pure coincidence'.

In this first movement we find the full-blooded rhetoric of romanticism wedded to a directness of utterance and economy of design that are truly classical. One could cite as an example of this superb craftsmanship the way in which the confident and assertive climax of the first group flows so swiftly and unobtrusively into the second. While in so many Romantic first symphonies the seams and joins in the structure are clearly visible, this transition is astonishingly smooth and accomplished. This first element of the second group (ex. 1b) later becomes the accompaniment to a second and more important motive (ex. 2), so that at the reprise Sibelius is able to telescope it all together. This second element also gives rise to some of the most powerful and compact writing in the development:

Ex. 2

[1]*Sibelius* (Oklahoma, 1954), p. 138.

Sibelius's mastery of transition can be seen in the finale, where he moves from one tempo to another with amazing skill. In his illuminating book on the symphonies[1] Simon Parmet points to the skilful transition from the *Allegro* to the *Andante assai* (the introduction of the contrasting theme) at fig. F in the score; both sections share a common pulse. This facility in handling contrasts of tempo acquires an added dimension later on; two contrasting tempos are maintained simultaneously in some of the later music, and seem to struggle for mastery before one or other gains ascendancy. The Seventh Symphony affords an excellent example of Sibelius's effortless virtuosity in this respect.

It is the slow movement of the First Symphony that most eloquently recalls Sibelius's debt to the Russians.[2] Whether or not Sibelius knew the work of Balakirev or Borodin at this time, he certainly felt a strong affinity to Tchaikovsky, whose *Symphonie Pathétique* was composed only six years earlier and had been performed in Helsinki both in 1894 and again in 1897. The lush opening theme of the *Andante* and the big tune of the finale suggest the higher, more feverish, emotional temperature of the Russian composer. The tune in the finale is unmistakably Tchaikovskian, an unafraid demonstration of melodic feeling. The fact remains that none of the other movements can be said to match the first in poetic intensity or organic cohesion. The melodic inspiration, though powerful on occasion, is less individual; the links which bind the part to the whole, the moment to the movement, are less securely forged. The scherzo, it is true, has a compelling physical excitement and some characteristic woodwind writing, and it is perhaps in the finale that the weaknesses become most readily apparent.

The movement begins with the clarinet theme which opened the work, though at a much higher level of intensity, being passionately declaimed by the strings. It also ends with the same two *pizzicato* chords in E minor as did the first; but here the similarity ends. The movement operates on an altogether different level, and the tension which it generates is that of melodrama rather than high tragedy; there is much thrilling orchestral detail, sudden and vivid dramatic contrasts, impetuous and declamatory outbursts of rhetoric, but the excitement is from moment to moment rather than the outcome of a cumulative increase of tension over a longer time-span. Although there is much that is characteristic in the last three movements and many pages of a stark and arresting beauty, the level of inspiration is distinctly inferior to that of the *Legends*.

Sibelius waited only two years before embarking on another essay in this

[1] *The Symphonies of Sibelius* (London, 1959), p. 6.
[2] There is a striking correspondence between the second group of the first movement of Tchaikovsky's *Souvenirs de Florence* and the figure at bar 84 of Sibelius's slow movement.

form. The Second Symphony breathes much the same air as the First, and in this work, too, it is the opening movement which makes the deepest impression. The air of apparent relaxation and effortlessness with which this sunny, genial music unfolds serves to obscure its immense strength; in the same way Sibelius's seemingly casual approach to his thematic ideas misleads the listener as to its intensely organic nature. Many of the ideas seem to belong to each other or derive from a common seed, though when they are more closely scrutinized their relationship becomes more elusive and less easy to define. But each motive evolves naturally from its predecessor, and even when one idea merely echoes another, as it does at the beginning of the symphony, it grows spontaneously and organically out of the texture and takes an independent life of its own. The horn motive, which punctuates the main woodwind theme, is an instance in point. How skilfully and unobtrusively Sibelius dovetails the first horn entry into the texture! It emerges from the theme not merely as an echo of the cadential figure (marked x) but as an idea in its own right:

Ex. 3

The use of a succession of thematic strands rather than long, predictable, obviously connected melodic paragraphs led Cecil Gray in his study of the symphonies to assume that Sibelius was breaking entirely new ground in his treatment of sonata form, whereas in actual fact he does nothing that cannot be explained in terms of traditional sonata procedure. Admittedly, one melodic idea does not appear to dominate either the first or second groups, though one of the elements of the latter does assume a more dominating role in the development. To speak of a second 'subject' in this context is therefore unwise (as it is, in fact, in so many classical works), and to isolate the oboe tune at fig. B, as Parmet does on the grounds that it is 'best suited to serve as the second theme, as it offers a greater contrast to the main theme than any other thematic idea',[1] belies in some measure the genius of this exposition. It is the amazing diversity of character contained in the second group that distinguishes it from the mildness of the pastoral first group. See ex. 4 for the motif in question.

Ex. 4

While this idea can be said to open the second group, the most important single element is the woodwind figure, in which a downward leap of a fifth is prominent. It will be observed that the accompaniment is that of the opening, though the tone is more emphatic and urgent, and by the end of the movement we are left in no doubt that there is an especially close relationship between the first and second groups in this piece (see ex. 5). A turbulent motif which springs from this and generates a good deal of excitement returns us to the dominant: the woodwind develop the downward fifth into an angry comment which is of some importance in the development.

The exposition is a fine example of the extraordinary freedom and assurance which Sibelius shows in his approach to sonata form. The fact that several authorities dispute the identity of the second 'subject', while yet another maintains that there is not one at all, speaks for itself; and

[1] Op. cit., p. 17

Ex. 5

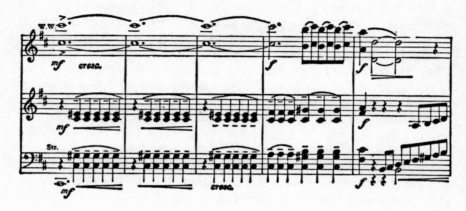

indeed, to dogmatize about this exposition in purely academic terms, with hard-and-fast divisions between the first group, the transition material and the second group, is impossible. One thing that will strike the student of Sibelius the closer he examines this symphony is the fact that no one fragment, idea or motif in the initial statement is wasted. In spite of the lushness of the idiom in comparison with, say, the Third and Fourth Symphonies, the movement betrays no less a degree of integration and cohesion; and it is certainly more remarkable in that respect than the corresponding movement of the First Symphony. There is no surplus flesh on this lithe Attic figure.

Take as an example the very opening of the development. Here the oboe begins with ex. 5, but from now on this melody is more often than not associated with the bassoon idea which darkly answers it. While the actual contour is new, this bassoon pendant has a close spiritual relationship to the horn motif attached to the first theme. It shares its first three notes and makes an allusion to the rhythm of its cadential figure. The use of the transition material is interesting. At its first appearance in the exposition it seems to bring the first element of rhetoric into the music, an element which is intensified with its impassioned, questioning pendant (marked x), from which the second group material so naturally arises (see ex. 6). The development itself largely tends to concentrate on exx. 3 and 5, and the material rising out of them; although oblique reference is made to it, the transition material is held in hand until, at the climax, the point of transition from development to restatement, it steers the music back into the tonic in a

Ex. 6

blaze of triumph. Here the persuasive rhetoric of the violins is exchanged for the massive and eloquent power of the brass.

This point, the opening of the restatement, offers a splendid example of Sibelius's powers of compression. The expressive pendant (ex. 6, x) is used as a counterpoint to the main woodwind theme of the first group: while a few bars earlier Sibelius had reinforced the bond we noticed between the first and second groups by weaving ex. 4 into the texture and again alloting it the role of a counterpoint to ex. 3. The remainder of the reprise pursues a fairly normal path, though, as reference to exx. 4 and 6 has been so recent, they do not return again. It is to ex. 5, and the material associated with it, that the recapitulation turns.

Again, as with the First Symphony, the other movements are by no means as highly concentrated or as perfectly proportioned. Nor, for that matter, do they show the same originality in the handling of the thematic substance, though the ideas themselves are individual enough. But none of these movements reveals so many subtleties on closer analysis as did the first. The second movement, for example, is far more loose-limbed and rhapsodic in feeling than its predecessor, though in layout it falls, roughly speaking, into a species of sonata form. It is of interest to note the modal feeling in much of the material. Modal influences are discernible in the whole of Sibelius's output from *En Saga* and the *Karelia* suite onwards. Needless to say, this can be largely attributed to the early assimilation of Finnish folk-music into both his melodic style and his harmonic vocabulary. But if the slow movement is rich in good tunes and impassioned in feeling, the scherzo is a brilliant foil with its highly effective virtuoso writing for the orchestra, much of it fiery and tempestuous. Possibly he was inspired by the example of Beethoven's

Seventh Symphony in adding to the normal ternary form an additional reprise of the trio, but the most striking feature of it is the final surge that brings us directly into the finale. Here we have a foretaste of the Sibelius that is to come, the architect of the massive climax, the master of the art of transition. The gentle oboe tune reinforces the pastoral undertones that one feels from the first movement: some have wondered whether this idea with its repeated notes is an echo of Gregorian chant, as a similar pattern occurs in the tableau from which the *Scènes historiques* are drawn, as the accompaniment to the liturgical rituals portrayed on the stage, while others have sensed folk origins. The Second Symphony has been the source of all manner of programmatic speculation which has now been authoritatively resolved in Erik Tawaststjern's study.[1] The nationalist gloss that Kajanus and Schnéevoigt put on it (the latter in a Boston Symphony programme note) as a symbol of protest, a musical portrayal of Finnish resistance to Russianization, is quite false. The lamenting figure on the wind in the finale was directly inspired by the memory of Sibelius's sister-in-law, Elli Järnefelt who had taken her own life, while the main theme of the coda came to him in Gallén-Kallela's exotic Karelian home. Here in the summer of 1899 he was sitting at the villa in Ruovesi and suddenly at one point leapt to his feet and said, 'Now I will show you what impression this room makes on me, its basic mood.' The finale itself is dominated by its opening theme, a simple, direct and strangely compelling idea that never strays far from the tonic. In form it is probably the most easily assimilated single movement in all the seven symphonies and operates at a less lofty level than the first. By Sibelius's standards, its sonata form is relatively unsophisticated; the two main ideas are strongly contrasted and their development not particularly subtle. Yet the overall effect is still eloquent and powerful and the peroration is undeniably stirring.

[1] *Sibelius*, vol. I (London, 1976), p. 244.

6

The symphonies – 2

Though both early symphonies spring from the soil of Romanticism, they offer convincing evidence of Sibelius's classical sympathies. The first movements are, in both cases, remarkable achievements by the highest standards; and even though the fevers of Tchaikovskian romanticism run high in some of the other movements, the musical ideas are erected on firm, solidly designed structural foundations. However, in terms of sheer originality both of conception and execution, of content and form, the early symphonies must yield pride of place to the symphonic poems. No movement in either symphony is as perfect in design and inspiration, or as rich in poetry, as *The Swan* or *Lemminkäinen in Tuonela*, and nowhere in these symphonies does the composer equal, let alone surpass, the taut, sustained, hair-raising symphonic finale of the *Four Legends*. With the third symphony, however, work on which occupied him from 1904 to 1907, this perspective began to change. This was the period of *Pohjola's Daughter* and *Night Ride and Sunrise*, as well as of the revision of the violin concerto; but it also saw the composer of masterly symphonic poems firmly launched on his conquest of the symphony.

Various claims have been made for the third symphony. It is certainly more classical in feeling and restrained in utterance than either of its predecessors; it is so cogently argued that one is reminded of Ralph Wood's comments: 'It is paradoxical but true that a work by Brahms or Dvořák or Tchaikovsky is a good deal easier to follow than one by Sibelius, not because there is more connectedness in any of the former but because there is less.'[1] Professor Abraham himself went even further in discussing the first movement of this symphony: 'In clearness and simplicity of outline, it is comparable with a Haydn or Mozart first movement . . . Nevertheless, the organic unity of the movement is far in advance of anything in the Viennese classical masters; and even the general architecture is held together in a way that had classical precedents but had never before, I think, been so fully developed.'[2]

Whether or not this is the case, the fact remains that there is no more

[1] In *Sibelius, a Symposium*, edited by Gerald Abraham, p. 43.
[2] Op. cit., p. 22

perfect instance of classical sonata form in all Sibelius than the first movement of this symphony. It is much simpler to analyse than the corresponding movement of the second, but the relationship between the various thematic elements is no less organic, the feeling of their belonging together no less intense; and the sense of inevitability is, if anything, more marked. The natural flow of the music is uninterrupted by moments of rhetoric, its contours are firm, its idiom is purer: the opulent orchestral colouring of the second symphony is abandoned for a more restrained palette, the glowing hues yield to subtler pastel shades. The actual composition of the orchestra in the two symphonies does not differ in essentials; both include double woodwind, four horns, three trombones, timpani and strings. The second symphony, however, calls for three trumpets as against two in the third and further reinforces its brass by the addition of a tuba. It is obvious that it is the approach to the orchestra and its treatment that differ. One thing is immediately striking: throughout the exposition practically all the important melodic material, including the first and second 'subjects', the closing idea of the second group, as well as the bulk of the musical argument, is given to the strings. In actual fact they are at no point silent during the exposition and, indeed, in the whole movement there are only sixteen bars where they are completely inactive. The pregnant opening bars, with their symmetrical, firmly sculptured outline and their measured rhythmic contour, leave the listener in no doubt as to the classic temper of the movement:

Ex. 7

74

As usual in Sibelius, there is no excess flesh on this vital, athletic body of a movement. An apparently insignificant idea (bar 17) generates a flood of semiquavers that sweeps the music onwards and periodically rises to a torrent that carries all before it. Another entry on the horns a few bars later is more than a climactic flourish; both in outline and rhythm it carefully prepares the ground for the second theme:

Ex. 8

Ex. 9

After the statement of the second theme the semiquaver figure returns as a kind of ostinato. From this texture the woodwind call up echoes of the second subject; and thus, as in the first movement of the second symphony, elements of both groups are united within the exposition. Either this passage or similar writing in the development 'is said to represent the composer's impression of fog-banks drifting along the English coast'.[1] Both the development and the restatement follow time-honoured, instinctive procedures. There is an undercurrent of melancholy resignation in the coda, a feeling which is more explicitly stated in the second movement. The actual theme of the coda is entirely

---

[1] Tovey, *Essays in Musical Analysis*, vol. ii (London, 1935), p. 123. This sort of remark, along with Sibelius's penchant for overtly programmatic symphonic poems, has encouraged some fanciful writers to try to find literary programmes for the symphonies. No task could be more fruitless, for few symphonies are laid on such sound structural foundations or can stand so firmly on their own feet. Sibelius's exchange with Mahler during the latter's visit to Helsinki in 1907 (the year in which this work was composed) bears this out: 'When our conversation touched on the symphony,' Sibelius told Ekman, 'I said that I admired its style and severity of form, and the profound logic that created an inner connection between all the motifs. This was my experience in the course of my creative work. Mahler's opinion was just the opposite. "No!" he said, "The symphony must be like the world. It must be all-embracing."'

new, though it seems related to the closing idea of the exposition; but, as is often the case in the symphonies, the relationship is not one of contour (though for the best part of three bars they share the same rhythmic pattern) but a less easily defined kinship of spirit.

The second movement is by contrast one of Sibelius's least complicated symphonic movements. It is a series of gentle ruminations on a supple wisp of a theme, much of whose charm derives from the metric interplay between 6/4 and 3/2. Those who are familiar with Kajanus's remarkable recording of this work made during the thirties will know that this movement runs a good deal deeper than one would imagine on hearing the average concert or broadcast performance. There is a note of gentle sorrow about the music which becomes very intense in the writing for divided cellos (fig. 6),[1] and the lightening of the atmosphere later on at fig. 10 is merely transient. The tonality centres on G sharp minor, a marked contrast to the outer movements, which are both in C.

From the point of view of structure the finale is the most interesting (and certainly the most original) of the three movements. It falls into two quite clearly defined sections, approximately equal in length; in this respect it might be regarded as a forerunner of the first movement of the Fifth Symphony, though there the two sections are not approximately equal. In the case of the Fifth, some writers (among them Parmet and Gray) maintain that the first movement does in fact constitute two separate movements, and they marshal impressive evidence for this. There can, however, be no question of this here. The first part can well be treated as the exposition and development of a straightforward sonata-form movement. The exposition lays out the two main groups, the second being in the relative minor; the two 'subjects' are both terse, pregnant ideas: the first moves stepwise, the second, on the other hand, makes use of triadic leaps and traces a bolder, more incisive outline. Sibelius makes the same material serve for both the second idea and the accompanying string ostinato from which it arises. This ostinato is trochaic in rhythm and recalls similar writing in *Night Ride and Sunrise*, which was completed at about the same time.

Before the development section the music momentarily returns us to C, almost in the manner of a rondo, and the first idea is again heard on the oboes. The fact that the development is dominated by the second theme, and that in its original form the first idea does not recur, may well explain its reappearance at this juncture.

The second part of the movement replaces the normal recapitulation section: it is concerned with a new idea, a theme of great power and

[1]Eulenburg edition.

eloquence, which gathers energy as it is reiterated in an atmosphere of growing excitement. The closing bars are worth quoting, for it is this segment which seems to drive the music forward relentlessly:

Ex. 10

The theme is at first stated gently by the strings, but later, as the tension mounts, they provide an ostinato while the woodwind and horns take up the melody. The theme, as is always the case in Sibelius, seems to have emerged quite naturally and spontaneously from the context of the movement; there does seem at first sight a connection with the horn figure which can be heard at the beginning of the development, but there is no direct rhythmic or melodic affinity. As a glance at ex. 10 will show, the fourth note of the scale is sharpened, and this, together with a tendency to move within a limited compass, is a feature of the first subject itself. The entire concept of this movement is strikingly unified and original; and the work as a whole is the first of Sibelius's symphonies that is throughout worthy of his genius.

If the Third Symphony sounds a note of classical understatement, it is the Fourth which, by general consent, enshrines the essential Sibelius. In this work he has distilled a language more economical and concentrated than in any other of his works (with the possible exception of *Tapiola*). The melodic language is more rarefied and allusive, the exploitation of tonality more subtle and complex, and the organization of the work is conceived far more as a totality than in the earlier symphonies. We have already observed that in the first two symphonies the mastery evinced in the first movements is not matched in the later movements; and even in the Third Symphony the middle movement, underrated though it is, is not pitched on quite the same level as the other two. With the Fourth Symphony, however, Sibelius's planning is far more comprehensive, the symphony being conceived as a whole much in the same way as the Seventh: each of the four movements is a member of one living organism.

Sibelius spoke of the Fourth Symphony as a reaction against 'modern trends', and there seems little doubt that he had in mind the large canvases and opulent colours of Mahler and Strauss. Certainly its restraint in using the full orchestra, the lack of self-indulgence of any kind, and the austerity of its musical language, place it at the opposite pole from Mahler. Its austerity earned it the title of the *Barkbröd* symphony in Scandinavia – a grim reminder of the hard days in the nineteenth century when starvation compelled some of its victims to eat the bark of trees. Although only three years had elapsed since the third symphony (the fourth was begun in 1910 and finished the following spring), the very opening bars emphasize the immense distance Sibelius had travelled in terms of self-discovery. The firm line, regular phrase structure and unambiguous tonality of the first bars of the Third Symphony contrast markedly with the dark brooding intensity of the Fourth. The confident, optimistic temper of no. 3 is laid aside: here the mood is despondent, the rhythm hesitant and the tonality obscure.

The first four notes come to assume considerable importance in the melodic thinking of the first movement: they unobtrusively outline three whole tones, C, D, E, F sharp:

Ex. 11

A minor is soon established, and the cellos and basses settle down to a slow, regular oscillation between E and F sharp, while a solo cello intones the main theme, the first segment of which is triadic in outline. The second group centres on F sharp: first, the brass insinuate themselves into the texture with some savage chords to which there is an impassioned response from violins and violas, in which ex. 11 is spread-eagled over an additional octave, giving it a certain rhetorical emphasis and a new colouring:

Ex. 12

Secondly, there follows a fleeting motive from the horns, a more tranquil fanfare in the subdominant of the new key; and thirdly, a figure of some majesty on trumpets and trombones. All three themes – or rather motifs, for they are so fragmentary in character – firmly establish the new tonal centre, and it is while we are still in F sharp that Sibelius makes further allusion to the first group material. Here the insignificant opening notes are seen to possess an importance that one had not imagined at their appearance. While the main theme is heard in the strings (softened by added thirds), variants of ex. 11 emerge on the woodwind. All this is a convenient procedure which enables Sibelius to transplant much of this section in the reprise, and thus telescope the initial statement of the first group. When ex. 11 recurs at the end of the movement it brings with it the severe, cold atmosphere in which the work began, though its key centre has been firmly anchored in the tonic.

The development itself contains some of the strangest music that Sibelius ever wrote. Echoing, perhaps, the tonal uncertainties with which the work began, the melodic line itself assumes an angularity unusual in Sibelius. The contrast in colour at the beginning of the development also serves to enhance the sense of mystery that inspires this music. The warmth of woodwind, horns and lower strings, together with the security of F sharp major, are abandoned for a bleak solo cello[1] and a tonality that is rapidly obscured:

Ex. 13

A little later the strings begin to rustle evocatively, and in the 'whole-tone' texture that ensues we can trace references to ex. 11, while flutes and clarinets, and later bassoons, cellos and double-basses, give ominous reminders of the tritone. A recurrent timpani pedal point on A serves as a preparation for the foreshortened reprise.

[1] In an article published in the Swedish-language Helsinki paper, *Nya Pressen* (7th June 1958), Harold Johnson floated the idea that the Fourth Symphony might possibly have begun life as a string quartet. Sibelius's scoring is at times chamber-like in its delicacy and, according to Tawaststjerna, (vol. II, p. 179) the cantabile theme of the *Largo* was originally laid out on the four staves of a quartet score. Sibelius set the symphony on one side several times to work on other projects, the last being a setting of Edgar Allan Poe's *The Raven*. These ideas eventually became part of the Fourth Symphony: the chorale-like second group of the finale was originally conceived for the Poe setting.

This remarkably concentrated movement (a mere 114 bars in length) is matched by a similarly terse scherzo. This even compresses the reprise of the scherzo section (initially some 250 bars in length) into a fleeting reference of six bars. The very opening of the scherzo emphasizes the point that each of the four movements reflects a different aspect of the whole; it is as if one were viewing the same magnificent edifice or vista from totally different vantage points. Here Sibelius begins on exactly the same note (A) as the first movement ended, but this tonic note is seen in a new light, that of F major, a key which had been avoided in the first movement. Over a string *tremolo* the oboe dances in a plaintive, pastoral fashion, avoiding for some time the note B flat; thus the tonality acquires a certain modal flavouring and the interval of a tritone inevitably appears. Later on in the movement the tritone comes to assume great importance, particularly in the menacing trio section, where the main thematic motif persistently hammers this interval against a characteristically Sibelian background of 'transitional harmonies' – a compound of shifting diminished chords, sustained trills that act as pedals in a general atmosphere of harmonic uneasiness where no definite tonality asserts itself.

The third movement may be said to represent the emotional peak of the work. It is contemplative in spirit, and is one of his most profoundly individual and deeply felt utterances. From the opening bars where two flutes icily ruminate through to the impassioned climax of the movement, where the main theme is finally and fully set out, there is no superfluous note. The rhapsodic character of the movement emerges at once when the flute soars against a vaguely imitative but highly purposeful bass line. Here we have the most austere yet poetic two-part counterpoint. As Ernest Newman put it: 'The sense of separation from the solid earth that this wide spacing gives us is increased as the flute theme ascends higher and higher and becomes more rhapsodical.' The passage in question is interesting, for it shows that Mahler was not the only composer to think in two widely separated lines bereft of harmonic support. The music makes several attempts to establish C sharp minor and state the lyrical burden of the movement, but the earliest entries of the theme disintegrate, and it is not until we are about half way through that the cellos succeed in stating the theme almost in its entirety, in a C sharp minor context (see ex. 14). The opening of the finale is in A major, but, as Robert Simpson has pointed out, it presents that key in the light of its relationship with C sharp minor, the key of the preceding movement. Thus the new key has a darker colouring than might have been expected. As in the case of the first two movements, the last two are linked by a pivot-note, the finale opening

Ex. 14

on the same C sharp with which the *Largo* ended. But the influence of the *Largo* is not confined merely to tonality: there is a direct thematic link between the first theme and ex. 14:

Ex. 15

This theme has a pendant which echoes the tritone cry that we heard in the first and second movements. This ejaculation is practically all that remains of the first group in the restatement, which is extremely compact. In this movement Sibelius lightens the texture by introducing the glockenspiel, which bears the abbreviation *glocken* in the score.[1] Another development that follows rapidly in the wake of the first group brings home the important dramatic role played by tonality in this symphony. After a longish stretch of 'cross-hatching' on the strings (in A major), the

---

[1]This has given rise to some confusion: Ansermet, Bernstein and Blomstedt among others interpret it as meaning tubular bells, but some years ago a copy of a letter in Sibelius's hand, dated

tonic is brought into direct apposition to its furthermost pole (E flat), when a woodwind cry of a third is superimposed on the texture (ex. 16*a*). This episode closes with a falling seventh (ex. 16*b*), and these two elements form the basic ingredients of the tragic coda which ends the work:

Ex. 16

It is interesting to note that at the restatement this tonal polarity is preserved, though the roles are reversed; this time the string ostinato is in E flat, a somewhat austere precursor of the finale of the Fifth Symphony, while it is the woodwind that insist on A. The woodwind in fact triumph and bring the music to a conflict involving considerable harmonic tension; this is only right and proper if one recalls that it is the tritone, the *diabolus in musica*, that is being resolved. This conflict has been avoided in the development (or at least postponed), since the music has largely concerned itself with the haunting second group, which rarely settles in one key for any length of time (though at its initial appearance it makes a hasty excursion into E flat). However, the whole of this section and the development move on tonal quicksands and the basic conflict is not brought to issue until the restatement. The coda contains some of the most desolate pages in all Sibelius. The material we have heard in ex. 16 forms the basis of the musical substance, though the atmosphere is transformed. There is a searching intensity here, a purity of utterance, and a vision and insight of rare quality.

15th January 1935, came to light, obviously written in response to an inquiry by the young English conductor Leslie Heward about the use of the glockenspiel in the Fourth Symphony: 'Concerning your two technical questions, I would suggest to you the using of Glockenspiel in the 4th Symphony and Stahlstäbe in *Oceanides*'. Furthermore, Sibelius corresponded with Sir Thomas Beecham about the score at the time of its first recording and Sir Thomas re-recorded it in accordance with his wishes. So we can take it that this reading comes very close to Sibelius's wishes – and that should largely take care of the argument about the glockenspiel and the tubular bells in the finale. According to Legge, a set of miniature bells were specially constructed that were more powerful than the glockenspiel to ensure their audibility on 78 r.p.m. records. The more cumbersome tubular bells were used only after his death by Ansermet and Bernstein and their weightier sonority inevitably thickens the texture and serves to slow down the pace. Moreover, Stokowski, Anthony Collins, Sixten Ehrling and Karajan all recorded the symphony during Sibelius's lifetime and had Sibelius wanted the tubular bells, he would have had no lack of opportunity to convey his wishes.

7

The symphonies – 3

The Fifth is undoubtedly the most popular of the later symphonies. In comparison with the fourth, with its spare orchestral texture, its colours are opulent and vivid, its mood is heroic, and its idiom easily accessible. The work, in particular its outer movements, is, however, no less fascinating to the student of Sibelius. Its genesis is both long and complex. As far as we know, it gave Sibelius more trouble than any other work, for he mentions the new symphony as early as 1912 in his diaries. After its first performance in 1915, when it was in four separate movements, it was withdrawn for revision; a second version, performed the following year, still left the composer unsatisfied. Sibelius planned a further revision for Armas Järnefelt to conduct in Stockholm in 1917, but the definitive score was not finished until 1919. The 1915 version has been pieced together with a set of orchestral parts that were found at Ainola and has been performed, but only a double-bass part survives from the 1916 revision.

Certainly the differences between Sibelius's first and last thoughts are striking, and pay tribute to the vitality of his artistic conscience. As Vaughan Williams remarked, Sibelius had the capacity to make the simplest C major chord sound wholly original. The chord A flat, E flat, F and C was one that he had made very much his own at the outset of his career in the first of the *Four Legends*. Oddly enough, both the first and second movements of the 1915 score begin with this chord. Not only is the scoring less expert but the ideas were slow to take shape. The second group (one bar before letter C), wrought it would seem from dark, solid rock, only reached its present form after a hard struggle; it loses much of its impact because of a strange upward contour at the end of the idea, and because it is given to violins without any doubling. The first movement begins to lose momentum and direction after the rough equivalent, say, of letter M in the 1919 version, and the scherzo begins at the point where the rehearsal lettering re-starts. It is not surprising to find the development the least unchanged, for it strikes one with the force of real inspiration when first one hears it, and seems to echo his diary entry of October 1914 concerning this symphony: 'My heart sings, full of sadness – the shadows lengthen.' In the scherzo section itself, the trumpet tune at letter D is given to the strings. Sibelius extended the coda considerably when he reworked this movement. The *Andante* is both paler and its sense of direction less firm in the 1915 score: incidentally, the reference to the horn theme of the finale which the double-basses introduced was evidently a conscious afterthought. The finale is much longer: Sibelius obviously felt it in need of tautening and strengthening. Interestingly enough, he recalls the second group (ex. 18) towards the end of the finale in a strikingly remote key, and the famous hammer blows that end the work come over a string tremolando to very little effect.

Most writers are agreed on the first unusual feature of the movement, the double exposition. There are four main thematic strands in the exposition, the first of which is probably the most important:

Ex. 17

The second, which develops quite naturally from the first, is a typically Sibelian woodwind motive in thirds, a discursive figure that prepares the ground for a change of tonality. Throughout the whole of the first group the strings are silent, which lends their intervention in the musical argument additional dramatic force. As it is, they plunge the music into G, the key of the second group, where yet again the

Ex. 18

woodwind ring out a powerful challenge (see ex. 18). The fourth element, more agitated and restless in mood, drives home the new key with some degree of urgency. The tonal scheme of the 'counter-exposition' is far less settled. The first reference to the main theme (on the dominant of G) soon

84

leads us through an area of some tonal uncertainty to the tonic; and it is in an affirmation of E flat that the whole exposition ends.

As in most organic processes, it is not always possible to say with any degree of dogmatism where one 'section' ends or another begins (nor, indeed, is there any real reason why one should want to). However, the transition from exposition to development poses no such difficulty, for the opening figure of the development emerges on the horns as the fourth theme gently subsides. This figure, which dominates the music for some time, is in fact the chromatic motif which anticipated the entry of the strings at the first appearance of the second group, though, characteristically enough, it was omitted in the counter-exposition. The writing that follows is among the most starkly original and imaginative in the whole symphony; the ever-shifting currents of the string harmonies, in some ways prophetic of *Tapiola*, provide a background for a long development of this chromatic motive, until the climax at letter L where the second subject (ex. 18) is heard in full.

A return of the first group in B major leads to the *Allegro moderato* (3/4), which began life as a separate if strongly related movement. Parmet described it as a toccata, while Gerald Abraham discerned its origins suggesting that the first hundred bars constitute a scherzo, the next eighty a trio, while the rest can be equated with scherzo-repeat and recapitulation. Yet at the same time, while not losing sight of its scherzo-like character, the fact remains that the 1919 version does correspond in broad outline to the recapitulation normal in sonata form. The tonic is re-established at fig. B and material derived from the first subject is brought under review; a new theme, closely related to the first group, is heard on the trumpet (see ex. 19). There is a good deal of animated, quasi-fugal discussion of this which digresses tonally. However, we soon return to the tonic, where the second subject is heard in a new and magical transformation. Another lengthy episode follows before the fourth theme is restated, again in the tonic, and a brilliant coda brings the movement to an end.

Ex. 19

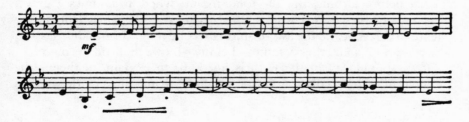

In comparison with this the *Andante* is a simple movement, though it offers ample evidence of the subtlety of Sibelius's thinking. It takes the form of a theme followed by a set of variations; among other things it is a model of the resource and skill with which Sibelius exploits pedal points. The movement is anchored in G major, the key of the second group of the first movement, but the undertone of turbulence and unrest there contrasts with the relaxed and sunny atmosphere that infuses this movement. Twice during the course of the movement Sibelius hints at ideas that are to come in the finale: the basses unobtrusively state the second theme of the finale (five bars after fig. F) and, as Ringbom has pointed out,[1] there are striking similarities between pages 83–4 in the slow movement and 99–100 in the finale.

None of Sibelius's finales offers so large a measure of sheer physical excitement as does the last movement of no. 5. None of the early symphonies can equal its sustained flow of energy; in fact, it is only approached in this respect by the last movement of the Third Symphony. Sibelius's approach to the problem of the finale is never the same, and although, as in the third, he does make extensive and masterly use of ostinatos and pedal points, it is the musical content that dictates the direction in which the music is to develop. As in so many of his movements, he moves with complete freedom and does not allow his imagination to be bound by any preconceived academic mould. Parmet calls it 'a kind of rondo', and gives its outline as main theme – second subject – a short working-out section – main theme – second subject –coda. Conversely, Abraham speaks of it as 'following the outline (though not the key-plan) of sonata form'. In actual fact the use of tonality is highly individual and effective in this movement. There are two main themes, the second of which opens with the famous horn theme which Tovey compared to Thor swinging his hammer.

Sibelius delays his change of key until the very last moment, so that the bulk of the exposition including the second group is in the tonic. The change to C is all the more effective, even though it is not long before the key changes yet again. The reprise begins in G flat with the subdued, mysterious whisperings of the first subject on muted strings. The second also follows in G flat before turning into the tonic minor, where it assumes a grave, melancholy splendour. The final return to the tonic is again heightened by being so delayed, and the awe-inspiring second theme brings the massive, glowing climax and the six famous hammer-blows that end the piece.

If the popularity of the Fifth is not hard to explain, neither is the comparative neglect of its successor, for the Sixth inhabits a world which is

[1]Op. cit., p. 139 n. (Swedish edition).

86

as far removed from the Fifth as that, in its turn, is from the Fourth. Like the Fourth, the Sixth Symphony has eloquent advocates. The days when one could say that it fell 'between the stools of the appreciation of the many and the appreciation of the few' have fortunately passed, at least as far as the few are concerned. David Cherniavsky speaks of it as 'the final stage in [Sibelius's] quest for, or in his spontaneous attainment of, complete unity', while Ralph Wood calls it 'a dazzling display of a technique so personal and so assured that its very achievements [are] hidden in its mastery and in its entire synthesis with its subject matter'. Neither claim is in the least exaggerated. Nevertheless the Sixth does not hold as firm a place in the affections of the general public as either the Fifth or the Seventh, for it lacks the heroic countenance of the one and the stern epic majesty of the other.

In spite of the addition of a harp to the normal Sibelian orchestra of double woodwind, four horns, three trumpets and trombones, timpani and strings, the scoring is more restrained than in any other Sibelius symphony. As in the Third, it is the strings that carry the main burden of the musical argument. The absence of virtuoso orchestral writing and the physical excitement of massive climaxes do not make for immediate popular appeal, and the refined modal flavouring of the work doubtless seems monotonous to the casual listener. It is clear that Sibelius was highly conscious of the enormous distance between this symphony and the glittering orchestral sonorities of Ravel and Strauss. While they were showing an ever-increasing preoccupation with subtleties of texture and refinements of the orchestral palette, he was working towards homogeneity of form and a greater purity of musical speech. Indeed, it was the feeling of being out of step with the values of his time that prompted his oft-quoted remark, apropos this very symphony, that, while other composers were concocting cocktails of various hues, he offered pure spring water.

In the thirties Cecil Gray hastened to connect the lofty suspensions and profoundly eloquent polyphony of the opening with Sibelius's known admiration for Palestrina, Lassus and the sixteenth-century English masters. He also maintained that its modal atmosphere was unusual in Sibelius's music. In actual fact Sibelius's melodic style bore traces of modal flavouring practically throughout his creative life. What makes the modality of the Sixth Symphony particularly striking is the greater degree of polyphonic interest at the opening and the greater frequency and impact of modal progressions and cadences.

The kind of symphonic thinking that we encounter in all the late symphonies, and particularly in the Sixth and Seventh, eludes the conventional analysis of the schoolroom. This music is essentially non-episodic, and is so highly integrated that the outward course it takes does not illuminate the vital organic processes that compel it on its path. But even a study such as that made by Parmet, who shows how the material of the symphony grows from what he calls the *kärnmotiv* or germinal cell, cannot illuminate this process in more than a limited sense. It is a process that is insusceptible to any method of verbal analysis. The sense of growth we feel in these symphonies takes place on more than one plane, and the growth and metamorphosis of themes is only one part of the process, though a highly important one. Some of the kinship one feels between two or more ideas cannot be explained solely in terms of similarity (indeed two completely contrasted ideas with no contours or rhythm in common often seem to belong to each other), and to relate each to an initial germinal cell to be found in the work itself, or in the sketches that precede it, or in the imagination of the analyst, is to do so on only one level. This kinship of themes and the feeling or organic cohesion is intimately related to other factors, including the overall tonal design of the work, and cannot be divorced from the constantly changing harmonic and rhythmic context.

In a sense the first movement follows the basic principles of sonata procedure, but it is characteristic of Sibelius's originality that, while agreeing on this basic formal outline, no two writers arrive at identical results. Parmet[1] implies that this is the first subject:

Ex. 20

and goes on to say that 'the exposition shows a remarkable irregularity in that the second subject, or something that might be regarded as equivalent, is missing'. He argues, too, that the *Allegro* proper, beginning at fig. B, is the section in which sonata form is used. Abraham,[2] on the other hand, calls this the first (and implies that it is the most important) element of the second group.

Certainly, since it begins an *Allegro*, the theme has the 'feel' of a first subject. Yet in the recapitulation it is the main Dorian tune that returns us to the tonic and assumes the role of first subject, while ex. 20 does not appear again. In its stead there is a new theme:

[1] Op. cit., p. 100–1.
[2] Op. cit., pp. 32–3.

Ex. 21

However, both these ideas have one thing in common, the descending figure x, Parmet's *kärnmotiv* from the very opening:

Ex. 22

This figure, as we can see, plays an enormous role in the growth of the symphony right until the impassioned outcry on the strings at the very end of the work:

Ex. 23

All this shows the futility of applying labels to the thematic strands in the late symphonies, for the role played by any one of them cannot be strictly defined in academic terms. Sibelius's mastery enables him to move with a freedom so complete that the musical events are dictated by their own inner necessity. They are not governed by any scheme or design imposed from without: that is why no two Sibelius symphonies are alike.

The slow movement (if it can properly be called a slow movement) could not be more characteristic of the composer both in its harmonic inflections and in its elliptical melodic line. The latter is far removed from the melodic style of Tchaikovsky to which Parmet compares it. Its scoring is wonderfully economical. The scherzo, too, is a *tour de force*: the pulse never seems to slacken. The menacing brass chords are used with a power similar to, but different in effect from, those in the Fourth Symphony. The finale, one of Sibelius's most perfect, opens with an introduction directly related to the opening *kärnmotiv*, just as the main *Allegro* idea takes the main theme of the first movement as its point of departure.

Sibelius planned the Sixth and Seventh symphonies at much the same time. This element from the first movement of no. 6 (ex. 24a), which plays a part analogous to a second group theme in both the exposition and restatement, is obviously hewn from much the same substance[1] as this lithe, sinewy figure (ex. 24b) from no. 7:

Ex. 24a

Ex. 24b

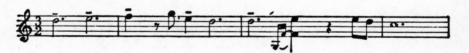

For some writers, among them Ralph Wood, the material of the Seventh Symphony seems less worthy of Sibelius: indeed in comparing the two Wood has gone so far as to describe it as 'a heroic failure'. The Seventh Symphony does, however, scale heights quite different from its predecessor, though in purity of utterance and harmony of spirit it does not match the Sixth.

[1]In an illuminating article, 'Some Aspects of Form in the Symphonies of Sibelius' (*Music Review*, 1949), W. G. Hill points out a large number of thematic correspondences between the various symphonies.

There is no reason why it should. Despite its intense concentration of matter, it is epic in character: its triumph is that of the human spirit struggling against immense odds on its quest of exploration. It is difficult, I think, to share Ralph Wood's verdict: 'After not only the beauty but the unsurpassable mellowness and fluency of the sixth symphony, Sibelius completed the heroic failure, a failure which the very indifference of some of the material proves to be the failure of a primarily technical feat, that 1924's Seventh Symphony is'.[1] The very history of the work makes it clear that it is no conscious exercise in symphonic integration: Sibelius did not set out to write a one-movement symphony. It so happened that he did so almost without knowing it. At the first performance the work was billed as 'Symphonic Fantasia'. Only after this did Sibelius number it among the symphonies. Nor can one readily agree that the thematic material of the work is indifferent.

As it stands, the Seventh Symphony is an example of symphonic metamorphosis so far-reaching and subtle that it would be impossible to do justice to it without countless music examples. In the First and Second Symphonies Sibelius had shown the extent of his mastery of normal symphonic practice, and even as early as the first movement of the Second we find evidence of a new, searching approach to form. From the Third Symphony onwards we never find him approaching the symphonic problem in precisely the same way, though there is, at the same time, no conscious formal experimentation: the material of each symphony dictates the course the music is to take. As Ernest Newman has said of *Tapiola*: 'The form is just the logical correlative of the ideas (or rather of the one idea that runs through it all). It is a form that relates only to that idea: it would be inapplicable to any other, and no "professor of composition" could deduce from it any "rules" that could be bottled and given to the student for home application.' With the seventh symphony we find that Sibelius had abandoned all the stereotyped formal conventions of keys, 'subjects', and so on, to achieve unity on his own terms, the form being 'the correlative of the ideas, and therefore, in the final result, not "a form" at all, but simply *form*, a way of setting about things and getting to the desired end that would hold good only of the particular ideas of the particular work'.

There is then no question of a preconceived mould into which musical material is poured, 'no first and second, no egg and no chicken, in the matter of the idea and the form: each just *is* the other'.[2] Although the symphony is in one movement and consists of a continuous and

[1]Abraham, op. cit., p. 89.
[2]Newman, *Notes for the Sibelius Society* (HMV, 1932).

expanding flow of ideas, the character and tempo of the music undergo many changes. These often seem to suggest the characteristics we normally associate with the conventional symphony; there are times when the music assumes the aspect of a scherzo and others where it seems like a sustained slow movement. The formal layout has been variously described: exposition, development, scherzo and so on, although there is general agreement that these are inadequate 'working labels' and that the symphony is a single indivisible organism. Formal analysis can however be of some help in recognizing some of the more obvious landmarks in the work when the terrain is still relatively unfamiliar. One obvious feature of the landscape is the appearance on three occasions of this theme:

Ex. 25

These appearances form the backbone of the symphony and enshrine its epic character. It has on all three occasions to superimpose itself on a texture of great complexity, and on each appearance the climax is stormier than the previous one. The theme, too, is an important reference point tonally. It always appears in C; in this sense alone, as in many other aspects of its tonal layout, the symphony is comparable to no other.

The process of metamorphosis is set in motion from the very opening bars, a rising scale on the strings. Out of this we come to an important idea which is almost immediately reduced to its skeleton form (x) after the repetition of the theme itself:

Ex. 26

92

Characteristically, too, the very opening and the second theme (ex. 26, x) are telescoped (seven bars after fig. E). One of the most individual fingerprints of Sibelius's craftsmanship is the use of apparently insignificant segments that serve to link more important thematic elements, as vital life-giving motifs on their own account later on. The little chromatic figure that links the first and second group in the first movement of the Fifth Symphony is a good case in point, for it assumes importance in the development. This turn (at fig. A):

Ex. 27a

is a case in point for it gives rise to this:

Ex. 27b

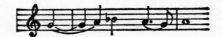

Who would suspect that the four descending notes that immediately follow would play such an important role in the heroic closing pages?

Ex. 28

Yet this gradually becomes the impassioned figure we encounter at fig. Z. Only a few bars after its first appearance it assumes a gentle, almost resigned, questioning air:

Ex. 29a

At fig. E we recognize the physiognomy familiar in the great final climax:

Ex. 29b   **Ex. 29c**

The sustained string passage which follows ex. 28 is one of the most remarkable examples of unbroken polyphony in twentieth-century music. From this idea the motif quoted in ex. 24b is obviously derived. It is in this section too that ex. 27 makes its impact felt:

Ex. 30

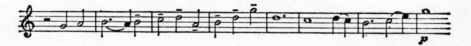

The way in which such themes are constantly renewing themselves is a never-failing source of wonder to the student of this symphony. No subsequent idea, however fresh it may seem, is unrelated to what has gone before. Whether or not Sibelius designed the Seventh Symphony as a symphony or as a 'fantasia sinfonica', the fact remains that he hardly ever composed a piece more completely original in form, so subtle in its handling of tempo, individual in its handling of tonality, or so wholly integrated in its thematic material. But it is not merely these virtues but the humanism that inspires this music that leaves the listener in no doubt that this symphony is a heroic work, life-enhancing and affirmative in spirit.

8

The symphonic poems

The symphonic poems are undoubtedly Sibelius's most important works apart from the symphonies. They span practically the whole of his creative career: the first, *En Saga*, was written in 1892, hot on the heels of the *Kullervo* symphony, while *Tapiola*, the last and greatest of them, dates from 1925. Were no other works to survive from his pen, we should still be able to form a fairly comprehensive picture of his development, for most facets of his highly idiosyncratic style are reflected in them. The full-blooded romanticism of his early works appears in *En Saga* and the first of the *Four Legends*; the more intimate, introspective aspect of his personality is revealed in *The Bard*; while the full extent of his mastery emerges in *Luonnotar, The Oceanides* and the monumental *Tapiola*. Even that aspect of his work which served more to gain popular favour and establish a worldwide reputation than it did to enhance his musical stature is represented by *Finlandia*.

Probably the most important function of the symphonic poem was to serve as a vehicle for Sibelius's interest in Finnish mythology. The symphonic poem had throughout the nineteenth century acted as a convenient outlet for composers discovering their national folklore. Their numbers, particularly in the Slav countries, were legion. But Scandinavian musical nationalism, on the other hand, was slow to develop. Both Gade and Berwald were far more conscious of their links with the classical tradition than they were of their national heritage. It was Grieg who first set Scandinavian nationalism on its feet after the first tentative steps taken by his countrymen, Kjerulf and Nordraak. But they were all miniaturists; Sibelius was the first, working in the larger forms, to show a profound and lasting interest in the folklore as opposed to the folk-music of his native country. The *Kalevala* exercised a fascination over him throughout his life, and this found its most natural (though not its only) outlet in the symphonic poem.

The symphonic poem, too, commended itself for purely musical reasons. Sibelius possessed in the most highly developed form the essential prerequisite of a great symphonist – the ability to conceive music organically. In all seven symphonies the long sustained paragraphs grow naturally one from the other, the main thematic elements are subjected to a subtle process of transformation, and the whole is informed by a sense of unity and a feeling of inevitability. It is not surprising that Sibelius's are the most 'symphonic' poems in the literature of music. In them he mobilizes all the artistic discipline of the symphonies along with a much greater freedom of poetic fancy. The matching of musical and extra-musical considerations is a delicate matter, and the one can easily overbalance in favour of the other. It is a tribute to Sibelius's mastery that programmatic considerations never outweigh musical ones. Moreover, such is the soundness of the musical edifice that our appreciation of the music is entirely independent of our knowledge of its programmatic aims.

The dividing line between symphony and symphonic poem had become blurred during the course of the nineteenth century; indeed, many symphonies of the period were little more than inflated tone-poems. With Sibelius the dividing line is clearly defined. However subtle the process of metamorphosis to which the thematic material is subjected, and however masterly the design, the symphonic poems do not match the weight of the symphonies in either content or form. The difference between the two is most clearly discernible in the range and variety of thematic substance. The symphonic poems, mostly intent on evoking some extra-musical image or mood and less ambitious in their purely musical organization, offer less diversity of melodic interest. This is particularly marked in *Tapiola*, which is virtually monothematic.

En Saga, on the other hand, is rich in melodic variety, although its themes are very different from the pregnant ideas encountered in the symphonies. As in the later symphonic poems, the work follows no direct programme but merely evokes something of the atmosphere of a Nordic saga. He told Ekman that it originated in an octet he wrote in Vienna but neither the score nor any contemporary reference to it in his letters are to be found. After *En Saga* was first performed in 1893, he withdrew it for revision and it is in this form that we know it.

The thematic variety we meet in *En Saga* is matched by considerable tonal freedom. The work opens in A minor and ends in E flat minor, its furthermost pole, while the most important key area of the work is C minor and its relative major, E flat. Apart from the coda which, like the introduction, is dominated by the first theme, there are two sections of relative tonal stability. In the first of these the remaining three themes make their first appearance (the last two being in E flat and C minor respectively). In the second the last two themes are restated, this time both in C minor, where after a short interlude of great poetry, an exciting ostinato heralds the re-entry of the first theme. It is characteristic of Sibelius's economy of means that the ostinato should be a subsidiary idea, which had already appeared as a foil to the fourth theme at its first appearance. This kind of creative thinking is typical of the symphonic writer. In the intervening period the music modulates with great freedom, touching keys as remote as E major, F sharp minor and G sharp minor.

In its original form, however, *En Saga* showed even more freedom of modulation.[1] Here is one example of the way in which the music plunged abruptly into a foreign key:

Ex. 31

When he came to revise the work Sibelius reduced the number and frequency of these modulations. He made the design of the work more taut and compact, reducing it from 952 to 810 bars. The intervening years had brought him much greater assurance and a very real mastery of the most complex problems of musical craftsmanship. Each transition is negotiated with consummate artistry and the seams that one encounters in the earlier version are no longer visible. The duration of pedal points is,

[1]See Nils-Eric Ringbom's study, *De två versionerna av Sibelius' Tondikt 'En Saga'* (Åbo, 1956), in which he compares the two scores.

strangely enough, much longer in the revised than in the original version; Sibelius was now confident that he could risk a greater simplicity of tonal structure than he felt able to ten years earlier.

In a sense the design of *En Saga* is analogous to sonata form in that there are clearly defined sections corresponding to exposition, development and reprise, but, as always in Sibelius, it is dangerous to append labels to the music. Sibelius possessed a sense of form so highly developed that it was always he who was the master. He never allowed the conventions of classical procedure to intimidate him: each work developed according to the nature and needs of the material with which he was working. None of the themes plays out the role that sonata form would impose on them; yet they are remarkably, indeed symphonically, integrated and seem to possess a close relationship with each other in spite of their differing character. Each is carefully prepared: the second, for instance, is introduced at its first appearance (bar 96, fifteen bars after fig. C) and accompanied by the first, while the third theme (bar 150, fig. F) embodies a nostalgic reference to the second. Evidence of Sibelius's contrapuntal ingenuity is very striking in the following example from the development, where we see how skilfully he combines various elements from his main themes:

Ex. 32

Sibelius's extraordinary feeling for the strings emerges at the beginning of the work. The opening bars are identical in both versions, though the magical (and highly original) effect he secures at bar 30 (five bars after fig. A) with his muted *divisi* strings is a product of the revision and his rapidly growing orchestral imagination. During the middle section we encounter similarly exciting effects, where all the strings play *tremolando* and *sul ponticello*. Even at this early age, as we see too in *The Swan of Tuonela* and *Lemminkäinen in Tuonela*, Sibelius showed an inborn genius for the orchestra; his imaginative and resourceful use of the strings is no doubt closely connected with his own not inconsiderable prowess as a violinist. But even his writing for other instruments is remarkable in its understanding of the potentialities of each. Here is no question of a young composer writing in terms of the keyboard and then translating his score into the medium of the orchestra. Like Berlioz before him, Sibelius thought directly and idiomatically in terms of orchestral colour.

As in Rimsky-Korsakov's *Skazka, En Saga* leaves the listener free to supply the programmatic content from his own fantasy. This is not the case with the *Four Legends* for orchestra, op. 22. All these pieces follow the stories from the *Kalevala* which they are supposed to illustrate. The first of them to be written was *The Swan of Tuonela*, begun in 1893 as the prelude to the opera *The Building of the Boat*, which he abandoned the following year. If the *Kullervo* Symphony, *En Saga* and the *Karelia* music showed commanding creative powers, *The Swan* is the first sign of something more. It evokes with icy intensity the lines inscribed on the score: these refer to *Runo* XIV of the *Kalevala*, where Lemminkäinen makes his attempt to shoot the Swan with his crossbow:

Tuonela, the land of death, the hell of Finnish mythology, is surrounded by a large river with black waters and a rapid current, on which the Swan of Tuonela floats majestically, singing.

The piece is a moving and expressive rhapsody dominated by the haunting timbre of the cor anglais, whose melody floats on an arctic sheen of strings. Beginning in A minor, the cor anglais line wanders widely, drifting from one tonality to another, often quite remote, before the music settles once again in the tonic. The writing for divided strings produces sonorities that are highly individual; even the opening A minor chords have no counterpart elsewhere. The slow and insistent harp ostinato in the closing section is one of the many touches of imaginative vision with which this score abounds. It underlines the brooding, evil beauty of this piece of tone-painting.

Its closing section, like many passages in *En Saga*, makes highly effective use of a sustained pedal-point, but nowhere is this practice more extensive than in the first of the *Legends, Lemminkäinen and the Maidens of the Island*, which was written in 1895 and revised two years later. This and its companion piece, *Lemminkäinen in Tuonela*, were not performed again until the 1930s, and did not appear in print until after the Second World War. Although he was a highly self-critical artist, Sibelius was in this instance moved to withhold them because of Kajanus's lack of enthusiasm. Inspiration runs high in *Lemminkäinen and the Maidens of the Island* not only just in the evocative opening bars. The thematic ideas fall into two categories, the one passionate and tender, and the other rhythmic and dance-like. The story comes from *Runo* XXIX of the *Kalevala*: Lemminkäinen is the typical hero of Nordic mythology, tough and fearless with more than a touch of Don Juan about him, and this episode tells how the young hero wreaks havoc with the hearts of the young maidens of the Island, until the return of the men from warfare prompts him to leave – much to their grief and his! To this the coda bears witness, and its woodwind cries seem to emulate the sound of the cranes and geese that Sibelius loved all his life. But the tone poem follows not so much the letter of the events unfolded in the poem but their spirit. Indeed, in all of the *Legends* Sibelius evokes atmosphere rather than portrays narrative; only two of his tone-poems, *Pohjola's Daughter* and *Luonnotar* are, like *Don Juan* or *Till Eulenspiegel*, in any way representational.

The two groups of themes alternate: the first represent Lemminkäinen and the second the dancing and other festivities on the island. Though neither *En Saga* nor *The Swan* reveals any trace of Russian influence, this work does. The first group includes a theme distinctly reminiscent of Balakirev's first symphony, full of tenderness and warmth. Other ideas, too, confirm the feeling that Sibelius is succumbing to the spell of the Russian nationalists (see ex. 33).

After the magical introduction (nothing could be more characteristic than these bars), the tonality gravitates towards E flat, where the second group of themes appears. There are three elements (the first at bar 44, the second at 63 and the third at 74), all of which have an important part to play in the proceedings. The tonality is anchored, often for long periods at a time in E flat, by the liberal use of pedal points. But there are some dramatic key changes. There is a daring and effective modulation in the following quotation (bars 197–206, see ex. 34), when we see how by means of a pivot note, enharmonically altered (C flat/B natural), Sibelius moves into a distant tonality with great ease.

Ex. 33

Ex. 34

There is a good example of Sibelius's economy of means in the coda, where, as the music dies away, fragments of the second group are heard; one of the repeated woodwind cries is itself a fleeting reference to the main theme of this group. As in so many other Sibelius scores, a fragmentary idea that sounds so new and fresh is found to tie up with motifs that have occurred earlier. Sibelius's was a mind that had the capacity, developed to a remarkable degree, of constantly illuminating the same basic material.

Lemminkäinen and the Maidens of the Island is a work of fresh poetic vision, and although it betrays some debt to Slavonic romanticism, from the very opening bars it immediately proclaims a new voice in music.

Its companion piece, *Lemminkäinen in Tuonela*, which was written and revised at the same time, is on a much higher level of inspiration. Its proportions are more finely judged and its material is more compelling and more thoroughly characteristic. The story again follows the *Kalevala* and tells how, in Runo XIV, one of the herdsmen from Pohjola kills Lemminkäinen as he is himself on the point of shooting the Black Swan. The dark waters of the River of Death bear Lemminkäinen's body to Tuonela. The opening bars set this mood with real poetic vision: *tremolando* strings insistently surge forward and convey an awe-inspiring image of the waters that are to bear the hero's body to Tuonela. Superimposed on this at bar 37 is a woodwind cry, a motif which never moves very far away from its initial note, and when it does, returns to it as if drawn by an irresistible magnetic force. The work, roughly speaking, falls into three parts, the outer two being largely concerned with this opening material. There are some immensely impressive and powerful brass suspensions which sear through the texture. The middle section is one of the most inspired passages in all early Sibelius, and it seems strange that the composer should have withheld music of this order for so long. We are plunged abruptly from F sharp minor into A minor with magical effect. The transition is beautifully contrived: the final element of the main motif (marked *a*) is transformed by the clarinet before being passed to the strings, who intone it with gentle, icy insistence (see ex. 35). This A minor idea is to be found among the sketches for *The Building of the Boat*, where Sibelius scribbled over it, 'the Maiden of Death'. In the opera she would have rowed Väinämöinen across the river to Tuonela. Here in the tone-poem she symbolizes the very opposite, the love of his mother whose ministrations return him to life. The essential contour of this melody is runic; it is accommodated with astonishing simplicity within the compass of the fifth and, as in so much of his music of the period (the 'Ballade' from the *Karelia* music, *Lemminkäinen's Homeward Journey*) and indeed later works such as *Pohjola's Daughter* and *Night Ride and Sunrise*, he studiously flattens the leading note.

What distinguishes *Lemminkäinen in Tuonela* from the other *Legends* is its use for dramatic effect of direct tonal constrasts: in no other symphonic poem is this so pronounced. The resumption of the material of the first section takes place without the remotest preparation (bars 276–7) and the effect is no less striking than the example quoted above. The closing pages of the work, too, are characteristic of the tonal ambiguity

Ex. 35

that Sibelius likes to leave with his listener here: it is by these means, and the dark, sombre orchestral colouring, that Sibelius evokes so powerfully the atmosphere of the legend.

Lemminkäinen's Homeward Journey tells how the hero, having been released from Tuonela with the remnants of his body sewn together by his mother's magic charms, makes his journey homeward. Sibelius fuses two separate episodes in the *Kalevala* which relate all the excitement that surrounds Lemminkäinen's progress as he gallops furiously through the wild forest landscape of the Northland. The piece is an exciting *moto perpetuo*: the opening three-note figure is a kind of seminal motive that fertilizes all the subsequent thematic material. A great deal of physical excitement is generated by means of the insistent ostinatos, and sustained semiquaver activity. Though none of the modulations is comparable in dramatic effect to those of *Lemminkäinen in Tuonela*, they do serve by means of their frequency (the rate of key change is naturally higher) to strengthen the illusion of a journey through constantly changing terrain. This is reinforced when, at the end of the work, which began in C minor, the colours brighten and the last part takes place in E flat major: one feels the terrain is a welcoming one. Some of the ostinatos[1] are reminiscent of those in *En Saga* and those which Sibelius later uses in *Night Ride and Sunrise*, a work which is not dissimilar in theme. In their effect, too, the closing bars curiously anticipate those of the first movement of the fifth symphony.

In between the *Four Legends* and *Pohjola's Daughter*, in which Sibelius again draws on the *Kalevala*, comes the tone-poem *Finlandia* written in 1899 and revised the following year. Feelings of national patriotism, however ardent they may be, hardly present the noblest aspect of mankind: such examples of musical nationalism as Elgar's *Pomp and Circumstance* marches or Tchaikovsky's *1812* overture, to name only two, do not show their composers in their most favourable light. Musically, *Finlandia* points backwards to the Lisztian inheritance: its gestures are dramatic (some might say melodramatic) and its structure simple and straightforward, and yet the pleading, patriotic tone of the woodwind theme is unfailingly effective. All the same it is no more fit to move in the company of the *Legends* or *En Saga*, let alone the later symphonic poems, than Elgar's patriotic pieces are worthy bedfellows of the Second Symphony or *The Dream of Gerontius*.

The symphonic poems that Sibelius wrote during the present century are among his very greatest works and, incidentally, among the greatest essays in this form. To each of them he brings a completely fresh approach; no two are alike in their treatment of the programmatic content or in their musical design. *Pohjola's Daughter* is on the face of it the most 'representational' of them. It comes from 1906, a particularly fruitful period in Sibelius's career. He had just completed the definitive version of the Violin Concerto and composed the incidental music for *Pélleas et Mélisande*; he was poised to write another – and very beautiful – score for the Swedish Theatre, for *Belshazzar's Feast*, while all the time the Third Symphony was busy forming in his mind. None of his tone poems *seems* more meticulously programmatic: the sounds of the maiden of the North seated on a rainbow at her spinning-wheel could hardly be more vivid, as are Väinämöinen's struggles with his impossible tasks. So it comes as something of a surprise to learn that he refers to it in his letters to Carpelan and his new publisher, Robert Lienau as *Luonnotar*. In May he

---

[1] pp. 38–41 of the miniature score published by British and Continental Music Agencies Ltd.

wrote to Lienau to say that '*Luonnotar*, the new symphonic poem is ready and it only remains to make a fair copy of the score'. And only a month later he speaks of *Luonnotar* to his brother Christian. Then suddenly, out of the blue, only a few days later he wrote again to his publisher, talking about 'a symphonic fantasia' on a completely different programme, the episode from the *Kalevala* about Väinämöinen and Pohjola's Daughter. At the end of June he mentions the new work to Robert Lienau, adding that he has not wholly abandoned the idea of a piece on the Luonnotar theme. At first Sibelius simply wanted to call the new piece, *Väinämöinen* but Lienau was doubtful about its appeal. In fact it was Lienau's idea to call the piece 'Pohjola's Daughter' and Sibelius who resisted the suggestion, because of the opera of that name by Oskar Merikanto. Sibelius's counter-suggestion, obviously inspired by *Ein Heldenleben* was '*L'aventure d'un héros*', but Lienau would not be dissuaded and *Pohjola's Daughter* it became.

The programme tells how Väinäimöinen is on his way home from the Northland when he meets the beautiful maid of Pohjola, seated astride a rainbow, busy at her spinning wheel. He immediately succumbs to her cool charms but she is not responsive to his importunings and declines to join him on his journey. To make an end of his wooing, she sets him a number of impossible tasks, such as making a boat from the fragments of her spindle and tying an egg into invisible knots. Väinämöinen sets about these with grim determination but they prove beyond even his magic powers and he is forced to continue his journey alone. Whatever the origins of its inspiration, no Sibelius work more completely fulfils both programmatic expectations and purely symphonic needs. The unity of the material strikes the listener most forcibly. But what we take as a vivid evocation of the spinning-wheel and the rainbow, could just as easily have been intended as the bird soaring above the oceans on its long quest in *Luonnotar*, which tells of the creation of the world as related in the first *Runo* of the *Kalevala*. There is the powerful brass theme which evokes Väinämöinen's sledge on its homeward journey. It is suddenly silenced by the vision of the beautiful maid of Pohjola and returns in the development section where he labours to perform the impossible tasks she has set him. All these could just as easily represent the energies unleased when the firmament was created. The cello theme which sets the mood of the saga, the cor anglais theme that grows out of it, are related in an organic way that is paralleled only in the symphonies. Yet the cello theme 'speaks' and intones, as it were, in much the same way as a narrator or runic singer in the *Kalevala*. *Pohjola's Daughter* is an unqualified masterpiece. It is the most ambitious and highly organized of Sibelius's essays in this form that he had attempted up to this time. As an example of programmatic art its achievement is fully commensurate with the finest of the Strauss epic tone-poems like *Don Juan* or *Till Eulenspiegel*, while as pure music it represents a degree of cohesion and integration even greater than Strauss's.

Pohjola's Daughter has overshadowed its immediate successor, *Night Ride and Sunrise*, which Sibelius completed in November 1908. Like so many pieces, it is very much at the mercy of its interpreter, and unless the cumulative effect of the long first section is realized in performance, the impact of the work tends to be greatly diminished. It is in fact a most exciting piece, every bar of which is characteristic of the composer. At first glance the ostinatos and the lengthy pedal points suggest that the work belongs more to his early period; indeed, the ostinatos are of a type that we have already encountered in *Lemminkäinen's Homeward Journey* and *En Saga*. Here, though, Sibelius makes even more daring use of these devices: they are sustained at greater length and managed with the greater simplicity of real assurance.

Night Ride and Sunrise falls roughly into the two sections suggested by its title. The first is almost entirely dominated by a trochaic rhythm, which settles down in E flat, though there are a number of gentle key shifts durings its course. This insistent rhythm well conveys the effect of an endless journey through a changing, shadowy landscape. Sibelius often heightens the tension and mystery by reducing the dynamics to a mere whisper. He holds back the most important thematic idea of the section for a considerable time: the tonality has moved to C minor and over an ostinato figure the woodwind give out this stirring motif:

Ex. 36

The trochaic rhythm gives way, almost imperceptibly, when the music moves into G minor. Now the scoring is reversed: the ostinato figure is heard on the woodwind while the violins announce the motif *sul* G. The skill with which Sibelius changes from the trochaic ostinato to equal semiquavers is no less evident in the transition to the second section of the work. This begins with some very eloquent writing for strings alone.

Afterwards Sibelius evokes with music of tremendous power and imaginative intensity the magical changes wrought by the sunrise in these northern latitudes. The simplicity of some of the thematic material serves only to underline the feeling of contact with nature. There is some magnificent writing for brass that adds to the growing warmth of feeling – a warmth, incidentally, that is unusual in Sibelius's later nature music. At the height of their glowing peroration the brass are suddenly interrupted by some chords that in their remote and mysterious beauty provide the most poetic touch in the whole work. Their cool pallor contrasts markedly with the rich E flat colouring of the context.

Night Ride and Sunrise has something of the tonal stability that marks off the later symphonic poems from *En Saga* and the *Four Legends*. Abrupt key changes become far fewer in the later tone-poems, and, though there are many excursions into related keys, the bulk of the action is played out in the area of E flat, just as for all its periods of uncertain tonality B minor is the basic anchorage of *Tapiola*. There are also many surprising touches of orchestration, including some marvellously splenetic bassoon comments derived from the opening orchestral out-burst. Indeed, *Night Ride* has many touches of real vision, and it is a pity that it is so seldom heard. Although it cannot match *Pohjola's Daughter* in its compactness of utterance and variety of ideas, any more than it can the profound imaginative intensity of *The Bard* or *Tapiola*, it is nevertheless a very fine piece.

The Bard (1913) shares with *Night Ride and Sunrise* the absence of any detailed programme, though a good deal of the latter is frankly pictorial. Nothing could be in greater contrast to *Night Ride* than this intense and contemplative work, Sibelius's first orchestral piece (apart from the *Scènes historiques*) after the Fourth Symphony. Whereas *Night Ride* is spacious, largely extrovert in feeling with a good measure of orchestral excitement, a number of easily recognizable melodic strands, and a glowing climax in the major key, *The Bard* is by contrast the shortest and most introspective. Its slow pace precludes any of the rhythmic excite-ment that the *Night Ride* offers; its melodic substance is slight and confined in fact to a few gentle wisps of melody. The scoring is for the most part soft and delicate, with a harp playing an important role in the proceedings. But despite its brevity and its static quality, *The Bard* is no slight work. Its cryptic thematic utterance matches its slender proportions and intimate musings. Superficially it falls into two parts, but the change in mood between them might well be compared to the shift in emphasis in the second part of a sonnet. Both parts are closely related in feeling, but the second and slightly shorter section raises the emotional temperature a little. However, composure returns with the reassertion of the gentle melancholy of the opening.

The very beginning of the work is full of poetry: the melodic strands from which it is woven are of the greatest simplicity. A descending sequence of chords on the harp and a semiquaver rustle from the violas provide the main substance of the music. The atmosphere evoked is both intense and haunting: it is quite unlike any of the other tone-poems in feeling:

Ex. 37

Sibelius returned to the theme of Luonnotar at this point. In 1910 he had been planning a setting of Edgar Allan Poe's *The Raven* for Aino Ackté, and sketches for this reached a fairly advanced stage. Ackté had hoped for a demanding concert aria that she could take on her 1911 tour of Germany but as Tawaststjerna has shown, the thematic substance of this finally found its way into the Fourth Symphony on which Sibelius was also working at the time. Hence Ackté was disappointed and it was a further three years before he set matters to right with *Luonnotar*. When in 1913 he was unable to fulfil a commission from the Gloucester Festival for a new choral work, he substituted the newly-composed tone-poem for voice and orchestra.

Luonnotar is one of Sibelius's most imaginative creations, whose exacting vocal part with its wide tessitura and ungrateful line has militated against its wider dissemination. The tessitura extends from the B immediately below middle C right up to C flat above the stave (exactly two octaves) and the vocal writing makes cruel demands on the soloist.

The line is often angular: there is an exposed entry (on B double flat above
the stave) against an accompaniment consisting of B flat, F, G flat and D
flat, while there are numerous other supported entries ascending to C flat,
one of them *pp*. The melodic line shows an uncanny feeling for the
language; although one occasionally feels on looking at the score that the
writing is instrumental, in performance, in the language for which it was
intended, it sounds perfectly judged. The opening idea is a gentle rustling
from the strings (F sharp minor), and the voice then enters with its
powerfully chiselled theme:

Ex. 38

The rising figure is an important part of the material; and though there is
no opportunity for orchestral development on quite the same scale as in
the purely instrumental symphonic poems, this does serve to announce

the cries of an ascending minor third one hears from the voice in the development. The secondary idea (in B flat minor) has a harp ostinato accompaniment and evokes an atmosphere even stranger than that of *The Bard*. The voice line again seems quasi-instrumental on paper, but once heard in the original language its vocal quality becomes apparent:

Ex. 39

Both these passages are restated, but as is always the case with the symphonic poems the process of development is continuous. Only this second idea is left virtually unchanged. It leads directly into what is perhaps the most mysterious of all Sibelius's codas. *Luonnotar* is among the most intense visions that Sibelius ever penned, surpassed only by the extraordinary world he conjures up in his last and greatest *Kalevala* tone-poem, *Tapiola*.

Unlike the brooding *Luonnotar*, *The Oceanides* does not draw on the *Kalevala*. It is Sibelius's only tone-poem to evoke the world of Homeric mythology. Although the title of the work is given as *Aallotaret*, Sibelius made it clear that this was but a translation into the terms of the Finnish sagas. The Oceanides were the nymphs that inhabited the rivers, streams and waters of classical antiquity. The work was written for Sibelius's American tour in 1914 and was apparently revised after his Atlantic crossing. The work is far more ambitious and highly organized in design than *The Bard*, and far more dramatic in content. The music is richer in melodic interest and more varied in mood. The greyish, ethereal opening very quickly merges into a much sunnier mood, though the sunlight is of the pale northern variety, all the more exquisite for being so short-lived. The proceedings are punctuated by the opening flute theme, and this lends the work something of the aspect of a free rondo. Towards the end of the piece clouds darken the horizon and the music builds up to a tremendous climax.

Several writers have commented on its 'impressionism'. Certainly the orchestral layout, with its liquid sounds from the harp and its delicate writing for the strings, produces an effect which differs from any of the previous tone-poems or, for that matter, any of Sibelius's other works up to this time. However, on closer examination *The Oceanides* can be seen to employ the normal Sibelian procedures and techniques. Its growth from the opening bars onward is profoundly organic, and its apparent independence from the rest of Sibelius's work is manifest only at a superficial level.

The Oceanides was the last of Sibelius's tone-poems to be written before the First World War. A gap of almost twelve years elapsed before his last and greatest symphonic poem was finished. It is indeed arguable that *Tapiola* is his greatest single achievement. Already in the thirties Cecil Gray made sweeping claims for it: 'Even if Sibelius had written nothing else, this one work would entitle him to a place among the greatest masters of all time.' There is no doubt that in *Tapiola* Sibelius exhibits the most subtle and complete mastery of symphonic procedure, in the sense that he achieves a continuity of thought paralleled only in the symphonies. *Tapiola* is unique even in Sibelius's output: its world is new and unexplored, a world of strange new sounds, a landscape that no tone-poem has painted with such inner conviction and complete sympathy. Nowhere, except possibly in Debussy's *La mer* and 'Nuages', is the feeling for nature so intense as to amount to complete identification. Yet though its world is unpeopled and the evocation of the unending sunless forests so powerful, there is, particularly in the closing pages, a longing for human contact.

Tapio is the god of the forest in the *Kalevala*. The score is prefaced by the oft-quoted quatrain which Sibelius himself supplied when asked by his publisher to explain the title:

Widespread they stand, the Northland's dusky forests,
Ancient, mysterious, brooding savage dreams;
Within them dwells the Forest's mighty god,
And wood-sprites in the gloom weave magic secrets.

The tone-poem is to all intents and purposes monothematic, since the material of the work is nearly all derived in some way or other from the opening theme. It was Ernest Newman who called *Tapiola* a symphony and drew attention to the extraordinary degree of organic cohesion that marks Sibelius's thinking in this work. It is in this important sense, though not in any other, that *Tapiola* can be called symphonic. The usual dramatic interest and contrast of key centres that we associate with the symphony are not in evidence.

Of all Sibelius's work it is *Tapiola* which shows the most profound originality in its handling of the orchestra. The sounds that he draws from what is merely a normal large orchestra without extra percussion or even harp are completely new. No one had ever before made the orchestra sound as it does in *Tapiola*; nor for that matter is so highly personal an utterance susceptible of imitation. All the familiar features of Sibelius's scoring are to be found here: the extraordinarily resourceful and imaginative use of the woodwind, the massive writing for the brass and the cross-hatch writing for the strings. But the demands made on all these are pressed to their uttermost limits, and the invention is inseparable from the instruments to a degree unsurpassed elsewhere in his work. A large amount of Sibelius's music, including the last four symphonies and many of the tone-poems, is so completely identified with the orchestral source of sound that it is impossible to conceive of them in other terms. Of no work is this more true than *Tapiola*. It is this score, too, that exhibits the most thorough-going and imaginative use of the pedal point in all Sibelius. More often than not it is a major second. As in the seventh symphony, we find the same mastery of transition and the same capacity to move simultaneously at two levels of tempo. One such transition is the passage beginning at bar 208 (fig. G) where the eerie scherzo-like exchanges between the wind and strings are accompanied unobtrusively by a pedal point which floats gently forward at a slower tempo (on horns, bassoons and clarinets): it is this slower tempo which by means of Sibelius's subtle alchemy comes to assume the greater importance.

One does not have to have experienced the vast forests of Scandinavia with all their variety of moods, colours and sounds, their immense loneliness, their magic, terror and majesty, for Sibelius's vision in *Tapiola* to make its impact. Its greatness communicates itself independently of its extra-musical intentions. Although it is as perfect an evocation of the forest as is *La mer* of the sea, its greatness lies in its impact in terms of pure music. In its homogeneity, concentration of utterance and intensity of vision it is a masterpice of the first order.

9

Other orchestral music

Although Sibelius's mastery of the orchestra was not fully attained until the first years of the present century, it is clear that right from the very beginning his approach to the medium was astonishingly original. Like most Scandinavian composers – Nielsen, Berwald and Grieg, to name only three – he writes superbly for the strings. This is only to be expected from a composer who was himself a violinist (as was Berwald) and was accustomed in his early years to writing for various string combinations. But it is interesting to watch the growth of his equally original wood-wind and brass writing – not to mention the percussion. Few modern composers have made so extensive (and, again, individual) use of the timpani. What is surprising is that his cross-hatch string writing, his woodwind in thirds, the powerful brass chords which immediately drop to *pp* and then gradually swell to *ff*, rarely seem to be mere mannerisms, so organically welded are they into his way of orchestral thinking. It is only when these devices are taken over by lesser composers – Dag Wirén is an example, or (nearer home) Moeran in his symphony in G minor – that they appear as non-organic figures of speech.

Sibelius's very first works for the orchestra date from his year in Vienna, when he was studying with Goldmark and Robert Fuchs. The earliest is an Overture in E Major. This and the *Scène de ballet* were originally to have formed the first two movements of a symphony. In April 1891 Sibelius sent them to Kajanus, who performed them later the same month, despite a subsequent telegram asking him to stay his hand. The Overture is a sonata-form movement with an appealing second group, very much in his *Karelia* idiom, which offers a distinct portent of the good things to come. The *Scène de ballet*, which Sibelius himself had already come to dislike by the time of *Kullervo*, makes a token gesture towards cosmopolitan sophistication with its castanets and dance-like rhythm, but Sibelius must have felt its inadequacy when measured against Strauss's accomplishments at the same age.

Most of the well-known works up to the first symphony have come down to us in revised form: *En Saga* and the *Four Legends* are obvious cases. Hearing his music played, and no doubt benefiting from the advice of Kajanus, Sibelius was able to adjust his scores to produce exactly the effect he wanted. The *Karelia* music (1893) is the very first of the well-known works to which he made no major subsequent alteration. Although its seams are far from invisible, the Overture, op. 10, is an enjoyable piece. The scoring is thicker and at tuttis brasher than in the Suite, where there is much less doubling, and the balance of the work is somewhat upset by the introduction of the famous tune from the *Intermezzo*. The second group is one of those melodies that were thought at the time to derive from Karelian folk-music. It seems on the surface to relate to the Russian 'Five'; yet both in the rhythmic inflexion of the line and its absence of squareness there is a distinctly Finnish flavour.

The Suite itself is much better known – and also much better! *Kullervo* had not only established Sibelius as a major figure on the Finnish musical stage, but had been acclaimed for its distinctively 'Finnish tone', so that it was inevitable that commissions of the kind that prompted *Karelia* would come his way. The pageant, a genre of entertainment that has passed from fashion in our more sophisticated times, depicted scenes from Karelian history, and from his score of eight numbers Sibelius published a suite of three pieces. The 'Intermezzo', which had originally depicted the Karelians passing in procession to offer tribute to a Lithuanian prince, opens with horn calls over tremolo *pp* strings. It is strongly reminiscent of Bruckner though it soon assumes a thoroughly Sibelian mantle. There had been Brucknerian echoes in *Kullervo* and there was (to quote one of Sibelius's most loyal advocates on the concert podium and in the recording studio, Herbert von Karajan) 'a much deeper influence, affinity, kinship – call it what you like. There is this sense of the "*Ur-Wald*" the primaeval forest, the feeling of some elemental power, that one is dealing with something profound.' In the pageant, the music of the second movement, the 'Ballade', originally portrayed the deposed figure of Karl Knutsson listening reflectively to a minstrel at Viipuri castle.[1] It is a gentle, reflective piece scored with much greater economy than the overture, and though its profile is less highly defined than that of its companions, its chaste, pastoral flavour makes a splendid foil to the outer movements. The modal writing occasionally sounds a little like Nielsen (and there is even a brief moment in the Ballet Suite in which chattering strings call to mind the Danish master). The third movement, the 'Alla marcia', follows a call to battle (Sibelius originally pencilled in the words, '*Marsch nach einem alten motif*' over the score). It is the most popular of the three pieces

[1] Karl Knutsson was Regent of Sweden but overthrown in 1464, after which he repaired to his lands in Finland.

– understandably so, for not only is the movement excellently proportioned, but its fresh, robust theme is one of which the listener never seems to tire.

Skogsrået (The Wood-Nymph), also known as *Ballade pour l'orchestre*, comes from the following year though it began life as a melodrama for speaker, strings, horn and piano to words of Runeberg, written for a concert in aid of the Finnish National Theatre. Like the pagaent, the melodrama has fallen into desuetude though the genre survived well into the present century (Debussy in the *Chansons de Bilitis*, Hindemith in *Herodïade* and so on). Tawaststjerna speaks of it as 'an experiment' but regrets that Sibelius did not wait before refashioning it as a purely orchestral tone-poem. He praises its 'splendid melodic ideas' and 'luxuriant and effective' scoring, not phrases that immediately spring to mind when listening to *Vårsång* (Spring Song). After its première in 1894 Sibelius revised it, omitting the final section, which was in a Spanish dance rhythm, transposing it all to his then favourite 'Nordic' key, F major. Its main theme is long-breathed but bland and, judged by Sibelius's exalted standards, it rarely rises above the commonplace. Be that as it may, the composer himself must have had some affection for both pieces, for in the periodic purges of his opus list they emerge unscathed. Moreover in the form in which we know it, *Vårsång* dates from 1903, while despite its early opus number, the first set of *Scènes historiques* are in effect much later than at first appears. There are also some smaller pieces worthy of mention: the *Menuetto* (1894), variously known as *Menuett-Impromptu* or *Tempo di menuetto* has a winning charm, though most Sibelians would be hard put to place its opening. Unusually for Sibelius it includes parts for tambourine and glockenspiel, and a few years later he re-used the piece in the incidental music to *King Christian II*, but did not feel disposed to include it in the Suite – or indeed publish it. There are one or two pieces from the 1890s for wind and brass: *Tiera* for brass septet and percussion is a tone-poem in name rather than substance. Tiera is a comrade-in-arms of Lemminkäinen, and the work belongs to those patriotic genre pieces Sibelius and Finland favoured at the turn of the century. It is short, barely five minutes in duration, and only intermittently characteristic. Nor is the much earlier *Preludio* fully individual: it does not wear its debt to Wagner lightly, but there is a genuine nobility that is imposing.

The Overture in A minor was composed for the concert in March 1902 at which the Second Symphony was given its première. It was said to have been written in an hotel room during the course of one night, a legend that gives some hostages to fortune. It sounds hastily put-together and has a certain lop-sided character. Sibelius never thought well enough of it to authorise its publication, though the opening fanfares are stirring and resonate in the mind: there is a mildly hilarious allegro which is far removed from the pomp of the opening and has little logical connection with it. Unlike the *Cassazione* of only two years later, it sounds as if it could have been written in the early 1890s. The *Cassazione*, or *Fantasy for orchestra*, does on the other hand sound as if it is from 1904 (though it misleadingly bears the opus number immediately preceding *Kullervo*). After its première Sibelius decided to revise it, which he did the following year but he never published it and the score bears a note 'to be reworked'. It has many felicities and is thoroughly characteristic, not so far removed from the world of the *King Christian II* music or the score for *Pelléas*, to which it is close in time (an idea for two clarinets prompts thoughts of 'The three blind sisters'). There are vague glimmerings of music to come (a clarinet figure even hints at *Pohjola's Daughter*) and there is also a solemn hymn-like figure on the strings which resurfaces in the Epilogue to the 1927 Helsinki production of *The Tempest*. Its weakness is not in the quality of the individual ideas but the thread that holds them together.

The *Scènes historiques*, op. 25 (1899), were all subsequently revised in 1911, while the second set, op. 66, was written the following year. The first is arranged from the music to various patriotic tableaux which Sibelius wrote for the press celebrations. The second is unconnected with the original score, although Furuhjelm wrote that one of the themes from 'At the Drawbridge' came from the third tableau.

The first scene, 'All' Overtura', originally formed part of a tableau which pictured Väinämöinen seated on a rock strumming his *kantele* while the Maiden of Pohjola was to be seen at her golden spinning-wheel in the sky. The work has a neo-classical simplicity of language which anticipates the Sibelius of the Third Symphony rather than the second, which had yet to be written. Its thematic material is not, however, as striking as that of the *Scena*, a more sombre work cast in a dark key (E flat minor) and again fully characteristic of the mature composer. Designed to accompany the tableau depicting Finland during the Thirty Years War, this seldom-heard piece has many highly dramatic moments in which the mysterious whisperings of the strings are heard (see ex. 40). A flute figure immediately after this passage is strikingly reminiscent of the Third Symphony. 'Festivo' is the best-known of all the six *Scènes historiques*, and it is the only piece in which Sibelius employs Spanish rhythms. Taken partly from the third tableau set in the sixteenth-century court of the Swedish governor of Åbo (or Turku), where festivities are in progress, the work has a gay, carefree character. It presumably acquires its Spanish

Ex. 40

flavouring from the duke's wife, Catharina Jagellonica, and makes use of castanets.

'The chase' is undeniably first class. Its powerful opening bars leave no doubt that it is set in a wild Nordic landscape: the horn calls echo one another under menacing, cloud-laden skies. No less characteristic is the way in which the dark textures quickly disperse and give way to an exciting *Allegro* whose sense of sheer physical momentum and exuberance makes one think immediately of *Night Ride* and *Lemminkäinen's Homeward Journey*. The 'Love song', the second of the later set, gives the lie to those who deny Sibelius's warmth. Horns and bassoons support a beautiful figure on muted violas *divisi*: this is a sustained threnody of great eloquence.

'At the drawbridge' is a masterly example of Sibelius's lighter music: it misses perfection only by a few bars, for it would gain immeasurably by being very slightly shortened. Two flutes lead an altogether delightful and often witty woodwind conversation over a sustained pizzicato accompaniment from the strings. There is a lightness of touch and texture about this which suggests a sun-filled landscape, and the horizon only darkens at fig. E, a pedal point over which a group of semiquavers on the strings and a questioning oboe and clarinet figure are heard (was this the idea Furuhjelm mentions? In another context it could well assume an Iberian flavour). These clouds gather from time to time, but never succeed in dispelling the atmosphere of lightness and gaiety. It is a pity that

Sibelius permits the syncopated horn chords to descend chromatically at fig. J; this crude passage and perhaps the very closing bars are the only blemishes on an otherwise beautifully judged miniature.

If the *Scènes historiques* show us the nature poet that Sibelius has become, the Romance in C major for strings, op. 42 (1904), belongs to the elegiac, Grieg-like tradition which he so magnificently transcended elsewhere. Even if we agree that the string writing is a model of effectiveness and of unextravagant and resourceful variety, the fact remains that the Romance in C is too mild-mannered a work, too lacking in concentration to rank among the finest Sibelius. Although it is vastly superior to the *Andante festivo* for strings (1922), which is given on State occasions in Finland, it lacks the ultimate ounce of poetic intensity that we find in *Rakastava*. *Rakastava* (The Lover), op. 14, extends the elegiac Scandinavian tradition well beyond its highly circumscribed and local boundaries: there is no doubt that it is one of Sibelius's most perfect compositions. To the strings of the Romance in C major Sibelius here adds percussion – timpani in the outer movements and a triangle in the innermost. The thematic substance from which the suite is derived comes from the choral work of the same name written in 1893, settings of poems from Lönnrot's *Kanteletar*. When Sibelius came to rearrange the work a year after it appeared in its original form for male chorus *a cappella*, he added strings.

In 1898 he rearranged it a second time for mixed chorus *a cappella*, but in 1911 he did a good deal more than merely rearrange. To follow the changes through which *Rakastava* passed would in itself provide a fascinating study of Sibelius's working methods and his feeling for voices. Nobody who was unaware of its origins would imagine that *Rakastava* was not wholly conceived in terms of the strings, so perfectly does it seem to belong to its medium. It would be difficult to place the work in Sibelius's output if one did not know its history. So perfect is its craftsmanship, so unified is each part to the whole, so balanced are the means and the ends, that it could only be by a master who had achieved as much as Sibelius had by 1911; at the same time, the ethos of the music belongs to the early years of his self-discovery and the thematic material has nothing of the brooding introspection of the Fourth Symphony. Yet as far as his feeling for the medium is concerned there is no doubt that this is as perfect as *Voces intimae*, with which it has more in common than its key. Just as the first movement of the quartet compresses the whole of a subtly masterful sonata drama into a comparatively short time, so *Rakastava* concentrates all its lyrical intensity and dramatic allusion into the most compact of frameworks. The delicacy and tenderness with which Sibelius touches on the feelings of young love with all its poetry, anguish and ecstasy, is indeed far removed from the Gallic conception of him as remote and detached. The melodic substance is of the very highest: yet, as with all Sibelius, it is subtly related to everything else in the music. This touching melody that opens the last movement, 'Good night – Farewell!':

Ex. 41

seems to arise naturally from a subsidiary figure in the first, 'The lover':

Ex. 42

There is no more wonderful tune in all Sibelius than that of the exquisitely wrought and moving second movement, 'The path of the beloved'.

At the present time *Rakastava* seems to have fallen out of the repertory, but one can confidently predict that this state of affairs will not continue, for it is a work of astonishing beauty. The neglect of *In Memoriam* (1909) is less difficult to appreciate. It belongs to that category of Sibelius's compositions that will always (and rightly) provoke division of opinion. *In Memoriam* is not among his finest work, yet at the same time to dismiss it as 'a pretentious conflation of the *Eroica* slow movement and the funeral march from *Götterdämmerung* but without the virtues of either'[1] is too easy a course to take and ignores the searching quality of grief that we find in such a remarkably comfortless passage as this:

[1]Ralph Wood in Gerald Abraham's *Sibelius, a Symposium*, p. 43.

Ex. 43

The angularity and starkness of the bassoon figure almost anticipate Shostakovich. Yet *In Memoriam*, for all its ring of genuine feeling, is not so personal an utterance as one would expect. It seems to have the quality of the sorrow one feels on the death of a well-loved public figure or a favourite writer or artist rather than the loss of a close and intimate friend. But the inexorability of its onward movement, the wave upon wave of descending chromatic lines, and the unrelenting martial rhythms, are not unimpressive.

There are three smaller works for orchestra written during the first decade of the century: *The Dryad* (1910) and the *Dance Intermezzo* (1904, revised 1907), which share the same opus number (45), and *Pan and Echo* (1906) also known as the *Dance Intermezzo* No. 3. Of these the most poignant is *The Dryad* which could possibly be viewed as a series of footnotes to the slow movement of the Fourth Symphony, or chips from the same block. It certainly shares something of its exploratory feeling and its sense of space. Tawaststjerna speaks of its 'free-floating quality . . . liberated from the rigid sense of bar lines' and the whole piece inhabits a weightless, dreamlike world. Its character can best be described as aphoristic; there is, as it were, a kaleidoscope of images rather than any real continuity of growth. At one point (bars 13–15) we are confronted with a clear reminder of the second group of the first movement of the symphony. Although there are many imaginative touches, the work as a whole does not seem quite to hang together. The *commodo* section at fig. E, for example, does not belong to the same world as the searching opening bars.

Ex. 44

Here is another instance of the effect of space produced by omitting the inner harmonic support. One of Sibelius's achievements between the Third and Fourth Symphonies was to show that he could work without this 'continuo' support. Mahler was arriving at much the same goal during the first decade of the century; the first episode of the finale of his ninth symphony is a perfect instance of this. *The Dryad* is scored for fairly large forces, though Sibelius takes (for him) the unusual step of omitting the timpani.

Its companion piece, the *Dance Intermezzo* is much earlier. In March 1904 he had conducted the *Musik einer scene (Ein Fichtenbaum träumt von einer Palme)*: he had been working on a tone-poem inspired by Heine's poem of a northern pine dreaming of a palm tree as early as 1897. The *Dance Intermezzo* first appeared in a piano reduction later that year and then in orchestral garb three years later, the four introductory bars being displaced by a harp glissando. It is unashamed light music and – *pace* earlier editions – not, I think, particularly good light music. It bears no relationship to *The Dryad* in character or in quality. *Pan and Echo* (or at least its opening half) is of finer quality and more characteristic even if the second half sails too close to banality for comfort. None of these pieces can really sustain the claims on our attention as the *Scènes historiques* or Nielsen's *Pan and Syrinx*.

Were it not for the evidence of the Sixth and Seventh Symphonies, *Tapiola* and *The Tempest*, one might assume, from the post-war orchestral works in smaller forms, a decline in Sibelius's creative powers. The Three Pieces, op. 96, find him in Viennese waltz mode, and pay tribute to Johann Strauss whose waltzes Sibelius admired all his life. The *Valse lyrique* has a certain appeal: the *Valse chevaleresque* has not! Both derive from 1921 and are transcriptions of piano pieces, though the *Valse lyrique* of 1919 exists in an earlier version as *Syringa*, and had originally been intended as the last of the op. 75 set. *Autrefois*, on the other hand, also from 1919, is a totally different matter. Unlike its two companions, the piano version is a transcription. It has a beguiling charm and is by far the most haunting of these pastiches. Sibelius introduces two sopranos (clarinets can be substituted in their absence) and their vocalise communicates a peculiarly fragile charm laden with nostalgia.

The two suites, op. 98, are frankly lightweight but not without charm. The first, *Suite mignonne*, is for flute and strings, and the criticism to which it has been subjected (including in earlier editions of this volume) has been unnecessarily harsh. It is like reproaching a charming if empty-headed flapper for not being a blue-stocking. There is a certain period quality about the 'Petite scène', a faint whiff of the tea-shop, of ferns and fans, and inexpensive perfume. True the opening sequences are a bit thin and feeble: the preparation for the entry of the main theme is not wholly convincing, but there is real charm. The opening of the delightful 'Polka' could easily come from a Tchaikovsky ballet, and the 'Epilogue', too, has balletic overtones. Though it is not Sibelius's best light music – far from it – neither is it negligible. The first movement of the *Suite champêtre* for strings alone is Tchaikovskian both in its rhythmic patterns and harmonic flavouring, and is slow to reveal its authorship though there is no doubt about that in the slow movement, the 'Mélodie élégiaque', whose darker overtones almost anticipate *The Tempest* music. The opening of the final 'Dance' suggests the world of the *Humoresques*, and one is tempted to view these as shavings from the same block. Of the two, the *Suite champêtre* is the more consistent. The last thing that the obstinately unmemorable *Suite*, op. 100, for harp and strings can be called is *caractéristique*. This is terribly thin, and the main idea of the finale with its empty-headed tune and oom-pah accompaniment is pretty cheap. Although the *Andante festivo* was composed in 1922 for string quartet in response to a commission from a factory, the version in which it is most often heard is Sibelius's transcription for full strings of 1930. It has a certain Purcellian solemnity and though its eloquence is very much that of an official national mouthpiece rather than the seer of *Tapiola*, it remains an affecting piece, particularly when played with the intensity the composer himself generated when he conducted it on New Year's Day 1939, the last occasion on which he stood before an orchestra, and the only example of his conducting ever to be recorded. On the other hand, the *Academic March* of 1919, written for a degree ceremony at Helsinki University, has a much stronger appeal and fully deserves a place in his catalogue.

10

Music for the theatre

One feature of the contemporary musical scene is the decline and debasement of light music. The eighteenth-century composer poured out functional music of this kind in great profusion; and although the collapse of the aristocratic order and the rise of a newly enriched *bourgeoisie* undermined standards of taste in light music, composers like Dvořák and Brahms could turn their hand to it in a way that is largely foreign to the twentieth century. There are exceptions: Poulenc, Ibert and Françaix wrote light music of great elegance. None of them, however, has to his credit the substantial symphonic works of Elgar and Sibelius; nor have any of their lighter pieces gained the wide currency of *Valse triste* or *Salut d'amour*.

Although his symphonies evince the highest quality of organic thought, Sibelius could think in the simplest musical terms and write in a comparatively light idiom. Pieces like 'The oak-tree' or the 'Chorus of the winds' from *The Tempest* are fired with an imaginative intensity worthy of the best Sibelius, yet they are essentially 'pattern' music: it is this kind of musical thinking that is the very stuff of light music. Most of his incidental music is a good deal lighter than the rest of his orchestral output, and even the best, such as *The Tempest*, contains music so light that it seems in positive danger of taking off altogether.

For much of his life Sibelius cherished operatic plans. Even as late as 1913 he was toying with the idea of an opera called *Blauer Dunst* (Blue Smoke), to a text by Adolf Paul and Birger Mörner, though *la commedia dell'arte* with a Spanish setting is hardly Sibelian territory. Like so many of his operatic ventures, it got nowhere. He took more seriously a suggestion from Ackté for an opera on *Juha*, but then decided against. (The subject was eventually tackled with conspicuous success by Aarre Merikanto.) Yet *Kullervo and his sister*, the centrepiece of the *Kullervo* Symphony, leaves no doubt that Sibelius had a powerful feeling for music drama and might in certain circumstances have become an operatic composer of some quality. But a good dramatic sense is not in itself enough: there must be a feeling for characterization, a feeling for movement on the stage, a sense of pace and much else besides. Sibelius abandoned his first opera, *Veneen luominen* (The Building of the Boat), after visiting Bayreuth in 1894, only two years after *Kullervo*, though, as we have seen, some of its material found its way into the *Lemminkäinen Legends*. Two years later came his only opera, *Jungfrun i tornet* (The Maiden in the Tower), performed in Helsinki in 1897 and never revived in the composer's lifetime. Operatic sirens beckoned from time to time – in 1912 he was toying with various projects – though none ever came near to fruition. Busoni was among those who consistently dissuaded Sibelius from straying from his symphonic path, and deep inside him Sibelius must have recognized the truth that his was not an operatic talent. In 1912 he refused Aino Ackté permission to revive *The Maiden in the Tower* at Savonlinna, ostensibly on the grounds that the libretto was unsatisfactory – which, indeed, it is! Its first revival in modern times came in January 1981 when the Finnish Radio mounted a performance conducted by the composer's son-in-law, Jussi Jalas.

The feeble libretto by Rafael Hertsberg has been blamed for the opera's failure but this is only part of the problem. It must be admitted that the quality of the musical invention is not consistently sustained. The plot does not rise above Victorian melodrama and the layout of the opera is somewhat bizarre. It falls into eight short scenes and lasts no more than thirty-five minutes. Its short Prelude is not unappealing but does not promise great things, any more than the ensuing scene between the Bailiff and the Maiden delivers them! But the orchestral interlude between the first two scenes is quite another matter. Here we have the real Sibelius, and the Maiden's Prayer in scene 2 is undoubtedly impressive: there are echoes of Wagner such as we find in some of the great orchestral songs of the following decade and the vocal line has the wide tessitura and dramatic flexibility of such masterpieces as *Höstkväll* (Autumn evening) and *Jubal*. Yet there are wonderful things in it: Sibelius is always at his best in evoking images of nature, and the choral writing at the opening of the third scene, which portrays the coming of spring ('Now in the forest the winds of spring are sighing'), is captivating and haunting. The lover's music in the fourth scene is also characteristic and interesting, and much of the music resonates in the mind afterwards. But there are many things that are best described as ineffective, and it is not only the libretto that is tarnished by naïveté. Ultimately it lacks something we find in Sibelius at his most characteristic – quite simply, a sense of mastery. Yet even if it must be admitted that this is neither good opera nor good Sibelius, there is enough musical interest to justify an occasional hearing.

125

Sibelius's involvement with the theatre as opposed to operas, was, however, lifelong. No reminder is necessary of the importance of the theatre in nineteenth-century Scandinavia as a forum for new ideas. Ibsen, Strindberg and Bjørnson are evidence of its extraordinary vitality at this time. The Scandinavian countries take the theatre seriously and there is hardly a composer of note who has not written for the stage. Of course, the days when the theatre could comfortably support permanent orchestras are long past. The end of the silent cinema and the subsequent rise of television has put paid to the convention of live incidental music, particularly on the scale of the celebrated 1926 Copenhagen production of *The Tempest*. In all, Sibelius wrote music for no fewer than eleven plays, mostly for the Swedish Theatre in Helsinki.

The first play for which he provided music was *King Christian II* by the Swedish dramatist Adolf Paul. This play was a great success at the time, though it has since disappeared from the repertory, leaving only the music to hold the public. The plot concerns the love of Christian II, whose dominion extends over all three Scandinavian countries, for a Dutch girl called Dyveke, who is a commoner. The famous 'Musette' was intended in the production to be danced by her.

According to Paul, Sibelius said:

> It should be for bagpipes and reeds, but I've scored it for two clarinets and two bassoons. Extravagant, isn't it? We have only two bassoon players in the entire country, and one of them is consumptive. But my music won't be too hard on him – we'll see to that.

This is a concrete reminder of the limited orchestral resources open to Sibelius at the time. He himself conducted the small ensemble consisting of two flutes, two clarinets, two bassoons, harp and strings, which were all placed behind the scenes. To the four movements that make up the original music – 'Élegie' for strings which prefaced the play, 'Musette', 'Minuet' and the 'Fool's song' – Sibelius was encouraged to add three for larger forces – 'Nocturne', 'Serenade' and 'Ballade'. This suite was his first orchestral work to appear in print, and introduced him to both the German public and the Anglo-Saxon world. It reached Leipzig in 1898, its year of composition, and Henry Wood introduced it in this country at the 1901 Prom season.

Like the *Karelia* music written some five years before, *King Christian II* belongs to the genre of Scandinavian national-romanticism, but in its quality of inspiration it moves on a much lower level. The *Karelia* music undoubtedly presents a far more individual profile. The elegy, beautiful though it is, is not far removed in spirit from the eloquent Grieg miniatures such as *Heart's Wounds* and *The Last Spring*. The minuet and the 'Fool's song of the spider' are conventional pieces with comparatively little individuality: it is 'Musette', gently playful and a trifle naïve, that is the most characteristic piece. Only the bars that return the middle section to the main idea seem unworthy of the composer. The three other movements, which are scored for a larger orchestra of double woodwind, four horns, two trumpets, three trombones, timpani and strings, are not first-rate Sibelius. The 'Nocturne' has many touches that are unmistakably personal, even though the main idea is not so distantly related to Mendelssohn's *Lieder ohne Worte*. It is one of the few ideas in Sibelius's orchestral music that could well be translated into keyboard terms without doing its nature real violence. The movement has a certain freshness and generosity of feeling, but the seams that join the various paragraphs are clearly visible. Yet for all its immaturity the *Nocturne* has something of the awkward charm of adolescence. Admittedly it is inferior Sibelius, but it is lovable in a sense because of its very faults.

The 'Serenade', which served as the prelude to the third act of the play, likewise has many touches that serve to establish Sibelius's identity without ever revealing his mastery. The big tune (thirteen bars after fig. C) on unison violins is pallid by comparison with the melodic sweep of the First Symphony written only a year later. The 'Ballade' is a rumbustious piece that is undoubtedly effective within its limits; but if it is put alongside pieces of a similar character such as *Lemminkäinen's Homeward Journey* and *Festivo*, or for that matter the finale of the symphony, to which there is a very superficial resemblance in places, its inadequacy becomes readily apparent.

If the *King Christian II* suite was the first orchestral work by Sibelius to make its way into the concert halls of Europe, his next essay in the realm of the theatre was destined to make his name a household word. This was the music to *Kuolema* (Death), a play by his brother-in-law Arvid Järnefelt. In the opening scene the central character, Paavali, is seen at the bedside of his dying mother. She tells him of her dream that she has gone to a ball. Later, while Paavali himself sleeps, Death comes to claim her and the mother, mistaking him for her dead husband, dances with him. When Paavali wakes up his mother is dead. It is in this context that *Valse triste* began the long life that took it into the tea-shops of Europe and America. It is difficult to imagine the effect this seductive piece made on its first appearance, so hackneyed has it become. It is associated now with so many improbable instrumental combinations that one tends to lose sight of the fact that it is an original miniature, despite the obviousness of some of its musical procedures. The middle section is commonplace by the side of the main idea.

The rest of the music to *Kuolema* is relatively obscure. Some of it cannot be transplanted into the concert hall, since it consists of simple musical devices designed purely to invoke a background mood. Two years after the production was first staged in 1904 Sibelius revised two scenes for concert use: The *Scen med tranor* (Scene with cranes), a highly evocative piece for clarinet and strings. Tawaststjerna quotes a diary entry of 1915: 'Every day I have seen the cranes. Flying south in full cry with their music. Have been yet again their most assiduous pupil. Their cries echo throughout my being.' This atmospheric piece is quintessential Sibelius. When *Kuolema* was revived in 1911, at the time of the Fourth Symphony, he added two new numbers, a *Canzonetta* for strings, and the *Valse romantique*, publishing them as op. 62. In the *Canzonetta* the strings are muted throughout and the music has some of the wistful, alluring melancholy of *Valse triste*. The sequences in the paragraph beginning at fig. A are particularly reminiscent of that famous piece. It is beautifully laid out for the strings and has an altogether greater distinction than its companion, the *Valse romantique*, scored for somewhat larger forces: two flutes, clarinet, horns, timpani and strings. Throughout his life Sibelius was haunted by the popularity of *Valse triste* and tried in vain to repeat its success, but the alchemy of popular success remains secret, and the stronger one aspires to it, the more signal is the failure. The longed-for success was never forthcoming and *Valse romantique* remains a *salon* piece with little real vitality to commend it.

Most of Sibelius's important music for the stage, apart from *The Tempest*, dates from the middle of the first decade of the present century. Hot on the heels of *Kuolema* came scores for *Pelléas et Mélisande* (1905), *Belshazzars gästabud* (Belshazzar's Feast) (1906) and *Swanwhite* (1908). Of these it is the music for *Pelléas* that is best known. Maeterlinck enjoyed an enormous vogue at the turn of the century: only three years earlier Debussy's opera on the same subject had been mounted at the *Opéra Comique*; Schoenberg embarked on his tone-poem the following year, and earlier, in 1897, Fauré had been commissioned by Mrs Patrick Campbell to compose music for a London production of the play at the Prince of Wales Theatre. *Pelléas et Mélisande*, in a Swedish translation by Bertel Gripenberg, was something of a relaxation during his struggles with the Violin Concerto and the Third Symphony, and in March 1905 Sibelius himself conducted the score in the majority of its fifteen performances. *Pelléas* is set in mythical Allemonde, the protagonists in the drama remain shadowy and we are left knowing little or nothing of their past background. Prince Golaud out riding one day discovers Mélisande, weeping and lost in the forest, and takes her under his protection. Maeterlinck's play charts her growing infatuation for his younger brother, Pelléas, and Golaud's ensuing jealousy.

The suite that Sibelius prepared for concert purposes consists of nine movements. Though few of them are as highly personal or inward-looking as the music for *The Tempest*, they are distinguished by immense polish and attractive thematic ideas. The best of them, the glorious 'Pastorale' and insistent, menacing 'Mélisande at the spinning-wheel', are as good as anything Sibelius wrote in this genre. The first, 'At the castle gate' (which has long enjoyed popularity as the signature-tune of a BBC TV programme, *The Sky at Night*), with its horn calls has an epic feel to it, and depicts the rise of the sun over the sea. Next comes a character portrait of Mélisande: although it is a trifle facile, the cor anglais melody that dominates it has a grave and haunting charm. After this, there is a short impressionistic evocation of the sea, running to some twenty-two bars, atmospheric and non-motivic, whose monotony is soon broken by darker shadows. 'By a spring in the park' is more carefree; the two protagonists feelings are still innocent. It is a wholly successful piece of pattern music which has no pretensions to any kind of musical development. The main tune is characteristic of the way in which Sibelius avoids the obvious. Many composers would have omitted the sixth bar in the interest of a well-balanced eight-bar phrase: Sibelius's melody fascinates because of its very asymmetry:

Ex. 45

'The three blind sisters' is a touching, strophic song of disarming simplicity. As it stands in the suite (the melodic line is again allotted to the cor anglais) its pathos provides an admirable foil to the 'Pastorale' which follows. The latter is one of Sibelius's most perfect miniatures: its luminous scoring evokes the delicacy of colouring of the gentle northern summer, and the lightness of texture almost suggests that the music was conceived *en plein air*. 'Mélisande at the spinning-wheel' is of a similarly high order of imagination. The writing for the violas is onomatopoeic in

function, as is that for the oboe, with its descending three-note chromatic figure, and the clarinets, whose halting melody admirably conveys the irregularity of the wheel's motion. The 'Entr'acte' is another superbly designed, unpretentious movement. Its mood is sunny and life-giving: the sense of movement generated by the quaver motion never ceases and the melodic line has a logic and sense of direction that seem almost classical. This is the kind of polished miniature which, because of its divertimento-like nature, is apt to be underrated even by the connoisseur of Sibelius: it radiates sheer joy in music-making. 'The death of Mélisande' is a beautiful piece too, though it is clearly related to the conventional Scandinavian elegiac style.

Sibelius's music to *Belshazzar's Feast*, a play by his friend Hjalmar Procopé, is by no means as well known as *Pelléas*. Yet it is a score of great quality. The play concerns the intrigues at the court of Babylon and is apparently of little interest; in fact one cartoonist at the time showed Procopé being held aloft by Sibelius. The suite that Sibelius drew up from the music is seldom heard in the concert hall and has been relatively neglected on record, so that *Belshazzar* is hardly known even to the Sibelius enthusiast. In a sense it is typical of the incidental music in that it follows a pattern formula and makes no pretence at development. Yet, despite its disarming simplicity, and indeed perhaps because of it, it has a poetic effect of great intensity. Least successful is the opening 'Oriental march', where the attempt to evoke the colours and atmosphere of an Eastern procession is greatest. This repetitive piece is no doubt effective in its theatrical context, but barely justifies its place in the concert hall. The other pieces are a totally different matter. 'Solitude', with its undulating whispered string ostinato, is a most poetic and affecting piece of outstanding beauty, and 'Night music' is no less searching and inspired. The last number of the suite is 'Khadra's dance', an exquisite little piece of a cool, fresh charm, punctuated by this haunting, affectionate oboe melody:

Ex. 46

As with many of Sibelius's slighter works, *Belshazzar's Feast* can easily be spoilt by a performance that falls short in imagination or affection; its delicacy and poetry are elusive.

Three years after the success of *Pelléas*, the Swedish Theatre commissioned music for Strindberg's fairytale, *Swanwhite*. Sibelius numbered himself among Strindberg's most fervent admirers and hoped that this would bring them together. However, their contact was confined to a brief exchange of courtesies and Strindberg, who died in 1912, never actually heard Sibelius's incidental music. From the fourteen scenes that comprise the full score, the composer made a suite of seven pieces. Generally speaking, the music to *Swanwhite* has a less sharply defined profile than that of *Pelléas*, and the poetic atmosphere that Sibelius distills leaves a stronger impression than its melodic substance. In Strindberg's 'Maeterlinckian fairy play for adults', as Evert Sprinchorn calls it,[1] there are strong parallels with the Tristan legend (A handsome prince is sent to bring Swanwhite home to marry the King and is accused of betraying his royal trust when they are discovered in bed by Swanwhite's wicked stepmother, but the prince has placed his sword between them. The first number 'The peacock', is characteristic Sibelius in that it bears his fingerprints clearly enough, but its invention is by no means of the highest quality. Nor is the finale, 'Song of praise', more than partially successful: the imaginative intensity of its opening is not really maintained, and the close (from fig. C onwards) seems comparatively lame and unresourceful. Best known is 'The maidens with roses' (its title, *Tärnorna med rosor*, is sometimes inaccurately rendered as 'The maiden with the roses', an alluring, lightly-scored piece which runs to no more than sixty-six bars. It has something of the same seductive quality as *Valse triste*, though it does not have the pronounced salon flavouring of its middle section. Only three of the movements are first-class Sibelius: 'Listen! the robin sings' is an imaginative piece, and its opening provides an interesting and novel variant of the beginning of 'La chasse', or the first of the four *Legends*. The texture has a space and freedom that recall the beautiful 'Pastorale' from *Pelléas*. 'The prince alone' is an eloquent piece, much tauter and more intense in feeling; the modal shape of the melodic line is not dissimilar to '*Night Ride and Sunrise*, which dates from much the same time. This and Swanwhite and the prince', the most immediately beguiling of all the movements, have a continuity of ideas and a simplicity of utterance that set them apart from the others.

There are four other scores for the stage before *The Tempest*: first, to Mikael Lybeck's *Ödlan* ('The Lizard') (1909); second, to Adolf Paul's *Language of the Birds* (1910); third, to Poul Knudsen's pantomime, *Scaramouche* (1913); and lastly, to Hofmannsthal's *Everyman* (1916).

[1]In *Strindberg As Dramatist* (Yale, 1982).

Interest was roused in the first of these when Sibelius wrote in a letter quoted by Ekman that this score was 'among the most full of feeling that I have written'. He began work on it after his return from England in 1909 and completed it by the October of that year. The play was not, however, successful when it appeared the following year and was taken off after only six performances. Scored for a small group of strings (Sibelius asked for nine players if possible, though agreed to a minimum of six), the music runs to forty-three pages of score; the first of the two sections consists of some thirty-seven bars in which the solo violin has an important role. The second is for the third scene of Act II; according to Rosas,[1] this is far more than a routine example of incidental music.

The Lizard bears the opus number 8, but Sibelius did not attach enough importance to Paul's *Language of the Birds* to number it at all. Apart from the 'Wedding march', there is apparently little extended writing of any moment. The music to Poul Knudsen's *Scaramouche*, on the other hand, is a work of some scale. Sibelius was exercised to discover that the book 'plagiarized', as he put it, Arthur Schnitzler's *Veil of Pierrette* and by fears that the final production would include spoken dialogue as well as mime. In all it runs to over sixty-five minutes of uninterrupted music and though there are some passages deficient in real inspiration, contains music that is touched by both distinction and vision. The dramatic argument is slender, and hardly the last word in subtlety: the story concerns Leilon who is presenting an entertainment in which his wife, the dancer Blondelaine, is the centre of attention. Blondelaine is dissatisfied with the music provided and coaxes the diminutive hunch-back, Scaramouche and his band of companions wandering musicians into playing for her. She succumbs to their seductive music and, when Leilon sends him packing, follows him into the forest where she is seduced. She returns the following morning to Leilon but when Scaramouche returns to press his attentions, she panics and stabs him, hiding the body behind the curtains. She dances but when she sees a stream of blood from underneath the curtains, she falls dead on Scaramouche's body, and Leilon is driven insane. If the music has undoubted longueurs, there are some moments of great poetic feeling, almost evoking the luminous colouring of the *Humoresques*, and much else of interest; glimpses of ideas that were forming in his mind for use in *The Oceanides* and, in the music where solo viola and cello depict Scaramouche's hypnotic viola playing (Act I, Scene 8), a figure that was to emerge in the Seventh Symphony. There are moments of genuine poetry and a wistful, gentle sadness that is both

[1]John Rosas, 'Sibelius' musiken till skådespelet, Ödlan' (*Suomen Musiikin Vuosikirja*, 1960–1).

132

touching and charming. There are moments that confirm the impression that it is Straussian, but the Strauss of *Le bourgeois gentilhomme*. Gray was dismissive in the 1930s and there is much in the score, particularly in the second act, that is thin. In later years Sibelius asked Jussi Jalas to make a suite of about twenty minutes preserving his original scoring which makes effective use of the piano. However, while the complete pantomime may not be effective, the Suite throws some of the lighter ideas into disproportionate prominence.

While *Scaramouche* is an extended work, though of uneven quality, the music to *Everyman* consists of sixteen numbers, some of which are only a few bars or are even confined, in the case of the first, to one chord: like *Swanwhite*, it is uneven. The *Allegro* that comprises the third number has considerable delicacy and lightness of touch (its material is more fully developed in the tenth section) but on the other hand, the simplicity of the fourth, a strophic song of greeting to Everyman, is not wholly convincing. Most evocative is the eleventh section, which accompanies the spoken dialogue between Everyman and Good Deeds. Here the writing is quite bold: chromatic wisps of sound weave a texture of subtle mystery.

Ex. 47

No. 14 contains an unusual stroke of colour: its opening bars are scored for the somewhat bizarre combination of piano, organ and strings.

Although he knew and read his Shakespeare, Sibelius did not match himself against many Shakespearean themes. True, he had spoken of a *Macbeth* Symphony in his youth and there are, of course, the two songs from *Twelfth Night*. But his score for *The Tempest*, his last and greatest work in the genre, was commissioned for a particularly lavish production of *The Tempest* at the Royal Theatre, Copenhagen, in 1926. The Royal Theatre is also the home of the Danish Opera and accordingly Sibelius was able to draw on larger forces than those normally available at the Swedish Theatre in Helsinki. The title-page of the score speaks of 'a small orchestra'; in actual fact the complete score consists of thirty-four musical numbers for soloists, mixed choir, harmonium and large orchestra. Fortunately, when arranging the orchestral suites, he replaced the harmonium with strings (the effect in the lullaby (ex. 49) is greatly to enhance the magical effect). When in 1927 it was produced in Helsinki, Sibelius replaced the final 'Cortège' with an Epilogue which draws on material he had used two decades earlier in the *Cassazione*. For all its visionary quality, there is a sense in which it could be said to be among the most uneven of Sibelius's dramatic scores, for the finest pieces, like 'The oak-tree' or the 'Intrada–Berceuse', are on so high a level of inspiration that the less inspired movements are thrown into greater relief. 'Miranda' and 'Caliban' are on a much lower plane, and it is difficult to reconcile them with the strange other-worldly vision of the 'Chorus of the winds'. In its entirety[1] the Prelude must be accounted one of the most effective and terrifying 'storms' in all music. Its effect is achieved by the quality of the texture alone, for it contains almost no passage of real musical development. It consists merely of a succession of rising and falling augmented fourths for the strings, chromatic figures in the woodwind, menacing brass entries and so on. Ralph Wood aptly called it 'the most thoroughly onomatopoetic stretch of music ever written'. This is no overstatement: the surging seas, strange distant lights and howling gusts of wind (horns, percussion) make an almost physical impact. It is a piece of the utmost virtuosity, and as sheer tone-painting is extraordinarily powerful.

One of the most hauntingly beautiful of the other pieces is 'The oak-tree'. The means it employs could hardly be more simple, yet the music is profoundly original. An anguished flute line moves over an eerie, insistent rocking ostinato figure which periodically changes position to great effect (see ex. 48). A pedal D is either heard or implied throughout the piece (its effect in its absence is no less extraordinary than its re-entries in providing subtle harmonic colouring); its persistence as well as the harmonic course the music takes at the very end of the piece is worth study. The piece is obviously inspired by the plight of Ariel, imprisoned by a witch for twelve

---

[1]In the second suite Sibelius included a shortened version of the Prelude, omitting the impressive closing pages and ending the piece abruptly (and less effectively) on a chord of E flat minor.

Ex. 48

years in an oak tree and threatened with like punishment by Prospero. The 'Humoresque', probably associated with Trinculo, belongs to the category of light music: its predictable (or almost predictable) tune has an underlying note of menace which, though never really strong enough to disturb its equanimity, is nevertheless present.

Both 'Caliban's song' and 'The harvesters' belong to Sibelius's lighter vein, though the percussion writing in the former (particularly the xylophone part) seems a trifle out of character and just a little strained. Sibelius did not think naturally in this kind of colouring, and in his attempt to convey the unpolished exterior and awkward gait of Shakespeare's character he forces a bizarre vein that seems unnatural to him. If one did not know its date, one would be tempted to place the 'Canon' along with the *Scènes historiques*: it has the exuberant classicism of middle-period Sibelius. The 'Scene' is a charming C major dialogue between wind and *pizzicato* strings, lightweight but admirably suited to its purpose, for its character is not so highly defined that it draws attention to itself. It is however the 'Intrada–Berceuse' that strike a deeper vein: the searing dissonances of the former subside after a mere half-dozen bars. These originally served to introduce Act IV in the original production, while the lullaby, a piece of grave and eloquent beauty, is designed for Act I, Scene 2, where Miranda sleeps. It is scored for two clarinets, harp and muted strings. Even if in character it suggests the dark black waters of the river of Death rather than an innocent lullaby, it is a movement of such rare magic and fantasy that it must be numbered among Sibelius's most inspired shorter pieces in any form. It could hardly be simpler in structure: set in E flat minor, a sombre enough key in all conscience, it consists of a melody whose phrases are punctuated by harp arpeggios thus:

Ex. 49

The 'Chorus of the winds' consists of a few sustained chords that do not look particularly impressive on paper, though their effect in performance is spellbinding. These wisps of chords of the seventh with their delicate colouring of woodwind and horns, the gentle wash of muted strings and harp harmonics, produce a sound that is as magical and haunting as it is individual. The E flat minor 'Intermezzo' into which it leads returns us to earth. Neither the 'Intermezzo' nor the charming 'Dance of the nymphs' has the rapt, breathless quality of the 'Chorus', though they are fine pieces for all that. The character portrait of Prospero is another of the inspired movements; its slow chordal writing has a Purcellian grandeur, but despite its assumption of Restoration trappings and its attempt at pastiche this could only be by Sibelius. As a study of Prospero, it is far more penetrating than the Miranda which we are given later in the same suite. There is a seductive quality about 'Miranda': the opening bars are very promising and the accompanying triplets are a telling stroke. But, alas, Sibelius gives way to a string of sugary sequences which bring unwelcome echoes of the *salon*, unworthy both of the composer and his subject. The remaining pieces, the two songs 'The naiads', and the final 'Dance episode' steer a middle course: they eschew the errors of taste we find in 'Miranda' but do not attain the level of inspiration that exists elsewhere.

The fact that in Copenhagen, the Royal Theatre was (and indeed still is) the home of the opera explains not only the size of the orchestral apparatus but the presence of a chorus. The complete incidental music is not really effective when played in concert form; many of the numbers are atmospheric but very short, and even were it practical to mount it in the context of the play, this view of Shakespeare is at variance with present-day dramatic taste. Yet to know *The Tempest* suites and to love them over many years (for all their lapses) compels one to contest Wood's dismissal of the work in his often penetrating essay. Comparing it unfavourably with *Scaramouche*, he writes that 'the Copenhagen commission was a switch that released a cascade of almost exhibitionistic virtuosity at last uncoloured by any tincture of creative impulse'.[1] In the face of 'Intrada'–Berceuse', 'The Oak-tree', the 'Chorus of the winds' and 'Prospero', this judgment seems wholly incomprehensible. Here, as is the case with most of his scores for the theatre, Sibelius's poetry and vision far outweigh any of the other reservations we may have about individual pieces. No other twentieth-century composer working in this field has surpassed his achievement.

[1] In Gerald Abraham (ed.), *'Sibelius: a Symposium*, p. 89.

11

Solo instrument and orchestra

As we have seen, Sibelius long cherished ambitions as a solo violinist and was an accomplished player. Indeed, for a time he even toyed with the idea of a solo career, abandoning it only in his early twenties. Even as late as 1915 he recorded in his diary, 'Dreamt I was twelve years old and a virtuoso'. His mastery of the instrument is clearly evident from the kind of music he wrote for it: in particular, the Violin Concerto and the unjustly neglected *Humoresques*, opp. 87 and 89, which may well have been afterthoughts of the Second Violin Concerto that he was planning in 1915, and for which the flute idea (five bars after letter A in the first movement of the Sixth Symphony) was intended. But the D minor Concerto is a superbly written piece, bristling with difficulties of the kind players enjoy overcoming, and whatever its standing may be with some of Sibelius's critics, it has a strong hold over the affections of both players and public alike. Its popularity can be judged by the fact that it is the most recorded concerto written in the present century.[1]

Apart from the Grieg, it is the only Nordic concerto to have attained classic status, and universal popularity for although he was not as good a violinist as Grieg and Stenhammar were pianists, his youthful ambitions provided him with a thorough understanding of the instrument. Display and virtuosity are the *sine qua non* of the concerto concept, and it is in the integration of contrasting and to some extent combative forces within a coherent artistic framework that its fascination lies. But from the concerto as a vehicle for display arose what one might call the heroic vision of Mozart and Beethoven in which the individual is pitted against society. 'Nothing' (to cite Tovey) 'in human life or history is more thrilling or of more ancient and universal experience than the antithesis of the individual and the crowd; an antithesis which is familiar in every degree from flat opposition to harmonious reconciliation.' In the lineage of Sibelius's concerto, the Beethoven was distant, and he did not hear the Brahms until January 1905 to which he responded with warmth though

[1] By 1990 there were seventy-three different recordings, including four by David Oistrakh and two by Heifetz.

he found it very different ('too symphonic') from his own. But like the Mendelssohn, with which he was familiar as a player, his was a soloist-led concerto.

The view has often been advanced that the Sibelius concerto never quite lives up to the promise of its opening and in earlier editions of this book I even went so far as to say that 'the theme is so superior in quality to the material that succeeds it that it seems a difference in kind rather than degree', a view which I would not now care to sustain. But though that might be an overstatement, the fact remains that the opening theme is inspired: Sibelius recognized it for what it was – a heaven-sent idea. It came to him much earlier than 1903. The concerto belongs to that select group of works among which *En Saga*, the *Lemminkäinen Legends* and the Fifth Symphony must be numbered, that underwent their birthpangs in public. After its disastrous first performance in Helsinki in 1904, in which as Tawaststjerna put it 'a red-faced and perspiring Viktor Nováček fought a losing battle with a solo part that bristled with even greater difficulties . . . than in the definitive score', Sibelius decided to overhaul it.

It was first heard in its definitive form in 1905 with Karl Halir as soloist and Richard Strauss, no less, conducting the Berlin Philharmonic. Sibelius's grip on his material is as firm as ever and the organic nature of his musical thinking is never in any doubt. The first movement is far more closely argued than its outward appearance would suggest and although its brilliant cadenza comes close to the language of the great virtuoso composers like Vieuxtemps, Sibelius breathes meaning into the empty rhetorical gestures they favour. He treats sonata form with great freedom and flexibility: none of the processes of the movement is handled mechanically. There are many flashes of real power in the orchestral writing that hint at the tough symphonic mind below the surface. Sir Donald Tovey was an early admirer:

> Of course, the greater concerto form of Mozart, Beethoven and Brahms is another story; instead of being lighter than symphonic form, it is perhaps the most subtle and certainly the most misunderstood art-form in all music. But in the easier and looser concerto forms invented by Mendelssohn and Schumann, I have not met with a more original, a more masterly, and a more exhilarating work than the Sibelius Violin Concerto.[1]

Even if the work as a whole is not one of the stature of the last four symphonies, *Tapiola* or *Luonnotar*, there is much in the score to justify

---

[1]*Essays in Musical Analysis*, vol. III (Oxford, 1936), p. 211.

Tovey. And, for that matter, the opening idea is of a level of inspiration that can warrant it keeping their company. Sibelius's grip on his material is as firm as ever. The wistful idea that follows the B flat minor idea (on page 17 of the Eulenberg miniature score) seems to come near to recapturing the high level of poetry that distinguishes the opening. The section beginning at fig. 2, the beginning of the second group in fact, though it is precariously poised between the tonic and B flat, is related to the first theme; the relationship, though obvious enough on paper, is sufficiently natural for the new idea to strike the ear as fresh. Subsequent developments proceed just as naturally. Whether or not one agrees with Wood's strictures on 'the cheap-tragic material' at fig. 3, with 'those plangent flattened melodic thirds and that relapse by the soloist into double-stopped sixths – how effective and how second-rate',[1] one cannot but admire the very continuity of growth that Wood denies it. There is a very real sense of movement and there are, too, flashes of real power in the orchestral writing: the menacing orchestral writing between figs. 5 and 6 is an instance in point. Many performances miss the dark strength and intensity of such passages.

It is difficult to conceive of a masterpiece in any other than its finished form. The impression the listener receives from Sibelius's Fifth Symphony, Stravinsky's *Le sacre du printemps* or Debussy's *La mer* conveys what Schoenberg called 'the illusion of spontaneous vision'. It is as if the artist had caught a glimpse of something that has been going on all the time and that he has stretched out and effortlessly captured it. Yet that illusion of spontaneity is often dearly bought (as it was in the case of the Dvořák symphonies), and nowhere more so than in this concerto and the Fifth Symphony. Sibelius realized the necessity to purify it, to remove unnecessary detail or ornament that impedes the realization of a cogent structure.[2] Erik Tawaststjerna goes into great detail about its genesis and the puzzling way in which Sibelius behaved towards Willy Burmester, who was to have given its première.[3] In the late 1980s the Sibelius heirs agreed to a performance and recording of the 1904 version of the concerto, thus bringing it out of its scholarly seclusion into the wider public domain and, in so doing, gave us an opportunity to see the familiar concerto struggling to get out of its 1903–4 chrysalis. Listening to Sibelius's first thoughts, one

[1] Op. cit., pp. 67–8.
[2] Erkki Salmenhaara takes the view that among the various factors it was not only the quality of the first performance that prompted Sibelius to withdraw it but Karl Flodin's adverse reviews, first in a leader in the cultural magazine *Euterpe* and subsequently in *Helsingfors-Posten*. Flodin was not only the leading critic of the day but had been consistently supportive, save in his 1897 review of the *Lemminkäinen Legends*, and Sibelius obviously attached some weight to his views.
[3] Tawaststjerna. *Sibelius*, vol. I (London 1976), pp. 270–87.

is at first brought up with a start by an incisive orchestral rhythmic figure at what would be fig. 1 of the 1905 score, whereafter the orchestra plays a more assertive role in the proceedings.

Ex. 50

In the unaccompanied cadenza 21 bars later there is a supporting rhythmic figure anticipating the main idea of the finale, which sounds crude, while to the next idea on cellos and bassoon (fig. 2 of the Eulenberg score), the soloist contributes decoration. But then seven bars before fig. 3, a delightful new idea appears which almost looks forward to the light colourings of the six *Humoresques*, opp. 87 and 89. Although it is a great pity that it had to go, there is no doubt that the structural coherence of the movement gains by its loss both here and on its reappearance later in the movement. It is the ability to sacrifice good ideas in the interest of structural coherence that is the hallmark of a good composer. There are other changes he must have regretted though not, one suspects, the second long and unaccompanied cadenza which bristles with fascinating difficulties but whose removal greatly improves the overall shape of the movement. There are some hair-raising difficulties early on in the finale and it is difficult not to regret the disappearance of a completely new and delightful idea starting at fig. 2. The fewest changes are in the slow movement which remains at the same length; the outer movements are both considerably longer. As in the case of the Fifth Symphony where the revision is even more extensive, the finished work tells us a great deal about the quality of Sibelius's artistic judgment, and that, of course, is what makes him such a great composer.

If the second is the most soft-centred of the three movements, the finale is undoubtedly the most brilliant and exciting. From the very outset its stunning impetus never slackens. Its rhythm is insistent and the interplay between 6/8 and 3/4 in the second theme is highly effective. It is this with its air of a rather ungainly abandon that brings Tovey's felicitous description to mind, 'a polonaise for polar bears'. The whole finale has an infectious and irresistible sense of momentum, and even in an inferior performance never fails to rivet the attention of an audience.

When we turn to the other music Sibelius wrote for violin, what is striking is not its inferiority but on the contrary the high level of its inspiration. Both the *Serenades* and the *Humoresques* are first-class; only the *Romance*, op. 78, No. 2, is a straightforward exception. This is an orchestral arrangement of the second of the four pieces, op. 78, for violin or cello and piano. It strikes an uneasy compromise between the sentimentality of the famous Svendsen *Romance* and the natural breeding and distinction of Stenhammar's genre pieces, like the *Sentimentalvals*, without really having any distinct character of its own. The result, at any rate, has the stale pallor of much Scandinavian *salon* music of the period, and is no way comparable in quality with the *Serenades* or the *Humoresques*. The other two pieces Sibelius wrote for this medium, *Cantique* (*Laetare anima mea*), op. 77, no. 1, and *Devotion* (*Ab imo pectore*), op. 77, no. 2, date from 1914–15 and fall short of the best without going so far as the *Romance*. Indeed, both are considerably more individual, particularly the second. The nobility of the *Cantique* has, however, a conscious rectitude that is reflected in its uneventful line, and it is the second with its searching modulations that is the more interesting. Neither compares with the *Serenades* or the *Humoresques*.

What is so striking about these is their totally unforced charm and spontaneity. They have a lightness of touch and a freshness and sparkle that make one wonder why they are not in the repertory of every violinist of standing. Both sets of *Humoresques* date from 1917, the year after the second version of the Fifth Symphony was completed, and both call for dazzling technique on the part of the soloist. The first set, op. 87, comprises two pieces and calls for a small orchestra of double woodwind, two horns, timpani and strings. Of the remaining four, op. 89, the first two are for strings only, the remaining two include some wind instruments. In these pieces the *Zigeuner*-like virtuosity that we meet in the Violin Concerto seems to have been wholly absorbed into the composer's stylistic bloodstream. In the second the soloist's part is full of the bustling scale figuration and large leaps we encounter in the Violin Concerto, but there is much greater delicacy of feeling and gentleness of colouring. The first piece has a similarly haunting flavour, and the writing for the soloist, while no less brilliant than in the concerto, has a far more individual character, as at fig. A for example. The phrase lengths are less predictable, and there is again a sense of onward movement.

The second set is no less fetching than the first. The third of this set has a captivating tune which once heard is difficult to get out of one's head. This is the most immediately attractive and lovable of the set, and one of Sibelius's most disarming compositions. In the *Humoresques*, wrote

Tawaststjerna, Sibelius 'captured the lyrical, dancing soul of the violin'; but not only do these pieces captivate, they have a poignant, wistful melancholy all their own. Indeed there are few pieces where the magic of the white nights of the Scandinavian summer is more keenly evoked. The lyrical invention is fresh, charming and (to my mind) irresistible.

Sibelius himself wrote that these radiant pieces convey something of 'the anguish of existence, fitfully lit up by the sun', and behind their outward elegance and charm, there is an all-pervasive sadness. This is even more intense in the two *Serenades*, which are glorious pieces and quintessential Sibelius. They are earlier than the Fifth Symphony (indeed they come from the period of *The Bard* and *Luonnotar*), and in addition to double woodwind call for four horns, timpani and strings. They are in no way less perfect than the *Humoresques*; both have great expressive poignancy and concentration of atmosphere in spite of their relatively modest dimensions. The opening of the first with the modal inflexion it acquires from its flattened seventh, as well as the airy texture, almost suggests Nielsen, though the passage beginning at fig. E could hardly be mistaken for anyone other than Sibelius. The second *Serenade*, in G minor, written a year later in 1913, is hardly less haunting and wears its sad charms with great elegance.

There remains only the slight but charming Suite for violin and strings, op. 117, a short three-movement piece written in the late 1920s at the time he was wrestling with the Eighth Symphony. At one time, it would seem that he intended to call it Serenade. Each movement bears a title in English, and although it lasts less than seven minutes, and is not top-drawer Sibelius, it does not quite deserve the oblivion to which the composer seems to have consigned it. The most touching of the three is the centrepiece, 'Evening in spring', which has something of the same poetic fantasy as the Humoresques. He put it on one side with the stern admonition 'not to be published' but it was recorded in 1990 by the Korean violinist Dong-Suk Kang.

12

Kullervo and the *Kalevala*

For Sibelius myth was a central preoccupation. It was of consuming importance to many nineteenth-century artists. Wagner's operas are all peopled by figures born of myth and, with the exception of *The Bard*, all the symphonic poems of Sibelius inhabit its shadowy world. Myth, after all, is the vehicle for universal truths about the human psyche, and the fascination it holds for mankind is an acknowledgment of its power. It is no accident that Maeterlinck's *Pelléas et Mélisande* attracted composers as diverse as Debussy, Schoenberg, Sibelius and Fauré, for it, too, has all the essential qualities of myth. The time and setting are not clearly defined, we know little or nothing of the background of the protagonists, which serves to throw the universal themes on which it touches into higher relief. To say that the *Kalevala* struck a responsive chord in Sibelius's sensibility would be an understatement: it was of crucial importance to the growth of his artistic personality. Indeed, it is no exaggeration to say that without the *Kalevala*, Sibelius would no more be Sibelius than he would be without the natural landscape of the North. It affected him far more profoundly than it did any other Finnish composer, and though themes in the *Kalevala* provide the points of departure for other Finns, they are 'cosmetic' rather than essential sources of inspiration. The reasons for its importance are not hard to find. These were the crucial years in which Finland was struggling to find itself and discover the beauties of its own language after so long a period of Swedish cultural domination and political servitude to an increasingly obdurate Tsarist Russia. Of course, it would be wrong to assume that his pre-occupation with Finnish mythology and its language is the whole of the story. There are other factors and other sources of inspiration. First and foremost is the Nordic landscape for which he had as strong a feeling as had Bartók for the natural world. Secondly, there is the nature poetry of the nineteenth-century lyric poets writing in Swedish, to whom he turned for the overwhelming majority of his solo songs. The Swedish nature lyricists he read in his youth left an indelible mark on him. The poetry of the *Kalevala*, on the other hand, calls for epic treatment, and this it received in *Kullervo*, the *Lemminkäinen Legends* and *Pohjola's Daughter*.

Had his mother not enrolled him in a Finnish-speaking school, he would not have been exposed to the rich repertory of Finnish folk-poetry either in the *Kalevala* or the *Kanteletar* until much later in his development. It fired his imagination throughout the whole of his career from *Kullervo* and the *Lemminkäinen Legends* in the 1890s through to *Luonnotar* (1913) and *Tapiola* (1926). However, the tone poems are not the only works inspired by the *Kalevala*: there are piano works like *Kyllikki*, choral pieces like *The Origin of Fire* and so on. And conversely not all the mythology to which Sibelius was drawn was Finnish: he spoke of *En Saga* being inspired by the world of the *Edda*, and the nymphs of *The Oceanides* come from the world of classical mythology. However, myth and the universal truths it enshrines undoubtedly meant much more to him than many other contemporaries, though it had undoubted importance for Stravinsky (*Oedipus Rex*), Honegger (*Antigone*), Szymanowski (*Mythes, Masques*, and *King Roger*), Milhaud (*Choéphores*) and many others. Nor, as we have seen, was Sibelius the first Finnish composer to find his way to the *Kalevala*: Johan Filip von Schantz (1835–65) wrote an orchestral piece called *Kullervo* and Kajanus had composed his *Aino* Symphony in the 1880s. *Aino* is more accurately described as a symphonic poem with a choral apotheosis rather than a symphony. It is a shortish work of about fifteen minutes duration and shows a certain indebtedness to Wagner. It does not show any strong creative identity, but one can well understand the impression it would have made on a young composer of Sibelius's then circumscribed musical experience.

But all these predecessors, Fredrik Pacius, the so-called 'Father of Finnish Music' who was German-born, and other even less familiar figures such as von Schantz, Aksel Ingelius and Sibelius's own teacher, Martin Wegelius, were nationalist in name rather than fact, their musical language deriving from European models. Such Finnish identity as there is, is grafted on to the surface. But if we were, for the sake of argument, to remove Sibelius from the scene, it is doubtful whether the wider musical public would have more than peripheral awareness of the *Kalevala*, so completely does Sibelius's art enshrine it (and so imperfectly do his contemporaries). Oskar Merikanto (1868–1924) cannot be said to have the measure of its atmosphere, and other works inspired by themes from the *Kalevala* do not bring it before our eyes in the same way. (His son, Aarre Merikanto (1894–1959) is a totally different proposition and a composer of real substance). But very few Finnish composers seem to have resisted its spell: *Kullervo* inspired an opera by Armas Launis (1884–1959) written in 1917, more than a quarter of a century after Sibelius's symphony. Though not a major figure, Launis was an authority on Finnish folksong, and a specialist on Finnish runic melodies. He was a pupil of Ilmari Krohn, himself a composer but better known as a musicologist: an authority on Finnish folk music and the author of an impressive two-volume study of the Sibelius symphonies. Erkki Melartin (1875–1937) who, as we have seen, supplanted Sibelius as Wegelius's favourite pupil in the 1890s (and also went on to compose seven symphonies) wrote an opera on *Aino*. There is also Sibelius's pupil, Leevi Madetoja (1887–1947) who had a distinguished enough musical lineage: he was also a pupil of Armas Järnefelt, and Robert Fuchs. His output is not dominated by the *Kalevala* in the way that many of his contemporaries were, but there are three choral pieces, *Sammon ryöstö* (The Capture of the Sampo) (1915), *Väinämöinen kylvö* (Väinämöinen's Sowing) (1919) and *Väinämöinen soitto* (The Play of Väinämöinen) (1935) as well as a tone-poem, *Kullervo* (1913), which precedes the first of his three symphonies. There are many others that spring to mind: the *Kalevala* Suite of Uuno Klami (1900–61), a good craftsman with a well-developed sense for orchestral colour, as one might expect from a pupil of Ravel. The *Kalevala* even cast its spell further afield: Dallapiccola drew on it in a choral piece *Liriche* and in his *Studi* for voice and orchestra.

But it is quite simply Sibelius whose art is so closely identified with it, and who penetrates it at a deeper level than his countrymen. His was, of course, the more profound and vivid imagination, and he liberated in music the very soul of the *Kalevala* and the Finnish psyche in much the same way as Musorgsky laid bare the Russian soul in his songs; secondly, and far more importantly, he absorbed its speech rhythms and melodic contours into his musical language. In his late forties Sibelius was at pains to stress to his first biographer, Erik Furuhjelm that he had visited Karelia *after* having composed *Kullervo*, but Tawaststjerna clearly established that Sibelius went to Porvoo (Borgå) *before* writing it – specifically to study the runic singing of Larin Paraske. He also explains Sibelius's reluctance on two grounds to have *Kullervo* performed in later life. First, he had intended to revise it but knew that it was basically a fully-realized if immature work which it would be difficult to improve upon without in some way damaging it; secondly, that he was 'at pains to appear as a unique phenomenon, uninfluenced by other composers or folk music'. This was a time when he was being presented to the English-speaking world by Ernest Newman and Cecil Gray as self-forming and unique. Yet influenced he undoubtedly was – and at a profound level not only by the world evoked by the *Kalevala* but by its verbal music. Simon Parmet, in his book on the symphonies, tells how the very inflections of the Finnish language affected Sibelius's melodic thinking in his orchestral works, and he cites *The Swan of Tuonela* in evidence. He quotes the absence of up-beats in Sibelius: the stress in Finnish tends to be on the first syllable.

There is little doubt that both in *The Swan* and in the *Kullervo* Symphony, the very character of Sibelius's melodic speech was shaped by his encounter with Larin Paraske's art. Paraske came from Inger-manland, the territory south of the Karelian isthmus, and she was brought to Porvoo in the autumn of 1891, when a new edition of the *Kalevala* was in preparation. This might well be an explanatory factor in his sudden emergence as a mature composer. For how, you might ask, was it possible for the composer of some two dozen relatively conventional chamber works such as the A minor String Quartet (1889) or its successor in B flat, op. 4, and the G minor Piano Quintet of the following year, to emerge almost overnight as a composer of such ambition, breadth and originality, as he did in the *Kullervo* Symphony? Its language is suddenly much more distinctive. Tawaststjerna even goes so far as to compare Sibelius's study of the runes of the *Kalevala* with Bartók's first encounter with Hungarian peasant tunes. But though 'runes and tunes' are very different, they are both at some level shaped by language. (The most often-cited example of the way in which the language of Finnish and Hungarian have affected two otherwise wholly dissimilar figures is *Fratricide* from the Finnish Peasant Songs where the two composers come closest.) Gener-ally speaking the runic melodies that Sibelius took down from Paraske comprise two more or less rhythmically symmetrical four or five beat phrases that are within the compass of the first five notes of the major or minor scale. The notes, sometimes extended to embrace the flattened sixth or the flattened leading-note, generally correspond with those of the five-stringed kantele. In some instances the kantele's third was so vague, that it is not easy to determine whether it is major or minor. The main melodic protagonists in *Kullervo* leave no doubt as to these runic influences. They persist throughout his career right up to *Tapiola*, whose basic idea falls within the compass of the kantele. So one can say without exaggeration that it is not just the mythology of the epic but the verbal music of the *Kalevala* that shaped Sibelius's music.

In ambition, scale and originality, *Kullervo* had no precedent in the then provincial world of Finnish music. It is in five movements, three of which are purely orchestral, while the third and longest calls for two soloists and male chorus. In all it takes about an hour and a quarter in performance, longer than the First Act of *Die Walküre* and not far short of the Second. No doubt because of its programme and the quasi-operatic nature of its central movement, Sibelius shrank from calling it a symphony. The title-page of the score describes it as 'a symphonic poem for soloists, chorus and orchestra'. It is, however, a symphony in much the same sense as is Mahler's *Resurrection* Symphony. In other words, it embraces concepts that, strictly speaking, lie outside the range of the normal classical symphony, though without sacrificing its essentially organic modes of procedure. The work employs comparatively modest resources (there is only double woodwind, for example), since larger forces were not to be had in Helsinki at this time. Its profile is by no means as developed as that of Mahler's symphony; but this is not surprising when we remember that Sibelius was only twenty-six when he composed it, and that apart from the Overture and Ballet Scene, it was his first serious attempt at writing for the orchestra. Mahler was seven years older when in 1894 he put the finishing touches to the *Resurrection* Symphony and had much greater experience in handling the orchestra, both as a composer and conductor. What is surprising is to find how innate is Sibelius's feeling for orchestral colour! Although his mastery is far from fully developed at this stage, his orchestral writing reflects an astonishing degree of assurance.

Like most early works it is clearly derivative in places; the shades of Tchaikovsky are present in the slow movement and the coda of the first. The first movement, 'Introduction', is generally descriptive of Kullervo's character and sets the scene in broad brushstrokes without dwelling on narrative detail. It is cast in sonata form and the striking thing about it is not so much the faltering proportions or inexpert scoring but his firmness of purpose and immediate sense of identity. The opening pages have a bold sweep that leaves no doubt that it is announcing a new voice in music. The opening offers us a magnificent tune over a characteristic ground swell (see ex. 51). There is no question of Sibelius's achievement in this movement whatever reservations there may be about the work as a whole. One can well understand the excitement of contemporary critics like Flodin: apart from the individuality of the ideas themselves, Sibelius handles his material with the authority of a master. The sense of forward movement which we know from the mature composer is already evident, and his handling of sonata procedure is confident. The second group opens with a dark horn theme (it reappears in ex. 52, marked *x*) and maintains the epic mood of the opening. This is less compact than

Ex. 51

Sibelius's mature melodic thinking, but is already the work of a born symphonist. Here is the passage where it bursts on to the dominant (B minor) with an emphatic *pizzicato* chord:

Ex. 52

The tonal scheme is straightforward but well thought out. The development plunges directly from B minor to E flat minor with dramatic effect. This, and the fact that the keys are (generally speaking) dark, like C minor, help to prepare psychologically for the E major opening of the restatement. In spite of the fact that the seams are clearly visible, the continuity of ideas even at this early stage is impressive. One is almost reminded of Bruckner's breadth and sense of mystery at the opening of the development, and certainly of his imaginative use of tonality when the music turns into C minor. The imitative treatment of the main tune produces effects of great spaciousness, and there are many daring and original touches: the quick, repeated B flats on the oboe maintained over a long period is one; another comes at the beginning of the recapitulation, where Sibelius hangs on to a chord of E major for a very long time indeed, the only activity being insistent, repeated *pizzicato* blows. This is highly effective, as is the long, sustained F minor chord at the close of the third movement. The modal flavouring that one finds in early Sibelius is also here: the accompanying figuration at the beginning of the development has a fresh modal quality that reminds one of *Karelia*, or Nielsen. Naturally the corresponding movement of the first symphony has much greater cohesion, and there is no doubt of the enormous strides made by Sibelius in the intervening years, or for that matter in the three or so years which separate this from *The Swan of Tuonela*. The greater compactness of the recapitulation of the first movements of the first and second symphonies is one obvious feature of his growing mastery.

The debt to Tchaikovsky is even more obvious in the second movement, which is subtitled 'Kullervo's youth', than it is in the unison string theme in the coda of the first. This movement, too, is purely orchestral, and at times offers fleeting hints of a world not far removed from that of the finale of the *Pathétique* symphony. Perhaps the fact that it is in B, hovering between major and minor, reinforces that impression. The main idea, on muted strings, has the tenderness and warmth we find in the slow movement of the first symphony:

Ex. 53

Its pendant is this violin figure which has a folk-like outline:

Ex. 54

Unlike the slow movement of the first symphony, however, this lacks concentration and a sense of direction. This may in some measure be due to the need to convey something of Kullervo's hapless early years (the story is set out in *Runos* XXXII TO XXXIV of the *Kalevala*) and to Sibelius's uncertainty in dealing with symphonic and programmatic elements in the same work. There seems little point-by-point adherence to the events described in the *Kalevala*, and, despite some eloquent string writing, the overall impression left by the movement is somewhat diffuse. One point of interest is Sibelius's use of a whole-tone figure, though there is no tonal

Ex. 55

ambiguity as there is later in the fourth symphony. This is inherited presumably from the Russian composers of the day, who had in their turn absorbed many of the modal usages of folk-music, including those which give rise to the whole-tone scale.

The opening of the third movement, the longest of the five, anticipates the epic, national strain we find in the familiar *Karelia* music. The movement is called 'Kullervo and his sister', and deals with the events described in *Runo* xxxv of the *Kalevala*. The first part concerns Kullervo's attempts to entice a beautiful girl he sees to join him on his journey. The trochaic rhythm conveys the motion of the sleigh to admirable effect later in the movement, though the momentum is nowhere so sustained as in later works like *Lemminkäinen's Homeward Journey* and *Night Ride and Sunrise*. Kullervo's dashing assurance is admirably captured in the opening (see ex. 55).

It is this central movement that introduces the two soloists, a soprano and a baritone, as well as a male chorus. The choral writing is mainly in

Ex. 56

unison, only rarely breaking into four parts; sometimes the parallel octaves are thickened by sixths or thirds, but for the most part the chorus is treated with a sturdy simplicity that is by no means ineffective. The setting of the words is fairly straightforward, more often than not syllabic. Most of the sheer excitement and interest of the movement lies in the orchestra, though the soprano's impressive *scena* when the identity of the two characters becomes known and the realization that their relationship is incestuous is apparent, has some dramatic power and makes one wonder whether Sibelius would not have made out very well as an opera composer. After her death, Kullervo's peroration, which abruptly insists on F minor and is punctuated by heavy orchestral *sforzandi*, has an unmistakably Slav ring about it (see ex. 56).

Despite its undoubted *longueurs* and the somewhat stiff choral writing, the third movement is redeemed by numerous imaginative flashes and the intensity of the soprano solo. With the scherzo and finale one feels that what Sibelius is doing here he was very soon to do much better and with greater economy of means in later works. The same is true of the slow movement. The opening of the scherzo, 'Kullervo goes to war', has the glowing colours and exuberance of *Karelia* and the *Scènes historiques*:

Ex. 57

But on this melody and an attractive later development Sibelius builds far too unwieldly a superstructure. Indeed, his very economy in all his later scherzos may well spring from the excessive length at which this tune is presented.

The finale, 'Kullervo's death', returns us to the tonic, E minor, but it never really lives up to the imaginative vision of its opening pages. Here ex. 52 (*x*) appears in the chorus under a string *tremolando*. Subsequently this melody, which Sibelius first introduced in the coda of the first movement, assumes an important role:

Ex. 58

This idea is fully characteristic of Sibelius's melodic style in his first period, embracing as it does the first five degrees of the minor scale and the flattened sixths. This kind of thinking recurs in *Night Ride and Sunrise*, but by then has been fully absorbed into his stylistic bloodstream; here, but more particularly in the coda of the first movement, it has a distinctly Tchaikovskian fervour. In the closing bars of the movement Sibelius pulls the threads together, as it were, by referring back to the very opening melody which, perhaps, in an unconvincing performance can sound contrived, but in the right hands it works convincingly. The *Kullervo* Symphony is more than just a work of early promise: it is pretty strong on fulfilment! It remains a rarity in the concert hall but on each hearing makes a stronger impression. Sibelius himself did not think well enough of *Kullervo* to allow it to be published, in spite of the fact that it was with this work that he made his breakthrough. Indeed he only parted with the manuscript in the early 1920s when he was short of money; otherwise it might have joined the Eighth Symphony and other autographs on the celebrated Ainola bonfires. The fact that it was already in the hands of the Kalevala Society prevented that, and his unbending attitude to it seemed to soften towards the end of his life. His son-in-law Jussi Jalas conducted its first performance in modern times in 1958, a year after his death.

A glance at the list of works at the end of this volume will show the extent of Sibelius's output for chorus with and without orchestra. Male-voice choirs are very popular in the Scandinavian countries so it is not surprising to find Sibelius writing extensively for this medium. *Rakastava*, one of his most inspired works, began life in this way, and his next choral opus, a set of partsongs written at various times between 1893 and 1904 offers music of real quality. Sibelius's opus numbering is something of a minefield and there is confusion about the order of op. 18. In these matters Sibelius was occasionally forgetful and did not remember what numbers had been assigned; some are given two numbers and others none. In Gerald Abraham's symposium and Lauri Solanterä's catalogue, only six are listed thus: their alternative numbers are in brackets here.

1. *Sortunut ääni* (The broken voice) (*Kanteletar I:57*), for male voices, 1899 (7)

2. *Terve kuu* (Hail, O Moon) (Boruttau) for male voices, 1901(8)

3. *Venematka* (The boat journey) (*Kalevala XL:1–16*), 1893; arr. mixed choir, 1914 (9)

4. *Saarella palaa* (Fire on the island) (*Kanteletar*), for male voices, 1895(3)

5. *Metsämiehen laulu* (The woodman's song) (Kivi), for male voices, 1899 (no opus number)

6. *Sydämeni laulu* (Song of my heart), for male voices, 1898; arr. mixed choir, 1904 (no opus number).

There are three others listed in Harold Johnson's book and earlier editions of this volume, albeit in the alternative numbering.

1. *Isänmalle* (To my country) (Cajander), for male voices, 1899; rev. version for mixed choir, 1900; arr. for male voices, 1908 (the alternative op. 18, no. 1; published without opus number).

2. *Veljeni vierailla mailla* (My brothers abroad), for male voices (also known as op. 18, no. 2; also published without opus number).

3. *Min rastas raata* (The thrush's toiling) (*Kanteletar: 219*) for mixed voices (probably written in 1898) (also known as op. 18, no. 4).

Most of them are short (some are less than two minutes) and many have an affecting simplicity, none more so than *Sydämeni laulu* (Song of my heart). This repertory deserves exposure outside Finland but the inaccessibility of the Finnish language for non-native choirs is an inhibiting factor. Also of some beauty is the op. 84 set dating from the period 1914–17 which is harmonically richer, particularly the searching chromaticism of the third of the set, *Ett drömackord* (A dream chord) to words of Fröding, which is echoed in the setting of Bertel Gripenberg's *Eviga Eros* (Eternal Eros) for baritone and male voices.

Most of Sibelius's works for male chorus are in Finnish, but *Sandels*, an improvisation for male chorus and orchestra, is an exception. It is a short piece of about ten minutes duration, and sets some lines of Runeberg who provided the inspiration for so many of the solo songs. Sibelius wrote it in Berlin in the winter of 1898, so it precedes the First Symphony. The theme was patriotic: Sandels was a celebrated Finnish General, who like our Sir Francis Drake finished what he was doing – in his case eating lunch – before confronting and vanquishing the enemy. In spite of the national climate at this period, the patriotic theme did not in itself prove a passport to success. The work was coolly received at its first performance in 1900 and much later Sibelius overhauled it – at about the time he was working on the first version of the Fifth Symphony. Its beginning has something of the spirit of the *Karelia* music, but some of the invention is conventional (Tawaststjerna calls it 'surprisingly tame') though the storm is quite effective. *Snöfrid* for reciter, chorus and orchestra to words of Rydberg comes from the same period and like *Islossningen i Uleå älv* (The breaking of the ice on the Oulu River) strikes a patriotic stance: Topelius's poem was in itself harmless and its sentiments generalized but in the climate of increasing repression, they assumed another significance.

Moreover the declamatory chords from the brass in the opening section foreshadow *Finlandia*. Patriotic sentiment is strong in two other Swedish settings of Wecksell, *Har du mod?* (Have you the courage?), and the *Song of the Athenians*, also known as the War Song of Tyrtaeus. Both are simple strophic songs with voices in unison, the latter for boys and men, to the accompaniment of brass septet and percussion, which bears a recognizable Sibelian stamp despite its oom-pah accompaniment. By his exalted standards, all three are pretty insignificant musically.

The Origin of Fire (1902) is another matter. Written for the opening of the National Theatre in Helsinki, it tells how Louhi hides the sun and moon in a mountain and steals the fires from the homes of Väinölä. News of this reaches the chief of the gods in the Kalevala, Ukko, who searches for them in vain. We hear then how he created fire and light and subsequently gave them into the precarious safe-keeping of the Maiden of the Air, who promptly dropped them. The text follows *Runo* XLVII of the *Kalevala*. The work falls into two sections: the first cast for baritone and orchestra; the second for chorus and orchestra. The latter begins at the point when Ukko forges light and fire from his sword. There is an impressive peroration, though the choral section as a whole is comparatively uninspired – the E minor tune does not show Sibelius at his best. However, there is some good first-period Sibelius in the opening section. In any event this is vastly superior to *The Captive Queen*, op. 48 (1906), a setting of a German translation of Cajander. The theme is patriotic; the queen is Finland and the captor Tsarist Russia, while the atmosphere is undoubtedly redolent of the Second Symphony. The theme faintly recalls the second group of the finale of the symphony and the cello figure at bar 25 offers another reminder of the same work (see ex. 59).

Oma maa (Our own land) comes from the period of the Finnish civil war, when he was still working on the Fifth Symphony. Yet its patriotic feelings are confident and serene, and there is a magical evocation of the wintry nights with *Aurora borealis* and the white nights of midsummer. It is a dignified and euphonious work, where musical and poetic considerations harmonize, and deserves to be heard more often outside Finland.

The flow of occasional pieces continued: *Jordens Sång* (Song of the Earth) was written for the inauguration of the Swedish Academy at Turku (Åbo) the following year, and in 1920 he produced *Maan virsi* (Hymn to the Earth), op. 95, to Finnish words. We find that he returns to an earlier style when he deals with the chorus: his writing for voices in no way reflects the ground he has won elsewhere. This may have been due to indifference, to the absence of first-class choirs, or perhaps because he felt some compunction about providing work beyond the capacity of his

Ex. 59

patrons. Certainly, if *Maan virsi* is typical, the neglect of the choral music outside Finland is understandable. The work begins in a characteristically dark and sombre fashion, but the promise of the opening is not maintained. As soon as the music shifts into the major the writing becomes commonplace.

Väinön virsi (Väinämöinen's song), op. 110 (1926), is an altogether finer piece, though even here the choral writing, to judge from the vocal score, particularly in the first section between figs. C and G, strikes the listener as differing remarkably little from the *Kullervo* Symphony. The choral writing is often in unison, or simply two-part, and dark in quality:

Ex. 60

Even when it is in four parts it is frankly homophonic. Admittedly the writing in *Maan virsi* is at one point more contrapuntal, but for the most part it would seem that Sibelius tends to avoid elaborate choral polyphony. For all his admiration of Lassus and Palestrina, the fact remains that there is no living tradition of sixteenth-century music in Scandinavia (outside Denmark), even though the choral works of the great Flemish masters were known and sung in the main Swedish centres and in Åbo. Scandinavia produced no master during the Renaissance: hence their choral tradition is of a simpler kind.

13

The songs

Were only the songs to survive from Sibelius's pen, we should form a comparatively incomplete picture of him. Sibelius the symphonist has, understandably enough, overshadowed his achievements as a song composer. In all he composed almost a hundred songs, most of them to Swedish texts, and made sketches for some three dozen more. These include more than one attempt at setting the same poem.[1] The earliest is a Runeberg setting, the *Serenade* (1888), but there are other songs from the same period, *Näcken* (The water-sprite) to an accompaniment of violin, cello and piano (1888), *Orgier* (Orgies) (1888–9), *Skogsrået* (The wood-nymph) to words of Rydberg (1888–9), and another Rydberg setting, *Höstkväll* (Autumn evening), completely different from the later setting (op. 38, no. 1). Song consumed much of his energy for the best part of his creative life: his first set of Seven Songs, op. 13, dates from the early 1890s, and the last, the Six Runeberg settings, op. 90, are from 1917 when Sibelius was still in the throes of the Fifth Symphony and Finland was poised on the brink of civil war. True, there are some later songs – Hjalmar Procopé's *Små flickorna* (The small girls) (1920) and the delightful setting of Bertel Gripenberg's *Narciss* (Narcissus) (1925); but to all intents and purposes, Sibelius's contribution to the *romans* repertory begins over a decade before the First Symphony and ends just before the definitive version of the Fifth. *Romans* is the Swedish equivalent of the German *Lied* or the French *mélodie*. Its foundations were laid early in the nineteenth century by such composers as Geijer, Almqvist and Lindblad, and its repertory through to Stenhammar and Rangström is enormously rich and still grievously neglected beyond its native borders.

When one thinks of Sibelius's extraordinary powers of compression, his ability to evoke a mood by the simplest of brushstrokes and the greatest economy of means, not to mention his highly developed sense of line, one might expect his songs to exhibit a mastery commensurate with

---

[1]Even *Höstkväll* exists in two versions, the first dating from his student years (1888–9). See Robert Keane, '*Höstkväll* – two versions?', *Finnish Music Quarterly*, (1900), pp. 62–5.

– even if it is different from – that of such orchestral works as *The Bard* and the Fourth Symphony. Many of them do, and – as far as the literature of song is concerned – Sibelius surely deserves a far more honoured place in the firmament than many commentators (even the present author) were inclined to accord him. Composers who have poured their inspiration solely into this medium, such as Yrjö Kilpinen[1] or those to whom it is central, rather than exclusive, like the Swiss master Othmar Schoeck, are a case apart. However, among others for whom song is not a primary preoccupation, Sibelius can more than hold his own. Nielsen's songs, for example, have none of the psychological subtlety of Kilpinen or the nature mysticism of Sibelius, but stem from the artless simplicity of Weyse.

But it is not just the celebrity of the symphonies and the tone-poems that has diverted attention away from Sibelius's music for voice; there are other factors, primarily the relative inaccessibility of the Swedish language as far as non-native singers are concerned. Flagstad and Söderström may have championed them, but the great lieder-singers of our day, Schwarzkopf, Fischer-Dieskau, Souzay, and Prey have fought shy of them, though Schwarzkopf did record *Säv, säv, susa* (Sigh, sedges, sigh). Moreover, like those of Musorgsky, Fauré or Grieg, the songs of Sibelius do not sound well in translation. Only a handful (quite literally five) of the songs are in Finnish, though these are among the most affecting of all; nine are in German, in which Sibelius was reasonably fluent, and one is in English, in which he was not; and another, the setting of Maeterlinck's 'Les trois soeurs aveugles' from *Pelléas et Mélisande* is in French (though even here the original setting was in Swedish). The vast majority of the songs are in the language with which he grew up as a child, Swedish.

Indeed, a reminder about language may be in order. As we have already seen, Sibelius was brought up in a Swedish-speaking home in Tavastehus or, to give it its Finnish name, Hämeenlinna where the language spoken by educated people was Swedish. Indeed, the young composer did not begin to learn Finnish until he was eight years old in preparation for school. Generally speaking, Sibelius's inspiration was best kindled by the nature poets writing in Swedish, be they Finnish, such as Runeberg, Wecksell and Tavaststjerna or mainland Swedish, like Karlfeldt, Fröding

[1]Kilpinen was trilingual, speaking Finnish with his father, Swedish with his mother and immersing himself in German as a student. He remained aloof from contemporary trends: his idiom is unexploratory and his harmonic vocabulary does not go much beyond Wolf, and yet at his finest he creates a strangely distinctive world. He is a master of the vignette and distills a powerful atmosphere and a keen psychological intensity with the greatest economy of means.

and, above all, Viktor Rydberg. It was to them he turned in his solo songs, while Finnish dominates the choral output. The lyric poetry he read in his youth left an indelible mark on him throughout his life; the poetry of the *Kalevala*, on the other hand, calls for epic treatment. Sibelius's setting of Rydberg's *Höstkväll* (Autumn evening) must be numbered among his very greatest and self-revealing songs. Not all of Sibelius's poets are of this stature but most of them are of quality, and all are linked by their highly developed feeling for the northern landscape and its desolate melancholy and grandeur. Runeberg was undoubtedly the poet he loved most deeply, an enthusiasm shared by Brahms, no less, and roughly a quarter of his output in the genre are Runeberg settings. Runeberg touched an especially sympathetic vein in his sensibility and he absorbed his language so completely that certain literary artifices one encounters in Runeberg's epic poetry find their way into Sibelius's diaries and letters. This body of poetry is little known outside Scandinavia and the bulk of the songs tends to be written off by many music-lovers, whose knowledge of them does not extend far beyond the popular handful, *Svarta rosor* (Black roses), *Flickan kom ifrån sin älsklings möte* (The tryst, or The girl returned from meeting her lover), and *Säv, säv, susa* (Sigh, sedges, sigh). Irrespective of their merits – and *Säv, säv, susa* is very beautiful indeed – it is they that one encounters in the concert hall rather than such strange and haunting masterpieces as *Jubal, Teodora* and *Höstkväll* (Autumn evening). And as with Grieg, the most popular of the songs are not necessarily the best and have served to deter some music-lovers from exploring the best.

Of course, the greatest of all Sibelius's works for the human voice is undoubtedly *Luonnotar*, half tone-poem half song-with-orchestra. If *Luonnotar* is not a symphonic poem in the normal sense of the word, it is on too extended a scale to be regarded simply as a song with orchestra or even a kind of *scena* like *Höstkväll*. Indeed, it is quite unlike anything in all music, a profoundly original work even by Sibelius's own standards. Its power and intensity are matched only in *The Bard* and *Tapiola*, and its atmosphere is unique in all his output. It was written for Aino Ackté, who possessed an exceptionally wide tessitura, and who gave the first performances of a number of other Sibelius songs (the *Arioso*, op. 3, another Runeberg setting, and *Höstkväll* (Autumn evening) also possess a wide if not so cruelly demanding a tessitura). However, the fact remains that in *Luonnotar*, Sibelius was working in his natural element, the orchestra, and he was also composing a work of symphonic proportions: *Luonnotar* is about the same length as the first movement of the Fourth Symphony, with which it is roughly contemporaneous. All the other songs are smaller in scale and are conceived with piano accompaniment, and even if commentators have dwelt on the limitations of his keyboard writing rather than its moments of strength, no one could reasonably argue that his mastery of the piano is remotely comparable with his genius for the orchestra. There is no doubt that the impact of many of the songs has been blunted by the apparent ineffectiveness of the keyboard writing. Sibelius himself recognized this by authorizing orchestral transcriptions of many of them by Pingoud, Hellman and Jalas, and making some himself.[1]

The *Serenade* (1888) to words of Runeberg, is the very first piece of Sibelius to have appeared in print, in an anthology of Finnish song, but he never assigned it an opus number. It is a charming song, though, unaffected and direct in appeal. His first opus, but by no means his first set of songs, is the *Fem Julvisor* (Five Christmas Songs), four of them settings of Zacharius Topelius, one of the Finnish poets for whom Sibelius had a particular soft spot. They are strophic songs of simplicity and charm dating from 1895 but, as we know them, the result of revision in 1913 made at the request of Horatio Parker, the American composer who was instrumental in encouraging Sibelius to go to the United States in 1914, for which journey *The Oceanides* was composed. Their directness of language reminds one of the tradition of the *Piae cantiones* or the simple Protestant chorale settings. Only one of them is to Finnish words, *On hanget korkeat* (High are the snowdrifts), and none betrays too many of the mature Sibelius's fingerprints.

His first important group, however, is the set of seven Runeberg songs, op. 13, composed in 1891–2. However, this is preceded in his opus list by *Arioso*, op. 3. In fact Sibelius did make two early attempts at Runeberg, both completely different from each other and the published op. 3, both during the same period (1890–2). *Arioso* itself has the grave air of melancholy that distinguishes the elegiac Grieg, and much the same intentness and conviction. It is much later than the opus number implies, and comes from the first decade of the present century, not from 1893 as we were originally led to believe. Being hard pressed for money, Sibelius sold this song to a Finnish publisher at a time when he was under an exclusive contract to Breitkopf & Härtel and explained its appearance in print by saying that it was an early work! One bar of the song with completely unrelated material survives from that year, so there was a grain of truth in his assertion. The setting of the words is

---

[1]In his article 'Sibelius's Orchestral Songs' Robert Keane reminds us that in 1946 Sibelius forbade the Finnish Radio to broadcast his songs other than in their original form. 'I don't want them orchestrated for they completely lose their individual character. One can't express little ideas by means of a large orchestra'.

totally free from artifice; in fact, the opening words are given almost equal stresses. There is a touching directness of utterance about this music and more than a hint of the wide-ranging vocal writing we are soon to encounter in *Luonnotar*:

Ex. 61

gos-sens ö - ga är dess vår - dag___ och min mo - ders är dess vin - ter

The op. 13 settings are also of poems by Runeberg and they come from the early years: indeed, they were announced in the press as early as 1892, the same year in which he had made his triumphant breakthrough with the *Kullervo* Symphony. They include *Våren flyktar hastigt* (Spring is flying) and *Drömmen* (The dream), which have established themselves in the concert hall, but some of the others are hardly less worthy of attention. Sibelius composed the first, *Under strandens granar* (Under the fir-trees) on his honeymoon at Monola in Lake Pielsjärvi in the summer of 1892. Runeberg had been inspired by a Serbian folk-song and his poem has something of the spirit of a folk-ballad: it tells how a water-sprite seduces a handsome youth by assuming various disguises, before he finally succeeds in the form of a young horse. Sibelius's setting makes use of some freely conceived recitative and the piano texture is obviously thought of in orchestral terms. The piano accompaniment consists largely of dark *tremolandi* in the bass clef that spring from the same world of fantasy as *Lemminkäinen in Tuonela* and the *Kullervo* symphony. The way in which the music sinks from a C sharp major chord by a semitone (bars 14–15) certainly recalls the former, and the harmonies in this passage are more advanced than in the companion songs (see ex. 62). Its rhythmic freedom and the uneven phrase repetitions posed problems for Finnish audiences brought up on Pacius and von Schantz, and the composer, Oskar Merikanto wrote of its first performance, 'Though the songs bear the imprint of the composer of *Kullervo*, the original use of rhythm and bizarre harmonies make a confusing and even tiring impression on the uninitiated ear'. Although the song is by no means wholly successful, it is undeniably powerful. The harmonies are certainly more advanced than in the companion songs. Astra Desmond speaks of it in her sympathetic and perceptive study published in Gerald Abraham's Symposium, as 'nearly a very fine song', though it is not as well wrought,

Ex. 62

even if it is more interesting than its immediate successor, *Kyssens hopp* (The kiss's hope). This song and *Hjärtats morgon* (The heart's morning) belong fairly and squarely to the Scandinavian *romans* tradition and do not step outside its conventions, though *Hjärtats morgon* is full of powerful feeling.

Våren flyktar hastigt (The Spring is flying) is a beautiful little song whose flexible, pliable phrases suggest the transience of the short-breathed seasons. The rapid changes of mood are well brought off in spite of the brevity of the song – indeed, it is one of Sibelius's most perfect miniatures. As is so often the case, its effect is greatly enhanced in the orchestral version Sibelius made in 1914. The opening figure, for example, breathes much more naturally in this version (two flutes, four horns, percussion and strings) that the transformation is beyond the fingers of all but the most sensitive pianist to convey. The rapid changes of mood are well brought off, though the more settled it becomes in E flat, the more it tends to be conventional. *Drömmen* (The dream), written in Vienna, bears witness to his growing interest in the *Kalevala* and the kind of speech rhythms and colours it has. It even makes oblique reference to a progression we later encounter in *Lemminkäinen and the Maidens of the Island*, and it has a dark and compelling quality. (For once, I would take issue with Astra Desmond who found this song uninteresting.) Its five-beat phrase lengths notated in 3/4 so that the upbeat of the second comes on the last beat of a bar show just how responsive he is to the speech rhythms of the Swedish spoken in Finland.

On the face of it *Till Frigga* (To Frigga), a love song, is another instance of an 'ineffective' piano accompaniment, using a restricted range of devices, yet in a curious way this limitation is turned to advantage, for this is a haunting song whose dark sombre hues and strength of feeling ring true. There is a poetic moment at the words, 'Säg, hvar fostrades du, leende angel, säg?' (Where do you come from, smiling angel?), when the accompaniment lends an almost luminous quality to the vocal line. There is 'something primitive and saga-like about it' (Astra Desmond) and one does not need to be too observant to note the anticipation of the Second Symphony. *Jägargossen* (The young huntsman) is a delightful song, Schubertian in feeling and full of character.

The *Serenade* (1895) for baritone and small orchestra is something of a discovery. Though it was first performed in April 1895 by Abraham Ojanperä with Sibelius himself conducting, it remained unpublished and unperformed for the rest of Sibelius's lifetime. According to his diaries he had intended to revise it, and it was only in 1984 that his heirs agreed to its publication on record. Though it comes from the period of the *Lemminkäinen Legends*, its musical language is quite different. A setting of Erik Johan Stagnelius, a Shelley-like figure in Swedish poetry, to whom Sibelius was much attached, it has the greatest delicacy and atmosphere, and its whispering pizzicato strings are wonderfully suggestive. Stagnelius's dithyramb tells of the lover's moods of yearning, hope and despair; only as the night falls, does he dare to approach in his thoughts and dreams the Olympia whom he worships. Not to put too fine a point on it, this is one of Sibelius's very greatest and most subtle songs both in its use of rhythm and colour.

The op. 17 set of Seven Songs was placed by Ekman, Solanterä and others in the 1890s but recent evidence shows it to be of later provenance. Certain references in letters and the dates of first performances supports the view that some of them are, in fact, much later and not written before the first years of the present century. Undoubtedly the earliest is *Se'n har jag ej frågat mera* (And I questioned then no further), a Runeberg setting which finds Sibelius at his most direct in melodic appeal and most powerful in emotional intensity. Its simplicity is affecting and it was with this song that Ida Ekman, accompanied by Hanslick, made so strong an impression on Brahms, so much so that he asked to hear the song again and sat down at the piano to accompany her himself. It was composed no later than 1894. The melodic line is drawn with firm but simple brushstrokes and the song strikes a deeper vein of feeling than anything else he had composed in this genre before. The next three settings are of Karl August Tavaststjerna (1860–98), the Finnish poet writing in Swedish, whose output is strongly national in feeling and shows an independence of such models as Runeberg and Topelius. (He is a distant relative of the composer's biographer, Erik Tawaststjerna.) *Fågellek* (Enticement) really does come from 1891 while he was studying in Vienna, and its simple alternation of pianissimo chords in the treble with arpeggiated writing, highlights the pathos of the vocal line. This is a touching song not wholly free from the influence of French models. *Sov in!* (Sleep on!) (1892) and *Vilse* (Astray) (1902) are typical examples of the *romans* tradition, the latter distinguished by a delightful rusticity and good humour which make an admirable foil to the delicacy of *Fågellek*.

The next song, *En slända* (A dragon-fly), dated 1894 in some sources and four years later in others, was first performed in 1904, and that fact, together with its more developed style would suggest that it was also written nearer that date. It is to words of Oscar Levertin, and the idiom is described by Tawaststjerna as 'more expressionistic' in texture and its harmonies as more Lisztian. It is one of the finest and most imaginative of the set, its line floating onomatapoetically, quivering like the wings of a dragon-fly itself. In some ways it anticipates the big songs such as *Jubal* though the recitative does not have quite the same boldness. The last two songs are to Finnish texts: *Illale* (To evening), sometimes sung in Swedish as *Om kvällen*), and *Lastu lainehilla* (Driftwood). Previously listed as coming from 1898, the second is almost certainly later, as a letter from Sibelius to his wife mentions his setting Ilmari Calamnius's poem during the summer of 1902. Both songs seem to me quite perfect in their purity of line, strength of feeling and complete simplicity. There is a total harmony of means and ends. It is interesting, too, that *Lastu lainehilla*, and another song written in Finnish at about the same time, *Souda, souda, sinisorsa* (Swim, duck, swim) have a strong affinity. The melodic character of each song is not dissimilar, the accompaniments are confined to the simplest filling in of harmonies, and the setting of the language is guided by its own verbal music. It needs no special knowledge of the language to see that Sibelius alters his approach to the voice when setting Finnish. The vocal line seems to carry so much of the music of the language itself: to hear *Illale* given in Swedish is quite a different experience. Finnish is a highly inflected language, rich in vowel sounds, and these songs reflect Sibelius's growing confidence in handling it. (Right up to the early 1890s he still made mistakes in writing Finnish). On a larger scale he handles Swedish more naturally, but later on, in the first decade of the present century, all this changed, and in *Luonnotar*, the actual sounds of the language and the vocal line are so perfectly matched as to be indivisible, and attempts to sing it in translation diminish its character and impact. *Souda, souda, sinisorsa* (Swim, duck, swim) is one of his most perfect in its handling of the verbal music of the poem by Forsman-Koskomies. Incidentally, at this time a number of writers, Forsman among them, abandoned the Swedish form of their names for the Finnish. Ilmari Calamnius whose poem *Illale* Sibelius set, adopted the name Kianto and Forsman 'fennicized' (if one can coin a phrase) his name to Koskimies, though to avoid confusion both forms are sometimes used hyphenated. *Sången om korspindeln* (Fool's song of the spider) comes from the same period and derives from the repertory of incidental music which Sibelius wrote in such profusion throughout his life. It comes from his score to Adolf Paul's play *King Christian II* (1898), the first of his works to find its way into the concert halls of England and Europe at the turn of the century. The fool tells of a spider, 'so large and black he captures the sunbeams and toils and twines . . . in its meshes he captures each living soul, and torments and tortures to death'. Its monotony conveys a sense of quiet menace, and at the time it was perceived as alluding to the tightening Tsarist grip on Finland. If it is 'perhaps a little too facile', particularly the closing bars, it creates a certain atmosphere and has the merit of memorability.

Before we come to *Jubal* there is *Koskenlaski an morsiamet* which was widely known in English as 'The ferryman's brides'.[1] This is the first of the two extended orchestral songs, the second being the tone-poem, *Luonnotar*. Neither in the boldness of the vocal writing nor in the musical inspiration itself does this work offer any real hint of what is to come in *Luonnotar*. Oksanen's ballad tells the story of Vilho, who takes his bride to watch him shoot the rapids at Pyörtäjä. The river-nymph, Vellamo, who cherishes a jealous passion for him, is driven to fury by the sight of his new bride and dashes a rock into the middle of the stream, thus drowning the pair. The poem ends by describing how the nymph sits mourning her love by the side of the very rock that destroyed him. Whereas in *Luonnotar* one wonders at the almost miraculous fusion of the words and the vocal line, *The Rapids-rider's Brides* gives little hint of this plasticity. Its idiom, not unnaturally considering its date, does not go beyond the national-romanticism we find from *Karelia* and *En Saga*

---

[1] A better translation would be 'The rapids-shooter's brides' or, more exactly, 'rapids-rider's brides' as these loggers 'ride' down the rivers jumping from one log to another.

down to the First Symphony; and the vocal line does not differ very much from the setting of Finnish that one finds in *Kullervo* on the one hand or *The Origin of Fire* written a decade later. Certainly there is little more flexibility than in either of these: Sibelius at this time seems rather more at home when dealing with Swedish texts. Admittedly *Souda, souda, sinisorsa* might be cited to the contrary, but this is a song of very modest dimension. Musically there are fine things in *The Rapids-rider's Brides* (notably the poetic passage at fig. E), but for the most part it does not show the composer at his most inspired.

Although *Jubal* is placed next in Sibelius's final opus list, ten years separate it from *The Rapids-rider's Brides*: all the famous songs of opp. 36, 37, and 38 precede it. It is worth looking at the freedom and mastery with which Sibelius handles the voice, which ranges over a compass of almost two octaves. The opening of *Jubal*, which tells how the hero sees a swan flying and swiftly draws his bow to shoot it, is a good instance of this dramatic power. Nothing could be further from the miniaturist we found in *Vilse* and the two Finnish songs of op. 17 (see ex. 63). It ranges with great freedom over a compass of almost two octaves; indeed, so intense is this writing and that in its companion, *Teodora*, and so full of dramatic fire that one wonders whether he would not have been an operatic composer of considerable note, had his inclinations not taken him so far in the direction of the symphony. *Teodora* will come as a revelation to many Sibelians for in its over-heated expressionism, it comes close to the Strauss of *Salome* and *Elektra*.

With the op. 36 set we come to Sibelius's most popular group of songs. Despite the later opus number they precede *Jubal* and *Teodora* by almost a decade, and were written at about the same time as the First Symphony. *Svarta Rosor* (Black Roses) is probably Sibelius's best-known song: its fascination undoubtedly lies in the darkening of the mood on the words 'ty sorgen har nattsvarta rosor' ('for sorrow has black-petalled roses'). This phrase is poised dramatically on the second inversion of the chord of C sharp minor before resolving on the C major tonic. Although it is a fine song, it pales in comparison with the second of the group, *Men min fågel märks dock icke* (But my bird is long in homing), to words of Runeberg. This has a simplicity of utterance, an immediacy of atmosphere and a sheer melodic sweep that earns it a high position in the Sibelian pantheon. Once again it is Runeberg's nature lyricism that seems to call on the deepest vein of inspiration in Sibelius, for not only is *Men min fågel märks dock icke* one of his most perfect songs, but it also ranks as one of the finest in the whole Scandinavian *romans* repertory. Tawaststjerna reminds us that the rising figure which opens it 'almost recalls the opening

Ex. 63

of *The Swan of Tuonela* and that, of course, the song itself begins by a reference to a swan!' Ekman gives 1899 for these songs but this is true only for the first three. Fazer and Westerlund, the Helsinki publisher, bought *Svarta rosor* for the then substantial sum of 370 Finnish marks, and it is obvious that the other Runeberg setting and *Bollspelet vid Trianon* (Tennis at Trianon) were included in the transaction. *Bollspelet vid Trianon* is a setting of Fröding. Not all of Sibelius's poets are of stature but most of them are, and Gustav Fröding certainly was. Most are linked by their highly developed feeling for the northern landscape and its desolation and melancholy. Fröding was five years older than Sibelius and was brought up in Värmland in central Sweden and studied in Uppsala. As a poet he was much influenced by the German romantics and also Byron. This poem obviously strikes a responsive chord, for the piano writing has great finesse and prompts one to call in question the general assumptions made about his understanding of the keyboard. Not that Sibelius himself is blameless in this respect, for he gave hostages to fortune by denigrating both the instrument and his understanding of it (in his conversations with Bengt de Törne, published as *Sibelius: a Close-Up*). *Bollspelet vid Trianon* shows a very considerable subtlety in the handling of contrast ('Noses turn up with well-bred refinement . . . but softly in the distance with heavy gait, goes the son of the dregs, Jourdan Coupe-tête') and the alternation between recitative and a pastiche pastoral style serves to convey the sense of bewilderment of the company as well as a sense of foreboding.

Säv, säv, susa is also to a poem of Fröding, a poem that is in itself so rich in verbal music that it must have represented an enormous challenge to the composer. Sometimes known in English as *Ingalill* after the heroine of the poem, it in every way deserves its considerable popularity. Sibelius heightens the music of the words by a gentle, sighing accompaniment of a harp-like character (indeed the harp plays an important part in the orchestral transcription he authorized by Hellman) and the return to this opening section is altogether magical. For the remaining two songs of op. 36, *Marssnön* (The March snow) and *Demanten på Marssnön* (The diamond on the March snow), Sibelius turned to Josef Julius Wecksell, a Finnish poet writing in the Swedish language whose work owes much to Heine. He is said to have something of the intensity of Shelley or, in Swedish literature, Stagnelius. At a relatively early age Wecksell succumbed to insanity, and both poems dwell on the theme of Death casting its shadows over the moment of fulfilment. *Marssnön*, as Tawaststjerna puts it, 'has nothing of the *Kalevala* about it: indeed, the melodic outline is more redolent of the Russian folk melody one encounters in Rimsky-Korsakov or at times Musorgsky', while in *Demanten på Marssnön* we have 'an example of the Finnish Biedermeier style'. *Var det en dröm?* (Was it a dream?) is a later Wecksell setting, and comes from the period of the Second Symphony. (There is an orchestral version by his son-in-law, the conductor Jussi Jalas.) Like *Höstkväll* (Autumn evening), *Var det en dröm* has a wide tessitura; the vocal line is reminiscent of the string cantilenas in the early symphonies, while the accompaniment evokes a dream-like atmosphere. These are appealing songs but do not chart new territory for Sibelius in the same way as do *Men min fågel märks dock icke* or *Bollspelet vid Trianon*. *Marssnön* is elegantly wrought but has been somewhat overshadowed by *Demanten på marssnön* which, for all its lyrical appeal, belongs to the more conventional among Sibelius's songs.

The op. 37 set is generally speaking less successful than either op. 36 or op. 38. Certainly *Den första kyssen* (The first kiss) fails to live up to the promise of the opening. Although the vocal line has a certain robustness, the unabashed self-indulgent romanticism of the music seems to spring more from the stock *salon* responses of late nineteenth-century song than it does from a genuinely felt experience. *Den första kyssen* seems to lack the inner vitality and freshness to survive transplanting outside its period. Sibelius's treatment of the words at the very end of the song, 'blott döden vänder ögat bort och gråter' ('only death turns aside to weep'), is redolent of Wagner. *Soluppgång* (Sunrise) is from 1902. Again, recent evidence has questioned the dating given by Ekman and others. In a letter to his friend, Axel Carpelan, in May 1902, Sibelius speaks of his working on Tor Hedberg's *Soluppgång*, which he describes as 'a slight but powerfully atmospheric poem'. This, indeed, it is, and it must be said that Sibelius's setting has great finesse. He himself thought sufficiently well of it to score it immediately. Another of the songs to be overshadowed by the Wecksell settings is *Lasse liten* (Little Lasse),[1] which Astra Desmond dismissed as 'marred by the excessive lowness of the accompaniment, which is almost exclusively in the bass clef'. Yet, oddly enough, its subtle rhythm, so completely attuned to the speech rhythm of Topelius's verse, strikes a note of conviction, and the dark colours evoked, convey an idea of the big wide world with all its attendant dangers that lurk outside the mother's sheltering embrace. Despite the odd reservation one might have, in none of the op. 36 settings does Sibelius's piano writing get in the way. On the contrary, its very simplicity in *Men min fågel märks dock icke* and *Säv, säv, susa* matches the quality of the inspiration of the song as a whole. The next of the op. 37 set, *Var det en dröm?* (Was it a dream?), carries an unimaginative and cumbersome piano accompaniment and, apart from some delicacy of feeling in the transition between the second and third verses of Wecksell's poem, this is *salon* stuff and cannot be numbered

---

[1]Lasse, incidentally, is a diminutive of the name Lars.

171

among Sibelius's better songs. Nor for that matter can the inordinately popular *Flickan kom ifrån sin älsklings möte* (The girl returned from meeting her lover), which shares more with the D flat major Romance for piano than just its key. It is true that the words of Runeberg's poem do not survive translation: what appears to be hack-work melodrama in English has in fact a restrained yet compelling ballad-like quality in the original Swedish. All the same Tawaststjerna speaks of the set as 'one of the finest lyrical collections in the whole of Sibelius's song output', though this is not to say that it matches opp. 35 or 38 in imaginative intensity and vision.

Placing them side by side, one would hardly guess that the songs of op. 37 and *Höstkväll* (Autumn evening) and *På verandan vid havet* (On a balcony by the sea) are by the same composer. Admittedly there are many individual fingerprints in *Den första kyssen*, but at no time do we glimpse the real Sibelius, the composer whose intensity of vision and spiritual stature are familiar from the great orchestral works. *Höstkväll*, on the other hand, comes from a totally different world: here is the grim, uncompromising nature poet at the height of his powers. *Höstkväll* is an astonishingly forward-looking song. Dating from 1903, the year of the first version of the violin concerto, its powerfully evoked atmosphere and magnificent sweep anticipate the world of *The Bard* and *Luonnotar*. The scoring gives some idea of the sombre colours: two oboes (no flutes), two clarinets, one bass clarinet, two bassoons, one double bassoon, four horns, three trombones, side-drum, harp and strings. Viktor Rydberg's poem seems singularly appropriate as a vehicle for Sibelius's own sympathies:

> The sun is setting, and the clouds are wandering mournfully across the sky low over the windswept lake while murmuring forests grow dusky . . . Alone in desolate nature among the rocks and spindrift, a wanderer stands transfixed, rapt and exultant. He feels his soul at one with the song of the wind in the starless night. Does his sorrow die like a cry lost in the autumn's mighty lament?

The song is in the unusual key of D sharp minor and the accompaniment is largely confined to the sketchiest harmonic support, dark sustained chords and pedals. Yet for all its economy this is extremely powerful, though its effect on the piano is greatly diminished. The vocal line has the wide-ranging compass and sense of freedom that we noticed in *Jubal*; though there is a trace of Wagner at times, the whole atmosphere of the song could hardly be more individual. The setting of the words 'falken dväljes i klyftans skygd' ('the falcon sits in the shelter of a crag') up to fig. 3 in the score is unmistakably Nordic, and its lineage seems to point to *Arioso*. Here is an example of the sheer sweep of the line: note Sibelius's word-painting, and the use of the side-drum (as in *Lemminkäinen in Tuonela*) to colour the string *tremolando* pedal:

Ex. 64

This is as self-revealing a song in terms of a basic human attitude as is Ravel's *L'Indifférent*. It is no accident that the loneliness of a stranger exalted by the mystery of nature and glorying in its power should strike a sympathetic chord in Sibelius's imagination. His own art suggests a greater involvement in nature and identification with it than it does a concern with the human predicament, even though the longing for human contact is often apparent.

If *Höstkväll* has the scope if not the dramatic power of an operatic *scena, På verandan vid havet* (On a balcony by the sea), is a good deal less ambitious in scale though it is every bit as intense in feeling. The poem is also by Rydeberg, and its brooding questionings are matched by the searching chromaticism of the music (see ex. 65).

The melodic line has much the same boldness as that of *Höstkväll*; since this is a much shorter song, however, the voice never takes flight so freely as it does in the earlier song. In the orchestral version the low menacing chords offer an oblique reminder of Wagner, but the whole mood and character of the song are profoundly Sibelian. As we have seen, Sibelius's relationship with Wagner is a more complex one than the composer admitted to, and the ghosts of his visit to Bayreuth in 1894 are surely hovering over these inspired and wonderful songs. The remaining

Ex. 65

Rydberg settings, *Harpolekaren och hans son* (The harpist and his son) and *I natten* (In the night), though not of the same calibre, are still evocative, particularly the latter. Indeed, Sibelius's use of the lowest register of the piano at the beginning of the song almost gives the lie to the notion that he wrote ineffectively for the instrument. The invention here is thoroughly characteristic and readers will recognize the familiar fingerprints. The last of the five songs in this set, *Jag ville jag vore i Indialand* (I would I were in India) to words of Fröding, is arguably the least interesting of the set. Sibelius scarcely matches the exoticism of the poem.

There are no songs after op. 38 that are of comparable stature to *Höstkväll* and *På veranden vid havet*, even though there are some fine if sadly neglected miniatures. The next set in order of publication is the six songs to German texts which date from 1906. German was, of course, Sibelius's first foreign tongue and it was natural that at a time when his music was beginning to find a welcome in Germany he should turn to a language that had wider currency than Swedish or Finnish. Two of the set, *Im Feld ein Mädchen* (In the field a maiden sings) and *Die stille Stadt* (The silent town) are among his loveliest and most powerful songs. *Lenzegesang* (A song of Spring), to words of Fitger, suffers from a cumbersome piano accompaniment which fails to blend with the voice; it is set too low in register with a resultant heaviness that is unappealing. The vocal part itself has exuberance and some measure of charm, and much the same goes for its immediate successor, *Sehnsucht* (Longing). This has the simplicity and finesse of the best Swedish settings, and the piano accompaniment has an affecting directness and economy. The piano part, gently adumbrated syncopated chords, lend the song a special pathos. The first of the Dehmel settings, a poet also favoured by Mahler, *Aus banger Brust* (O, wert thou here, or From anxious heart) is an impassioned one, but the real masterpiece here is its companion, *Die stille*

174

Stadt. This has the concentration and atmosphere of a tone-poem: indeed, its serenity, beauty of line and sense of repose mark it out from the others. It is grievously neglected, to judge from its infrequency in the concert hall, but it has great distinction and refinement of feeling, and its subtle shifts of harmonic emphasis resonate in the memory. It is worthy to rank alongside some of the best of the smaller-scale Swedish settings, and has far stronger claims on the repertory than the oft-performed *Demanten på marssnön* and *Flickan kom ifrån sin älsklings möte*. The last of the set, *Rosenlied* (Song of the roses), though not by any manner of means in the same league, has great charm and an almost Viennese lilt.

There are two other songs to German texts, *Erloschen*, (The fire has died out) also from 1906, *Segelfahrt* (Sailing), both at one time thought to come from 1918, but the latter would seem to be of earlier provenance (1899). Sibelius only ventured once on a French text, though not the French language, in the course of his incidental music to Maeterlinck's *Pelléas et Mélisande* (1905). '*Les trois soeurs aveugles*' was originally set in Swedish translation. Less familiar is his setting of the *Hymn to Thaïs*, to words of Arthur Borgström. The *Hymn to Thaïs* is in fact Sibelius's only attempt to set the English language (the two settings of Shakespeare's *Twelfth Night* were in Hagberg's Swedish translation). Borgström suggested the theme during a telephone conversation in 1909 when the words 'Thaïs, she who cannot be forgotten' resonated in Sibelius's mind. When he sent a sketch of some bars to Borgström, the latter responded with a poem of ten lines. On reading it, Sibelius started again from scratch though setting English, a language which he read but in which he was far from fluent, posed problems for him. However the result is a piece of no mean dignity and eloquence.

The eight Josephson settings, like the two from *Twelfth Night*, op. 60, come from 1909, a crisis year in Sibelius's life, two years after the composition of *Jubal* and *Teodora*, and the same year as the *Voces intimae* Quartet. Ernst Josephson was celebrated not only as a poet but a painter, too. After his studies in Stockholm, he went to Paris where he came under the influence of Manet. He spent most of his life in France and his work as a painter has to some extent overshadowed his achievement as a poet. *Älven och snigeln* (The snail) tells how a snail made its home in the rushing river water. It has many felicitous touches but cannot be numbered among the finest of the set. Similarly, the persistence of the pedal note in the accompaniment rather spoils the effect of *En blomma stod vid vägen* (The wildflower). *Kvarnhjulet* (The mill-wheel) offers some charming effects at the very beginning but neither it nor its successor, *Maj* (May) call for special comment. By far the loveliest of the set is the fifth song, *Jag är ett träd* (I am a tree), which has a much bolder sense of line than its companions and a much more powerful and deeply characteristic atmosphere. Not that there can be any doubt about the authorship of *Hertig Magnus* (Duke Magnus), though its feeling is that of early rather than later Sibelius. Were one to discover that it dates from the early years of the first decade and was contemporaneous with the Second Symphony and the Violin Concerto, it would entail no surprise. *Vänskapens blomma* (The flower of friendship) leaves much the same impression but it is a very appealing song with a genuine breadth to it. *Näcken* (The water-sprite) is an interesting song, too, touched with moments of dark poetry that are striking. On the whole the Josephson settings cannot be numbered among the finest Sibelius, although they contain some felicitous touches. Like the German settings they are modest in range, though none of them approaches the eloquence of *Die stille Stadt*.

The two Shakespeare settings, op. 60 are among his greatest songs. In *Kom nu hit, död* (Come away, Death) the contrast between the chord of E minor and the G sharp minor triad (the D sharp of the latter is the leading note of E minor) lends a particularly macabre colouring to the word 'death'. One expects it to end in E minor but it is death (and G sharp minor) that claims the last word. The words fit the Hagberg translation which Sibelius set: the vowel sounds, the speech inflexions and rhythm are different from the English, and as a result the song has an undeniably alien flavour when given in English. This is even more true of its companion *Och när som jag var en liten smådräng* (When that I was and a little tiny boy), an elegant little piece of great character. When sung in English it sounds somewhat comic because of the numerous false stresses that arise, but Sibelius's melody fits the rhythm and the inflexion of the Swedish text like a glove. Death was, of course, uppermost in Sibelius's mind in 1909 when he lived in fear of the throat tumour that had developed the previous year and whose symptoms Rosa Newmarch noticed during his London visit of 1908. It is ironic, too, that his thoughts returned to this song in 1957, the last year of his life, when he made a transcription of *Come away, Death* for strings and harp.

During the composition of the op. 61 set, Sibelius was wrestling with the Fourth Symphony, and the songs not unnaturally show him at his most advanced stylistically. As Tawaststjerna puts it, 'late romantic in outlook with a strong element of impressionism, they are far removed from the expressionist world of the Josephson settings'. Where, he asks, has Sibelius composed a more eloquent and elegiac vocal line or wrought so intense and evocative an accompaniment as in *Långsamt som kvällskyn* (Slowly as the evening sun), which opens the set? This and *Vattenplask* (Lapping waters), a Rydberg setting of great power, are remarkable songs by any standards. The latter is thematically related to the Largo of the symphony and has an accompaniment that is on paper questionable but which proves highly effective as well as original in performance. Rydberg's image of the sun-tanned youth from Venice is common enough in the Nordic countries '. . . we sense Princes when our eyes dwell on children but among adults we find no Kings'. *Långsamt som kvällskyn* is the greater song, perhaps, and it haunts the listener with its concentration of mood and atmosphere. It is a setting of Tavaststjerna, to whom Sibelius turns for four other poems in this set: *När jag drömmer* (When I dream), *Romeo, Romans* (Romance) and *Dolce far niente*. If none is quite so searching and inward in feeling as that remarkable piece, it must be said that they find the composer at his most individual, and I was far too dismissive of their achievement in the 1965 edition of this monograph. Indeed, the only poem which discovers him in conventional vein is Bertel Gripenberg's *Vårtagen* (Spring spell), though this has no want of charm. *När jag drömmer* has some wonderful ideas in it and a marvellously austere opening. Tawaststjerna finds it 'not altogether successful in integrating the recitative-like, somewhat expressionist introduction with the more rigid inner section'; it must be admitted that the mood changes are abrupt, but what quality there is in the individual sections. However, it is not as masterly as *Romeo*, a subtle and brilliant song which offers evidence of his study of Debussy, or as concentrated as *Romans* (his diaries record that Sibelius had been studying both Debussy and Rakhmaninov at about this time). In *Romans* a captive Prince sings from his prison to his Princess, and the troubadour style is most effectively conveyed. Only one of the songs is to words of Runeberg, *Fåfäng önskan* (Idle wishes) about which Sibelius himself would seem to have had ambivalent feelings. He spoke of it with pride in a letter to Axel Carpelan as 'intense and grand', yet a diary entry calls it 'sloppy' and the piano part 'second-hand Chopin'. The 'countless waves' ('*otaliga vågar*') are represented by arpeggio figures that span the whole compass of the piano and make an effect that is in its way highly personal.

The remainder of the songs come from the war years: the Songs, op. 72 with one exception date from 1915. There were originally two settings of Rydberg, to whom Sibelius was particularly responsive. However, only one of the settings, *Kyssen* (The kiss) survives. The other, *Vi ses igen!* (We will meet again), together with *Orions bälte* (Orion's girdle) to words of Topelius, did not survive in Breitkopf & Härtel's vaults after the war. Of the four that did, *Kyssen* is a touching song with an attractive and direct language, while its imediate neighbour, *Kaiutar* (The echo-nymph) to words of Larin Kyösti, is another rare instance of a solo song to a Finnish text. The melodic line is expertly tailored to meet the text: the opening words are a case in point, and their gentle rise and fall are sensitively matched in Sibelius's subtle line. *Der Wanderer und der Bach* (The wayfarer and the stream) is less characteristic than the Runeberg setting, *Hundra vägar* (A hundred ways), which ends the group. In this poem, the maiden asks forgiveness, for in church her thoughts are so often full of her beloved: 'A hundred ways my thoughts take, but when they most turn to Thee, they are almost all of him.' The song begins in 5/2 time and, as one would expect, Runeberg draws inspiration of real quality from the composer. The line is dignified and impassioned, yet eminently supple. The song is much earlier than the others and dates from 1907, the year of the Third Symphony.

The Six Songs, op. 86, come from the following year and opens with a setting of almost Schubertian charm and directness of appeal, Tavaststjerna's *Vårförnimmelser* (The coming of Spring), though it is the next, *Längtan heter min arvedel* (Longing is my heritage) to words of Karlfeldt that touches the deepest vein of feeling. It, too, is of great simplicity and is all the more affecting on that count. It must be regarded as one of the greatest of the songs of the war years, beautifully matching the mood and the verbal music of one of the great poems of the period. *Dold förening* (Hidden union) has a tender, wistful charm that is irresistible, and the very simplicity of the piano accompaniment enhances its delicacy of feeling. The poem tells how two water-lilies, separated from each other by the waves, are still united by their common root below the surface. Astra Desmond calls its successor, *Och finns det en tanke?* (And is there a thought?), another Tavaststjerna setting, an 'exquisite little miniature' and this it surely is. Indeed, together with *Längtan heter min arvedel*, it is one of the masterpieces of these years. There is the same tenderness and poignancy of the *Humoresques* for violin and orchestra which are roughly contemporaneous. Neither of its two companions, *Sångarlön* (The singer's reward) and *I systrar, I bröder* (Ye sisters, ye brothers) are of comparable quality.

The two remaining sets of wartime songs draw on two poets, Runeberg and Franzén, and it must be admitted that of the two, it is the op. 90 Runeberg settings that deserve to be heard, even if some of the op. 88 set have charm. *Blåsippan* (The blue anemone) certainly has that in abundance but it is relatively conventional as, for that matter, is the next Franzén setting, *De bägge rosorna* (The two roses). *Vitsippan* (The star-flower) has a touching melancholy and is the most memorable of the

Franzén songs and superior, I think, to the next two Runeberg settings, *Sippan* (The anemone) and *Törnet* (The thorn) or even *Blommans öde* (The flower's destiny). For once Runeberg seems not to have fired his imagination. However, the first of the op. 90 songs is another matter: *Norden* (The north) is the most celebrated of the group and as in all the nature poetry of Runeberg, touches a special vein of inspiration in the composer. A steady, gentle syncopated figure is sustained throughout and serves to focus attention on the changing harmonies and the eloquent vocal line. *Hennes budskap* (Her message) prompted Astra Desmond to write somewhat patronizingly of 'a pathetic little song of a kind that is apt to appeal more to Northerners than to us' – of which I am doubtful. None of the remaining op. 90 songs is of the same order as *Norden* and only the last, *Vem styrde hit din väg?* (Who brought you here?), shows Sibelius at anywhere near himself. *Narciss* (Narcissus) to words of Bertel Gripenberg, dating from 1925, is a beautifully wrought miniature, highly responsive to the Swedish language; it possesses strong atmosphere and a melodic line of haunting delicacy.

It is in the great nature songs that Sibelius's mastery most fully emerges, above all in *Höstkväll*, but there is no question of his standing in the field of Scandinavian song. His achievement has been partially obscured by the popularity of *Svarta rosor* and *Flickan kom*, (just as *Jeg elsker Dig!* and *En svane* have served to hinder the cause of Grieg), but even many Sibelians are not fully aware of the scale and range of his output in song or conscious of its quality. The publication of a virtually complete recording of them in the 1980s and the prospect of another in the 1990s should give them the recognition they so fully deserve.

14

Chamber and instrumental music

Although Sibelius was one of the greatest masters of the orchestra it was not until he was in his mid twenties that he wrote his first orchestral piece. All his earlier works (and they are numerous) were written for various chamber groups. Yet so much has the 'silence from Järvenpää' monopolized the attention of the musical public that his subsequent lack of interest in the more ambitious chamber forms has aroused comparatively little comment. After 1892, the year of the *Kullervo* symphony, Sibelius wrote only one string quartet, a sonatina for violin and piano, along with a handful of insignificant miniatures for the same combination, whereas before that we know (or know of) some twenty or more youthful works that reached various stages of completion, including three string quartets and two violin sonatas.

The reason why his youthful energies were turned into chamber music is obvious enough: they were intended for his own immediate family circle and their friends. Indeed, the very composition of some of these groups leaves little doubt as to their *ad hoc* domestic origins. A quartet for the improbable combination of violin, cello, harmonium and piano is an instance in point. This was composed for the Sucksdorff family in Lovisa, whose music room accommodated both a piano and a harmonium. Tawaststjerna speaks of its melancholy having 'a somewhat Schubertian ring about it compounded with a touch of Nordic romanticism'. Another instance among the dozen or so chamber works that survive in fragmentary condition is a quartet for violin, cello and piano four-hands. Apart from this kind of home-made music there was little else to be had in nineteenth-century Finland. Although there were periodic concerts, Helsinki did not possess a permanent symphony orchestra at the time Sibelius was born. The impact of regular orchestral concerts when he became a student in Helsinki (by which time Kajanus's orchestra was well under way), and more particularly in Berlin and Vienna, was enormous. With the discovery in the nineties of his inborn flair for the orchestra it is not surprising that he temporarily laid chamber music aside. What is surprising, however, is the fact that to all intents and purposes he returned to chamber music on only one occasion, the composition in 1909 of *Voces intimae*. Although he continued to write music for domestic use, into none of it did he pour ideas of significance or real inspiration. It is as if the medium reminded him of the provincialism of his early years, and plans for two further quartets at about the time of the Fourth Symphony came to nothing.

Drawing of Sibelius by Eero Järnefelt

Now that the family vaults have been opened, the full extent of his early creativity is apparent. Once he had acquired enough technical expertise on the violin, he explored with family and friends the quartets of Haydn, Mozart and Beethoven; later on the chamber music of Schubert and Mendelssohn. His early music sees him stretching his creative powers in their footsteps. The E flat string quartet (1885) shows that Sibelius knew his Haydn well.

Ex. 66

The writing is well-schooled and the ideas are not without charm, but the music gives little indication of what was to come, whereas from the vantage point of hindsight, one can hear overtones of the 1890s in the slow movement of the 'Lovisa' Trio, so-called because it was written in the summer of 1888 in the small town of that name. Rosas quotes Sibelius's secretary Santeri Levas as saying that in all his correspondence with the Sibelius Museum in Turku (Åbo), the composer was at pains to emphasize that these chamber works were neither to be published nor performed – even after his death. He did ask to see the score of the 'Lovisa' Trio, which the Museum had acquired from Adolf Paul in the 1930s as he had completely forgotten it, and he eventually allowed it to be performed when the Museum was inaugurated in 1952. (Although they have obvious curiosity value and fill in the picture of his artistic growth, he would probably not be best pleased to see any of these pieces gaining the currency of commercial recording.)

Of his student compositions before the two string quartets of 1889 and 1890, mention should be made of the Sonata in F major, for violin and piano, previously ascribed to the period 1886–7 but in fact written during the summer of 1889. It obviously took as its starting point the Grieg Sonata in the same key, but the Andante already points to the future, to *Kullervo* and *En Saga* (see ex. 67). Another prophetic piece, particularly in its use of pedal points, had been performed earlier that same year: this was the five-movement Suite in A major for string trio, which caused quite a stir. The first three movements survive but only the viola and cello parts of the Air (Andante sostenuto) and a draft of the final Gigue. It is possible that the Andantino for string trio dating from the same year was originally intended as its first movement but then discarded.

For a long time the A minor String Quartet, also from 1889, existed in an even more fragmentary state: only the first violin part survived together with a few bars of the score of the scherzo. But in the early 1980s,

Ex. 67

the remaining parts were discovered in the library of Sibelius's brother, Christian. There are many prophetic touches as well as plenty of what Tawaststjerna calls 'the fragile Nordic melancholy linked stylistically to Grieg'. Grieg's own G minor Quartet, which was to influence Debussy's, was still new music, and barely a decade old. There is also an unexpected harmonic audacity in the Scherzo, where an A major triad cuts across some writing in a predominantly C minor context. However there is a breadth and sense of scale that is impressive; the 'Razumovsky' quartets are a probable model. Earlier, in the slow movement, there is a mysterious and imaginative episode that almost calls Dvořák to mind. (It was this quartet that the composer took for comments to Busoni, who 'sat down at the piano at once, played through the quartet from beginning to end without for a moment having had the chance of looking at it beforehand. And *how* he played it!', Sibelius wrote.)

Later, in the summer of 1889, before he left for his studies in Berlin, Sibelius embarked on a successor, in B flat, op. 4, but put it on one side, completing it the following autumn. It is evident from the title-page of the op. 4, which he calls Quartet no. 2, that he thought of the A minor as his first. The obvious influences are again Beethoven and Schumann in the first movement as well, of course, as Tchaikovsky, whose harmonic language had surfaced in earlier student chamber works, including the A minor Suite. The slow movement is a set of variations on a lyrical Finnish folk tune, that could be spiritually a distant antecedent of *Rakastava*. (In its very first choral form, *Rakastava* was composed only three years later.)

Ex. 68

The scherzo proper (in D major) is wonderfully vital and inventive, and the trio comes close to the Schubert of the A minor Quartet, albeit a tone lower. Although they will never (and perhaps should never) be repertory works while such masterpieces as Dvořák's op. 34, to take but just one example, are so seldom heard, they are more than just student works of interest to the Sibelian. They are finely wrought and already touched with mastery. It is interesting to see that highly developed feeling for form we recognize from the mature Sibelius is already evident. New ideas emerge at just the right moment (with the possible exception of the rather primitive fugal episode in the first movement of the A minor) and the music is excellently paced. Sibelius was sufficiently happy with the latter to assign it an opus number (and in his subsequent purges of his early opus lists allow it to stand), though he discouraged its performance.

He was a good deal more critical of his next major chamber work, the Piano Quintet in G minor (1890). In his last months as a student he had taken part in a performance of the Schumann Piano Quintet with Busoni, and it was he who encouraged him to write a large-scale quintet. The work itself was probably inspired by (and is to some extent modelled on) the Sinding E minor Piano Quintet, which he had heard when Busoni played it with the Brodsky Quartet in Leipzig. Busoni, indeed, took part in a performance of the first and third movements (together some 22 minutes) in Helsinki early in May 1890, when the quartet was led by the Norwegian violinist and composer, Johan Halvorsen. Sibelius had finished it in April and there was not enough time or, possibly more to the point, inclination to prepare all five movements. It is an ambitious, albeit not wholly successful piece some forty minutes in length, and substantial fare. Whatever reservations one might have, Sibelius was undoubtedly too harsh in dismissing it so savagely (in a letter to his friend, Werner Söderhjelm), 'You can well believe how I have felt since the realization struck me that my quintet is absolute rubbish'. It is far from that even if it is not quite the equal of either the A minor or the op. 4 quartets. Wegelius made much of the poverty of his piano writing, but although it is less effective than it might have been had Sibelius been a better pianist, this is not a major obstacle. Nor, incidentally, was Wegelius wholly fair in speaking of there being 'no flow – just one section tacked on to another' (although he thought the structure of the first movement impressive). In many ways the first movement is the finest though Busoni's description of it as 'wunderschön' is rather overdoing things. The Andante, too, has a lot of good music in it but is badly let down by a threadbare, march-like second theme. The scherzo is attractive and though the finale is less satisfactory in terms of structure, it has a good deal of spirit and some memorable ideas.

In the following year we have the C major Quartet for piano, two violins and cello. This is a modest piece, written in Vienna, and consists of a slow introduction leading to a theme and variations. One of the motifs in the second half of the introduction looks forward to the finale of the Second Symphony. Apart from an *Adagio* for string quartet written at about this time, we find that Sibelius's interest in chamber music slackens abruptly just as he begins to flex his newly discovered orchestral muscles. After this there are virtually no instrumental pieces of note until we come to the *Voces intimae* Quartet, with the exception of the *Malinconia* for cello and piano. In spite of the fact that he was close to his brother, who played the cello in their family trio, Sibelius wrote only two pieces for the instrument, a *Fantasia* probably written in 1889 and the *Malinconia*, op. 20. Early in 1901 a typhus epidemic broke out in Kerava and Sibelius's daughter, Kirsti was one of the victims. The *Malinconia* was written soon after her death though it could well have been inspired by Magnus Enckell's painting of that name. It was written for Georg Schnéevoigt, better known as a conductor, and his wife Sigrid. The *Malinconia* was also at first called *Fantasia* and listed as op. 25 in a handwritten catalogue dating from 1909, but in one of his periodic purges Sibelius removed the opera *The Maiden in the Tower* from the list and reassigned its opus number to *Malinconia*. Its ineffectiveness (particularly of the piano writing) probably owes much to the limitations of the Schnéevoigt partnership, and the piece does not show him at anywhere near his most characteristic.

Voces intimae is not Sibelius's only quartet but it is the only one that matters. There were reports at the time of the Fourth Symphony that he was working on two others, but they came to nothing, and *Voces intimae* remained his last word in the medium. Its very opening has something of the quality of that discourse of inner voices the title evokes. The violist Alan George has spoken of the 'very real sense of inward communion among the four voices', and by the side of the Second and Third Symphonies there is something intensely private. There are allusions to earlier works, such as the Overture in A minor, which turns up in the finale, and one feels at times close to the scurrying semiquavers of *Lemminkäinen's Homeward Journey*. The way in which the first and second movements are fused is remarkable, albeit less radical than in the Fifth Symphony a decade later. Both Gray and Ringbom mention its similarity in layout with Haydn, but Tawaststjerna reminds us that its symmetry is 'disturbed by the intimacy with which Sibelius's *Vivace* is linked to the opening sonata movement' and suggests that he is closer in design to the late Beethoven quartets and those of Schubert. Its concentration and sense of flow are never forced; on the contrary the music hides its compelling and muscular argument under a surface that seems wholly relaxed. Yet it is a remarkably taut piece with no spare matter. Much has been made of its modality: indeed Gray accepted the view that the Dorian mode is a distinguishing feature of Finnish folk-music.[1] The opening is pure D minor but the idea that immediately follows is Dorian in inflexion:

Ex. 69

Sibelius makes particularly impressive use of the contrast between the modal and the tonal: the frank A major of the second group has a wonderfully smiling quality about it and the unforced momentum of the line itself is irresistible. Another magical touch is the way in which, almost without one realizing it, Sibelius moves from the exposition into the short development. So great is the sense of continuity that we are left unaware of this process of growth at the actual time it happens. There is almost a

[1]This was dealt with by Andersson in his article *Tonaliteten och det nationella i den finska folkmusiken* some fifteen years before Gray's book appeared, and in other articles where he showed this to be characteristic of Scandinavian folk-music as a whole, and not especially of Finland.

beatific quality about this movement: it is one of the purest utterances in this medium since Schubert. The slow movement is more than the centrepiece of the quartet; it enshrines its essence.

The scherzo that follows is hardly less masterly: such is his alchemy that one is scarcely conscious of its close relationship with the first movement until the very closing bars, which directly quote the second group. However, the thematic substance is entirely drawn from the first movement. Although there are many beautiful ideas in it, including its inspired opening, judged by the yardstick of the first movement it lacks the compelling concentration we expect. It is from this movement that the work apparently acquired its title: Ringbom tells us that the composer pencilled in the words *Voces intimae* over the three *ppp* chords of E minor at bar 21 in a copy of the score belonging to a friend. The passage immediately following this seems to look back nostalgically to first-period Sibelius. For all the relaxed rumination of this movement this kind of introspection seems worlds apart from the profound and bitter spiritual experience of the Fourth Symphony, begun only a year later. That they are near in time, however, might possibly be deduced from this figure:

Ex. 70

The *Allegretto ma pesante* is a fine movement possessed of a Haydnesque honesty of utterance and sanity of outlook. Commentators have not been slow to point out the skill with which Sibelius transforms and comments on his material. The passage at bars 22–3 of the *Adagio* rears its head five bars after fig. 1, and the main theme itself is obviously a near relative of the first group of the movement (see ex. 71).

The finale strikes the epic note of the tone-poems, and in fact moves with a sense of momentum that almost reminds one of *Lemminkäinen's Homeward Journey*. It is an exciting and exhilarating movement.

The only other substantial piece is the sonatina in E major for violin and piano, op. 80, which, like the op. 78 and op. 79 pieces for the same combination, dates from 1915. This is a slight work, modest both in aim and achievement; it does, however, stand head and shoulders above the other violin and piano pieces. Sibelius's writing for the violin is never less

Ex. 71

than highly accomplished, and, as we know from the concerto and the *Humoresques*, it is often very much more than that. In the thirty or so pieces he wrote for this combination he is handicapped by his less than perfect command of the keyboard. The sonatina, however, though not ideal in this respect, is much more successful than some of his smaller pieces; the piano writing is never obtrusive, and is on the contrary often very effective in its own way. The invention is delightfully fresh and spontaneous and there is never any doubt about the identity of the composer — witness the main theme of the first movement. The middle movement has a delicate, reticent charm.

Most of the other pieces from the Op. 2, which Sibelius revised in 1912, down to the *Three Pieces*, Op. 116, written in 1929, are well laid out for the instrument but are for the most part of little real moment. Of the op. 78 set the *Impromptu* and *Rigaudon* are slight, genre pieces, while the wistful charm of the *Romance* might entitle it to be called a Nordic *Salut d'amour*. The best of the set is the *Religioso*, a piece of simple dignity written for his brother Christian, a circumstance that explains its existence (and that of the whole set) for cello and piano. The *Berceuse*, op. 79, no. 6, is a *salon* piece but has a gentle, sad allure that is quite appealing. Neither the opp. 115 nor 116 sets contain great music, but they are much finer than they were given credit for in the 1965 edition of this book. Both 'On the heath' and the 'Ballade' of op. 115, nos. 1 and 2, have a certain innocence that almost call to mind the *Humoresques*. In particular 'The Bells', op. 115, no. 4, is a rather cryptic miniature and its companion, the *Scène de danse* with its striking tonal juxtapositions is a kind of Finnish equivalent of the Bartók *Romanian Dances*.

15

Sibelius and the piano

Composers who are not themselves pianists seem to experience difficulty in writing idiomatically for the keyboard. The greatest masters of keyboard writing have themselves been executants of considerable prowess or even virtuosity, and have developed in their early years an approach to the instrument that has become almost instinctive. Only in a few cases, such as Chopin or Medtner, does this seem to preclude the development of a comparable mastery of the orchestra. Certainly those composers who have not been brought up at the keyboard, and who think directly in terms of orchestral sound, either evince little interest in it or, if they do, show some degree of ineptitude in their handling of it. Berlioz and Mahler are good examples of the former. While it may be going too far to say that Sibelius falls into the second category, all but the fanatic would concede that he seemed unable to draw from the piano sounds that do justice to its genius or to his. Only rarely is sheer virtuosity in the handling of both media to be found in the same composer as it is in Debussy or Ravel.

It is true that Berlioz's genius for the orchestra developed even more rapidly than Sibelius's; but unlike Berlioz, whose keyboard writing is strictly confined to three pieces for harmonium and the odd accompaniment for songs (most of which he later orchestrated), Sibelius wrote for the piano at regular intervals throughout his life. Altogether his output comprises a sonata, the *Kyllikki* pieces, the three sonatinas, and over a hundred and twenty small pieces, the earliest, *Au crépuscule*, dating from 1887, and the last, op. 114, from 1929. Yet even at his best, and with the exception only of the sonatinas and a handful of other pieces, he is never completely at ease; there are too many ingrained orchestral habits of mind to inhibit him. Bengt de Törne quotes Sibelius as follows:[1]

> The orchestra is a huge and wonderful instrument that has got everything – except the pedal. You must always bear this in mind. You see, if you don't create an artificial pedal for your orchestration there

[1] *Sibelius – A close-up* (London, 1937), pp. 31 and 33.

will be holes in it, and some passages will sound ragged. Many composers, even great geniuses, either never discovered this or entirely forgot it – Liszt, for instance . . .

A little later he describes the effect obtained at the piano when pressing the pedal, striking a *fortissimo* harmony and letting it die away:

In the orchestra an analogous effect may be obtained by giving the beginning of the chord to trumpets, trombones, horns and woodwind, all *fortissimo*. A *diminuendo* follows and gradually the stronger instruments are dropped, leaving only horns and clarinets, flutes or bassoons to finish their *diminuendo* on the subtlest *pianissimo*. Thus you will achieve a thing of ideal beauty; it will be like a thought, born under a heavy sky and trying to reach purer regions.

Once a chord on the piano has been struck, however, it cannot be modified except by the pedal: it merely dies away and the pedal can only affect its length in so doing. Part of the genius of Sibelius's orchestral writing is the way in which a chord will suddenly be subdued in volume only to make a gradual *crescendo* afterwards. This he could not do on the piano. Yet many of his orchestral habits were carried over to the keyboard: his supporting texture is often concentrated in the lower half of the keyboard, roughly where the brass, horns and lower woodwind would normally operate. In addition he made little or no attempt to range over the whole of the keyboard: he never exploits the kind of effects obtainable at the extremities that Debussy and Ravel were masters of; nor did he appreciate the percussive possibilities of the instrument as Bartók did.

Sibelius's first piano work to be dignified with an opus number is the set of six *Impromptus*, op. 5, which date from the early nineties. Even Erik Tawaststjerna, the most enthusiastic champion of Sibelius's piano music, admits that 'to his continental contemporaries these must have appeared highly amateurish'.[1] There is a certain folk-like directness of utterance about some of the pieces, particularly the third and fourth, but for the most part they are feeble and uninventive. Tawaststjerna assumes they are preliminary studies for the F major sonata, op. 12 (1893), but it is only fair to say that the sonata, inept though much of the piano writing is, stands head and shoulders above most of Sibelius's early piano music both in quality of invention and the growing mastery of form it evinces. This is not to say that it can take its place alongside Sibelius's other music

[1] *The Pianoforte Compositions of Jean Sibelius* (Helsinki, 1957), p. 28.

of this period; it is, as Eric Blom pointed out,[1] as orchestral as Grieg's early sonata, though there is probably more in Grieg that is conceived in terms of the keyboard than there is in Sibelius.

Despite its immaturity and uncertainty, there is a good deal to admire in this sonata. The first movement is in sonata form and, although most of the seams in the structure are clearly visible, there is a genuine sense of movement and often some attractive melodic invention. The key scheme of the movement is by no means conventional: it is evident that Sibelius's powers of thinking in terms of long paragraphs are developing. Most of the ideas are not particularly personal; they are born in the world of pale Scandinavian nationalism – Kjerulf, Grieg, Gade and Sjögren.

The op. 24 set, which follows the sonata, comprises ten pieces written at various times between 1894 and 1903. The best of them are probably more personal than the sonata. The first two were for many years believed to be transcriptions from *Skogsrået*, written at about the same time. The *Impromptu* certainly betrays orchestral habits of mind and poses the question whether some of Sibelius's piano pieces did not begin life as orchestral sketches. It is certainly more characteristic than many of the later pieces, such as the third, *Caprice*, or the ninth, the hackneyed Romance in D flat, with its stale rhetoric and trite, *salon*-like tune. The most characteristic, however, in its melodic outline is the tenth, the *Barcarola*; the opening tune cries out for violins unison *sul* G (it is interesting to observe that Sibelius does not take the line below G for the first twenty-six bars). The eighth, too, called *Nocturne*, is highly individual. The harmonies are recognizably Sibelian, though the music evokes the sound of the strings; the left-hand melody seems designed for the cellos.

Kyllikki (1904), which most writers on Sibelius seem to regard as one of his best piano pieces, speaks much the same harmonic language as the Second Symphony and the Violin Concerto. It derives its title from the *Kalevala*. Kyllikki is one of the maidens of Saari; Lemminkäinen abducts her, loves her, and finally leaves her in order to try his hand with the better-known daughter of Pohjola. On the whole this is an unsuccessful piece with few attractions. One or two of the ideas are characteristic: the full-blooded opening melody is impressive (or would be in orchestral colours), and so is the *tranquillo* section in the third and final movement, which comes from the same stable as the trio section of the scherzo of the Second Symphony. Glenn Gould[2] described it rather engagingly as 'a

[1]In Gerald Abraham (ed.), *Sibelius: a Symposium* (London, 1947), p. 98.
[2]Glenn Gould, 'The Piano Music of Jean Sibelius', in *The Glenn Gould Reader*, Tim Page, (ed.) (London, 1984), pp. 103–6.

slightly giddy mix of Chopin and Chabrier'. However the actual piano writing is, by the exalted standards Sibelius himself set elsewhere, limited in resource.

Between *Kyllikki* and the sonatinas comes the set of ten pieces, op. 58, dating from 1909. They are at best undistinguished, though the first, 'Rêverie', and the fifth, 'The evening', contain unmistakably Sibelian touches. But the three sonatinas, op. 67, are an altogether different proposition. Written in 1912, a year after the Fourth Symphony, these are probably Sibelius's most convincing keyboard works. They are compact in design and economical in utterance: they eschew any attempts at the kind of 'effective' piano writing which Sibelius made in the op. 24 set. None of the movements is very long; they average less than two minutes in duration, so that there is no time for any development along the lines familiar in the bigger works.

The first – in A major according to the title-page, though it is in fact in the relative minor, F sharp – is linear in style: the texture is much more spare than we find in *Kyllikki*; this is a feature that is common to all three sonatinas. Indeed, not only in matters of keyboard layout but also of the suitability of the ideas to the medium, this sonatina shows a considerable advance over Sibelius's earlier work. This idea, for instance, is memorably pianistic and falls conveniently under the fingers:

Ex. 72

In addition this and the other two movements are recognizably Sibelian. Not only is the texture *dépouillé* but the proportions are most skilfully balanced. Sibelius rests content with one short idea which is never developed *in extenso*. Yet despite its brevity the finale of this sonatina still retains his characteristic sense of forward movement.

The F sharp minor sonatina is the most perfect of all his piano works, but the remaining two, in E major and B flat minor respectively, are very nearly as fine. The canonic imitation in the first movement of the E major is wholly successful: there is no sense of strain, no feeling that too scholarly an apparatus is imposed on too lightweight a substance. There is an enviable harmony of means and ends in these three pieces, for the texture is always lightened to match the melodic character of the music. Though they do not look effective on paper, they come off remarkably well in performance. The third and last, in B flat minor, employs related thematic material in all its three movements. The *Andante* is the most vulnerable from the pianistic point of view, but in the hands of a sensitive player even its bare octave writing can be made to sound effective. The melody itself has vague overtones of Rimsky-Korsakov.

The sonatinas score on the grounds of their sheer economy of ideas, layout and form. When Sibelius attempts more ambitious concentrations of keyboard sonority, as in the opening bars of 'The Village Church', op. 103, no. 1, or in the 'Romance', op. 101, no. 1, he does not wholly succeed in banishing thoughts of the orchestra. Immediately following the sonatinas and closely related to them in character are the two *Rondinos*, op. 68. Eric Blom's theory that these may have been intended as movements for incomplete sonatinas seems highly probable. The reflective and very beautiful G sharp minor *Rondino* could well be a slow movement to an unfinished sonatina. Its expressive leaps of a minor ninth and its plastic improvisatory line are poetic and recall a vaguely Scriabinesque mood, even though the harmonic language is less complex. The *Rondino* in C sharp minor would make a delightful finale to a work of this kind.

The sonatinas and *Rondinos* were published in 1912, and can be regarded as a relaxation from the world of the Fourth Symphony, *The Bard* and *Luonnotar*. The next batch of pieces comes from 1914, when the war forced Sibelius into publishing sets of potboilers. Between them, the three sets, op. 74, 75 and 76, comprise no fewer than twenty-one miniatures. The *Four Lyric Pieces*, op. 74, have been overshadowed by the comparatively popular op. 75, the superiority of which is generally undisputed. The first, *När rönnen blommar* (When the rowan blossoms), is a delicate piece that has been compared with the first *Rondino*, though it misses its wayward poetic quality. *Den ensamma furan* (The lonely pine) has a genuine nobility, though it is easy to hear the weight of the unison strings in the triplet quavers in bar 10. Similarly, in the fourth piece, *Björken* (The birch), the second half cries out for muted strings with perhaps the delicate rustle from the side-drum that accompanied the middle section of *Lemminkäinen in Tuonela*. The last piece, *Granen* (The spruce), is far more pianistic, even though the arpeggiated writing marked *risoluto* is not wholly effective. By far the best of the set is the third, *Aspen*

(The ash), an eloquent piece with a feeling of resigned melancholy that is thoroughly individual and memorable.

It is difficult to share Tawaststjerna's enthusiasm for all of the op. 76 set. None of the thirteen pieces seems as good as *The Ash*, save perhaps the magnificent *Twinflower of the North*, an original piece that at first glance looks Schumannesque on paper. Of the others, the second, *Étude*, maintains an amiable but brainless patter in the style of so much children's music. A similar study is the *Pièce enfantine*, which one would never imagine in a thousand years to be the work of Sibelius. A great many of the earlier sets, op. 34 (1914–16) and the *Pensées lyriques*, op. 40 (1912–14), seem equally unworthy, though there is at least one outstanding exception, the *Pensée mélodique*, op. 40, no. 6. This is a haunting piece whose frequent modulations are as charged with melancholy as the Szymanowski *Mazurkas*, op. 50. This piece is worthy to rank alongside the first of the *Rondinos* and deserves a place in the repertory.

The next batch of pieces, op. 85, dates from 1916. These all bear floral titles and have considerable charm. Most delightful is *The snapdragon*, which despite its apparently platitudinous sequences has an alluring quality that belies the notion that Sibelius lacks humour. Whatever their shortcomings these pieces are characteristic Sibelius, which is more than can be said for the later piano pieces, op. 94 (1919), op. 97 (1920) and op. 99 (1922). More personal, though by no means Sibelius at his most interesting, are the two sets, op. 101 (1923) and op. 103 (1924). They seem far closer to the world of the *Suite mignonne* and *Suite champêtre* than they do to the Sixth and Seventh Symphonies. 'In mournful mood' (the pieces have English titles) from op. 103 is as trivial as 'The storm', its immediate predecessor, is ineffective. By far the most imaginative piece is the *Scène romantique*, op. 101, no. 5, which has an atmospheric opening, even though this level of inspiration is not really maintained.

There is little doubt that Sibelius is not really at home in piano music. A comparison with the piano works of Nielsen is very much to his disadvantage. Nielsen's *Chaconne*, the *Theme and Variations*, op. 40, the *Suite*, op. 45, and the late op. 59 pieces are bigger in scope and forward-looking in technique. They make use of devices and sonorities which Sibelius never attempted to employ. It is significant that a composer of his stature, who could think more organically than any of his immediate contemporaries, should have confined himself to miniatures where the keyboard was concerned. Nielsen made none of Sibelius's pianistic blunders; his writing is admirably balanced though often difficult to play. His textures are never overweighted in the bass by thick chords when the right hand is relatively light (even confined to a single line). The fact is that Sibelius's music for the piano yields a handful of miniatures that have genuine charm, as well as the three sonatinas which show evidence of real mastery. They enjoyed the advocacy of Wilhelm Kempff and Glenn Gould among others. Whatever reservations one might have, one must recognize the validity of Gould's verdict, 'Sibelius never wrote against the grain of the keyboard'. And as his contemporary Selim Palmgren, who wrote effectively for the instrument, put it, 'even in what for him were alien regions, he moves with an unfailing responsiveness to tone colour'. Were they, however, the only work to survive we would have no inkling of his real stature. Sibelius's evident reluctance to undertake a big work in this medium suggests his recognition of this shortcoming.

16

Afterthoughts

Taste is never static: composers accepted as masters during their lifetime, like Telemann and Spohr, quite often recede into relative obscurity only a few years after their death. Unfortunately it is not only the second- or third-rate composer who is subject to these shifts in public interest and huddled off to comfortless neglect. Even the great masters are not exempt. At the end of the nineteenth century Bernard Shaw could write of the scandalous neglect of Mozart in London, while Mendelssohn, who reigned supreme in Victorian England, enjoyed a comparatively inferior status in the 1940s. Bach was neglected for almost a century after his death.

Sibelius was fortunate in receiving during his lifetime veneration and fame on a scale that few other composers have enjoyed. However, as his critics were quick to point out, apart from Finland and the Scandinavian countries, his music gained a real hold over the public only in the Anglo-Saxon countries. Although his admirers in France were few, Marc Vignal's study in the series *Musiciens de tous les temps*[1] paved the way for a growing interest in his music. Thanks to him and writers such as Harry Halbreich, Henri-Claude Fantapié and Pierre Vidal, the climate in the 1990s is quite different from the days of Nadia Boulanger. In the 1950s the wider French musical public still did not embrace Brahms, let alone Mahler and Bruckner. And when Sir Thomas Beecham programmed the Third Symphony of Sibelius in the late 1950s, a work that had been slow to reach Paris, public indifference forced him to replace it!

In Germany during the years following World War II Sibelius was slow to win an unchallenged place in the permanent repertory though he had distinguished advocacy from conductors such as Hans Rosbaud and Herbert von Karajan. The resistance to Sibelius may well have been in part due to his excessive exposure during the war when he was presented as a kind of symphonic equivalent of Wagner; it was certainly fuelled by figures such as Theodor Wiesengrund Adorno who had taken refuge in

[1] Éditions Seghers.

196

Oxford during the war and resented the way in which Sibelius overshadowed Mahler in England. (Thomas Mann responded similarly though less vehemently in the United States.) It is a measure of Sibelius's low standing that when Karajan was appointed to the Berlin Philharmonic, one of the conditions he made was that the first concert should comprise the Fourth Symphony, unthinkable at the time, together with Beethoven's Seventh. But post-war Germany, so long the centre of the European tradition, was slow to re-admit outsiders like Sibelius, Elgar or Delius, all of whom had been frequently played in Wilhelmine Germany, or composers such as Roussel, Nielsen and Vaughan Williams.

As far as the French are concerned, their reluctance to accept Sibelius may be in some measure temperamental. Sibelius's is a world that is as personal as Berlioz's. Indeed the parallel with Berlioz is worth pursuing, for he, too, is a composer who has kindled the most profound controversy – hailed by his admirers as a great master and denounced by others no less vehemently as an amateur and a charlatan. It is, strangely enough, in Britain, too, that Berlioz has the most vocal and devoted following, and where he enjoys at the present time a measure of public support that is not surpassed even in his own country. Both Berlioz and Sibelius are profoundly original composers, self-forming, uncompromising and new; indeed, if originality were the sole criterion of greatness in music, Berlioz would probably be counted as the greatest master of them all. Just as Sibelius met with little response in France during the 1950s and 60s, Berlioz was equally underrated in the Scandinavian countries. In both cases, perhaps, ignorance of their work facilitated the erection of artificial barriers which the wider dissemination of repertory that has characterized the LP and CD eras has in part broken down. Temperamental disaffinity also plays its part: the impulsive flow of invention, the white-hot, feverish temperature, the asymmetric melodic thinking, the vivid colouring and the absence of reticence in Berlioz are elements which strike the Scandinavian sensibility as theatrical. Similarly the regional flavouring of much of Sibelius's nature poetry, identified so intimately with the northern landscape, the icy intensity of some of the inspiration (which obscures for the casual listener its profound inner warmth) and the non-episodic nature of his thinking do not win *immediate* favour.

England, however, responded warmly to Sibelius's music from the very beginning, when his work was introduced by Richter, Bantock and Henry Wood in the early years of the century. It was in the 1930s that the round of Sibelius festivals, the formation of the Sibelius Society and the constant appearance of his music in concert programmes led to his recognition as a classic. That his standing would come to be questioned after his death in the 1950s was inevitable in the natural course of events: the claims made by Gray that Sibelius would 'ultimately prove to have been, not only the greatest of his generation, but one of the major figures in the entire history of music' were bound to be re-examined. The climate of critical opinion in this country hardened against Sibelius during the 1950s; Mahler, on the other hand, began to make greater headway. During the 30s Mahler had fewer champions among conductors and critics in England and his work was expensive to mount. After the war, when the BBC Third Programme and the gramophone companies made available authentic performances of his work, he began to win a considerable public following.

After the arrival of William Glock as the Controller of Music at the BBC, Sibelius enjoyed considerably less exposure. Attempts were even made to dissuade Hans Rosbaud from including the Fourth Symphony in his programmes as guest conductor with the BBC Symphony Orchestra – unsuccessfully as it so happened. The reaction against Sibelius was equally strong in the United States but, as in England, it was generally confined to a small group of impresarios and critics rather than the general public. His representation on record remained strong throughout the 1960s and grew apace during the 1970s and 80s. In the early 1960s, Benjamin Frankel, himself a powerful symphonist could say, 'Sibelius's public was on the way to his less popular side when a sudden change of critical climate absolved them from the necessity to trouble further.'[1] But only a decade or so later, the wider musical public had moved on from the Violin Concerto and the Second and Fifth Symphonies to such relative rarities as *Luonnotar*, *The Bard* and *Kullervo*, which began to claim a place in the record catalogues.

From the vantage point of the 1960s when serialism and the post-serialist movement became Establishment and tonal post-national music moved into neglect, Sibelius occupied a peripheral position. For the critic who equates the complexity of harmonic language and a higher norm of dissonance with the idea of musical 'progress' (an essentially nineteenth-century concept), Sibelius is not as great a composer as Schoenberg or Bartók, simply because he was content to leave the language of music very much as he found it. He used an already existing vocabulary as Bach did, but in so highly idiosyncratic a manner that no attempt to imitate it can succeed. The self-styled 'progressive' will dismiss him much in the same way that the contemporaries of Bach tended to relegate him to the second rank because he was 'old-

---

[1]Benjamin Frankel, 'Sibelius and his Critics', *The Listener*, 29 June 1961.

fashioned'. This is to confuse language and style. There are few greater masters of musical syntax than Sibelius: what is extraordinary is his capacity for making a simple chord sound his own.

Yet admirers of Sibelius must concede that, in contradistinction to Palestrina or Bach, his world has circumscribed limits and a less-than-universal appeal. To a large extent it can be explained in terms of centrality of experience. Sibelius has an acutely developed sense of identification with nature and a preoccupation with myth that at one and the same time define his unique strength and his basic limitation. These preoccupations override his involvement in the human predicament, except in so far as it affects man's relationship with nature. This is not to deny that as a nature poet he expresses feelings that can be shared by all, a sense of nature's awe and power, even though the very nature with which he is concerned is regional. There is a strong feeling for nature in Mahler, but it is not the predominant factor in his musical make-up as it is in Sibelius. What makes Sibelius's achievement the greater, in spite of Mahler's centrality of experience, his greater warmth and his dramatic awareness, is that as a symphonist he imposes a greater degree of order on the materials of the symphony and exercises a greater discipline in the selection of these very materials. Mahler, whose sense of form is not to be underrated, was still prepared to offer, as it were, the raw materials of experience as if they were in themselves a finished work of art. The compulsion they exert is that of the poignant human document that overwhelms because of the variety and intensity of its emotional climate. Sibelius's way is fundamentally more classical because he refuses to treat certain states of mind and feeling in the context of the symphony. Without wishing in any sense to belittle the achievement of other masters of this period, such as Mahler, Strauss, Elgar and Debussy, there is little doubt that none of them had the highly developed sense of form that Sibelius had. 'What distinguishes genius from talent is condensation, which is related to brevity, but not identical with it,' as Einstein put it in *Greatness in Music*. Or to quote Benjamin Frankel, 'Sibelius is the true post-Beethoven symphonist in the same way that Mahler is the true symphonist post-Wagner.'[1]

All were masters of the orchestra. Debussy's achievement in terms of new sonorities and enrichment of language is greater than Sibelius's. His command of the media in *La mer, Pelléas et Mélisande*, the sonata for flute, viola and harp, and the *Préludes* for piano witnesses greater virtuosity; his debt to inherited tradition was even less than Sibelius's.

[1]Op. cit.

Debussy was capable in the *Petite Suite* of writing light music that is every bit as perfect as that of Sibelius in his *Pelléas* or *Humoresques* for violin and orchestra; but he was incapable of turning out the quantities of third-rate light music that poured from Sibelius's pen in such embarrassing profusion. Yet even in Debussy's greatest works we find a reliance on short phrase patterns that are repeated. *Nuages* is an obvious case of Debussy constructing a highly poetic mosaic of repeated two-bar phrases; rarely do we find anything remotely resembling the kind of growth that we meet in Sibelius. But so unique is his inspiration and so integrated is his musical personality that these two-bar patterns and their repetitions never disturb us as they do on occasion in the work of another noble nature poet, Janáček. On the other hand, nowhere in Debussy do we find the elevated heroic spirit of the Seventh Symphony.

Sibelius's capacity for what one might term 'continuous creation' in the symphonies and symphonic poems has few parallels; to find them one has to look among the composers of the very first rank. When Gerald Abraham wrote of the Third Symphony's first movement that it was comparable only with the great classical masters, he was in no sense exaggerating. This, together with the last four symphonies, shows a feeling for form that never fails to astonish, however often one analyses them. W. G. Hill, who confessed a temperamental disaffinity for Sibelius, and investigated his art from the point of view of an uncommitted if not hostile critic, was led (albeit reluctantly) to a growing admiration for its breathtaking formal mastery.[1] Why, then, as total experiences are they not in the final resort as great as the symphonies of Beethoven or Brahms? It must be admitted that, great though he is, Sibelius does not belong to the 'super-giants' of the order of Bach, Handel, Haydn, Mozart, Beethoven and Schubert, whose numbers barely exceed a dozen. These masters record a greater wealth, range and depth of experience; theirs is an inexhaustibility of spirit, and what they say has a universality of application that seems untied to any particular time or place. It is arguable whether a master of this order has yet come to light in the present century.

While Sibelius can be said to transcend the period in a way in which a highly self-conscious figure like Stravinsky does not, he cannot be said to be independent of place in a way that Stravinsky is. What Sibelius has to say is intimately related to the atmosphere and sensibility of northern Europe – just as Musorgsky is related to the Russian ethos. In that lies his strength. Sibelius does, however, respond to nature in a way that unites

---

[1] 'Some Aspects of Form in the Symphonies of Sibelius', *Music Review*, 1949.

two traditions – that of the nineteenth-century tone-poem together with the classical tradition with its concern for tonal change and dramatic contrast. This primary concern with nature has universal application but at the same time excludes some areas of feeling. But I was wrong in 1965 to say that there was little sense of the transience of human experience (think of 'Solitude' or 'Night music' in *Belshazzar's Feast*, *Rakastava* or the *Humoresques*) and understated the capacity for suffering one finds, say, in *The Bard*, or the closing pages of the Sixth Symphony. In *Rakastava* he reveals a vulnerability and innocence that is comparable with that of Schubert. And among the twentieth-century masters from Debussy and Bartók to Stravinsky, the quietism of the Sixth Symphony or the profoundly searching *Tapiola* has no parallel. Apart from dedicating his Fifth Symphony to him 'without permission and in sincerest flattery', Vaughan Williams paid Sibelius another tribute. 'It has been well said that the most original genius is the most indebted man. Sibelius has followed the direction pointed out by the great masters of the past. He is the heir of all the ages. It is for this very reason that he gives us with a new voice a message that has never been heard before and his voice will remain new through all the changes and chances of freak and fashion.'[1] At its greatest Sibelius's art seems timeless: he creates the illusion that it has always been in existence, and that the composer has merely served as the instrument to bring it to us. Few other composers of the twentieth century achieve this. He captured the soul of the North as no composer before him had done; and his achievement as a symphonist is unique.

[1] In a broadcast on the BBC Home Service recorded on 23 November 1950.

Appendix A

Calendar

Year	Age	Life	Contemporary musicians and events
1865		Born in Hämeenlinna, 8 Dec	Albeniz 5; Arensky 4; Balakirev 28; Berlioz 62; Berwald 69; Bizet 27; Borodin 32; Brahms 32; Bruckner 41; Chausson 10; Debussy 3; Delius 3; Dukas born, 1 Oct; Dvořák 24; Elgar 8; Fauré 20; Franck 43; Gade 48; Glazunov born, 10 Aug; Grieg 22; Halvorsen 1; d'Indy 14; Janáček 11; Kjerulf 50; Lyadov 10; Liszt 54; Magnard born, 9 June; Mahler 5; Musorgsky 26; Nielsen born, 9 June; Nordraak 22; Puccini 7; Rimsky-Korsakov 21; Ropartz 1; Rossini 73; Saint-Saëns 30; Sinding 9; Smetana 41; Strauss 1; Svendsen 26; Taneyev 9; Tchaikovsky 25; Verdi 52; Wagner 52; Wolf 5; Ysaÿe 7.
1866	1		Busoni born, 1 Apr; Nordraak (23) dies, 20 Mar.
1868	3	Father's death (31 July).	Bantock born, 7 Aug; Berwald (71) dies, 3 Apr; Kjerulf (52) dies, 11 Aug; Rossini (76) dies, 13 Nov.
1869	4		Berlioz (66) dies, 8 Mar; Dargomizhsky (55) dies, 17 Jan; Järnefelt born, 14 Aug; Pfitzner born, 5 May; Roussel born, 5 Apr.
1870	5		Lekeu born, 20 Jan; Novák born, 5 Dec; Florent Schmitt born, 28 Sep.
1871	6		Skryabin born, 25 Dec; Stenhammar born, 7 Feb.
1872	7		Alfvén born, 1 May;

			Moniuszko (53) dies, 4 June; Vaughan Williams born, 12 Oct.
1873	8		Rakhmaninov born, 20 Mar; Reger born, 19 Mar.
1874	9	First regular piano lessons.	Holst born, 21 Sep; Ives born, 20 Oct; Franz Schmidt born, 22 Dec; Schoenberg born, 13 Sep; Suk born, 4 Jan.
1875	10	First attempts at composition, including *Vattendroppar*.	Bizet (36) dies, 3 June; Glière born, 11 Jan; Ravel born, 7 Mar.
1876	11	Entry into Hämeenlinna *Suomalainen Normaalilyseo*.	Falla born, 23 Nov.
1877	12		Dohnányi born, 27 July.
1878	13		Palmgren born, 16 Feb; Schreker born, 23 Mar.
1879	14		Respighi born, 9 July.
1880	15	Begins study of the violin with Gustav Levander.	Bloch born, 24 July; Pizzetti born, 20 Sep.
1881	16	Studies Marx's *Lehre von der musikalischen komponisten*.	Bartók born, 25 Mar; Enesco born, 19 Aug; Myaskovsky born, 20 Apr; Musorgsky (42) dies, 28 Mar.
1882	17	Piano trio in A minor.	Kodály born, 16 Dec; Malipiero born, 18 Mar; Stravinsky born, 17 June.
1883	18		Bax born, 6 Nov; Casella born, 25 July; Szymanowski born, 21 Sep; Wagner (70) dies, 13 Feb; Webern born, 3 Dec.
1884	19	Andantino for cello and piano.	Rangström born, 30 Nov; Smetana (60) dies, 12 May.
1885	20	Passes *studentexamen* (15 May) and begins law studies at Helsinki; completes String Quartet in E flat.	Berg born, 9 Feb; Varèse born, 22 Dec; Wellesz born, 21 Oct.
1886	21	Abandons law studies to devote himself entirely to music.	Liszt (74) dies, 31 July; Schoeck born, 1 Sep.
1887	22	Becomes second violin in Helsinki conservatoire's quartet.	Borodin (53) dies, 20 Feb; Madetoja born, 17 Feb; Fartein Valen born, 25 Aug; Villa-Lobos born, 5 Mar.
1888	23	*Svartsjukans nätter* composed, violin pieces, op. 2. Friendship with Busoni (22).	
1889	24	String Quartet in A minor performed. Begins studies in Berlin with Albert Becker.	
1890	25	Engagement to Aino Järnefelt (autumn). Performance of String Quartet in B flat, op. 4. Journey to Vienna, where he makes first	Franck (67) dies, 8 Nov; Gade (73) dies, 21 Dec; Frank Martin born, 15 Sep; Martinů born, 8 Dec.

		attempts at orchestral composition.	
1891	26	First sketches for *Kullervo* Symphony.	Prokofiev born, 23 Apr.
1892	27	Successful first performance of *Kullervo* symphony (28 Apr); composition of *En Saga*. Marriage to Aino Järnefelt (10 June) and appointment as teacher of composition at conservatoire.	Honegger born, 10 Mar; Yrjö Kilpinen born, 4 Feb; Milhaud born, 4 Sep; Rosenberg born, 6 June.
1893	28	*Karelia* music, *Swan of Tuonela* and Piano Sonata in F completed.	Tchaikovsky (53) dies, 6 Nov.
1894	29	Visit to Bayreuth. Choral version of *Rakastava*. Abandons opera and starts works on the *Four Legends*.	Moeran born, 31 Dec; Piston born, 20 Jan.
1895	30	Continues work on the *Four Legends*, op. 22.	Hindemith born, 16 Nov.
1896	31	*Jungfrun i tornet* composed and first performed (7 Nov).	Bruckner (72) dies, 11 Oct.
1897	32	Award of annual pension from Finnish Government: begins work on *King Christian* suite.	Brahms (63) dies, 3 Apr; Saeverud born, 17 Apr.
1898	33	Performance of *King Christian* (24 Feb). Visit to Berlin.	Roy Harris born, 12 Feb.
1899	34	*Scènes historiques I*, and First Symphony (26 Apr). *Finlandia* and the songs, op. 36, composed.	Chausson (44) dies, 10 June; Poulenc born, 7 Jan; Revueltas born, 31 Dec. Tsar Nicholas II suspends Finnish constitution, 15 Feb
1900	35	S. visits Paris during tour with Helsinki Orchestra (July–Aug).	Burkhard born, 17 Apr; Copland born, 14 Nov; Klami born, 20 Sep.
1901	36	S. visits Rapallo (Feb) and Prague, where he meets Dvořák (60) and Suk (27); conducts his own music in Germany. He revises *En Saga* and begins Second Symphony. Relinquishes teaching post at Helsinki.	Kalinnikov (34) dies, 11 Jan; Rubbra born, 23 May; Verdi (87) dies, 27 Jan.
1902	37	Second Symphony performed (8 Mar).	Shebalin born, 11 June; Walton born, 29 Mar. First performance of Debussy's *Pelléas et Mélisande*.
1903	38	Completes original version of Violin Concerto (summer) and *Romance* in C for strings.	Berkeley born, 12 May; Blacher born, 3 Jan; Wolf dies, 22 Feb.
1904	39	Moves to Järvenpää and begins Third Symphony (Sep). Songs, op. 38, including *Höstkväll* and *På verandan vid havet*; *Kyllikki* for piano.	Dallapiccola born, 3 Feb; Dvořak (62) dies, 1 May; Petrassi born, 16 July. Assassination of the Tsarist Governor-General of Finland in

			Helsinki. Russo-Japanese War.
1905	40	Conducts Second Symphony in Berlin (Jan). Composes music to *Pelléas et Mélisande* (spring). Revised version of Violin Concerto first perf. with Strauss conducting (Oct). First visit to England.	Hartman born, 2 Aug; Lambert born, 23 Aug; Tippett born, 2 Jan; Dag Wirén born, 15 Oct. Debussy's *La mer* and Strauss's *Salome*. General strike in Russia. Increasing tension between Norway and Sweden leads to the dissolution ('oppløsningen') of the Union between the two countries, Oct.
1906	41	Composes *Belshazzar's Feast* and *Pohjola's Daughter*.	Arensky (44) dies, 25 Feb; Shostakovich born, 25 Sep.
1907	42	Completes Third Symphony (perf. 25 Sep); Mahler visits Helsinki (Nov).	Grieg (63) dies, 4 Sep.
1908	43	Second visit to England, where he conducts Third Symphony at R.P.O. concert (20 Feb). Composes music to *Swanwhite* at Järvenpää. Operation in Helsinki (May) and visit to Berlin. Begins *Voces intimae*.	Rimsky-Korsakov (64) dies, 21 June; Messiaen born, 10 Dec; Larsson born, 15 May.
1909	44	Completes *Voces intimae* in London. Songs, op. 57 and *In Memoriam* composed.	Albeniz (48) dies, 18 May; Holmboe born, 20 Dec. Strauss's *Elektra*.
1910	45	Works on Fourth Symphony and composes songs, op. 61.	Balakirev (73) dies, 29 May; Barber born, 9 Mar; William Schuman born, 4 Aug.
1911	46	Concert tour in Sweden and the Baltic States (Feb). Completion and first perf. of Fourth Symphony (3 Apr). Visit to Berlin (Oct) and Paris (Nov), where he hears much new music. *Rakastava* for strings and percussion completed.	Mahler (50) dies, 29 May; Svendsen (70) dies, 14 June.
1912	47	Invited to become professor at Vienna. Second series of *Scènes historiques*, three sonatinas for piano. Visits London, where he conducts Fourth Symphony.	
1913	48	*The Bard* and *Luonnotar* composed.	Britten born, 22 Nov. Stravinsky's *Le Sacre du Printemps*.
1914	49	Visit to America (May) where he receives honorary degree at Yale; composes *The Oceanides* and begins sketching the Fifth Symphony.	Lyadov (59) dies, 28 Aug; Magnard (49) dies, 3 Sep. Outbreak of war between Russia and the Central Powers, 1 Aug.
1915	50	First version of Fifth Sym-	Skryabin (43) dies, 27 Apr;

		phony completed; sonatina for violin and piano, op. 80, settings of Fröding, op. 84; concert tour in Scandinavia.	Taneyev (58) dies, 19 Jan.
1916	51	Revised version of Fifth Symphony performed (Dec).	Ginastera born, 11 Apr; Reger (42) dies, 11 May.
1917	52	Runeberg songs, op. 90.	Finnish Independence declared, 6 Dec.
1918	53	Finnish civil war. Järvenpää searched by Red troops (Feb). S. moves to Helsinki (Mar).	Debussy (55) dies, 25 Mar. Finnish Civil War, Jan–May. End of First World War, 11 Nov.
1919	54	Definitive version of Fifth Symphony (autumn).	Niels Viggo Bentzon born, 24 Aug. Death of Axel Carpelan.
1920	55	*Maan virsi*, op. 95, orchestral pieces, op. 96, *Six Bagatelles* for piano, op. 97. Invited to become head of the Eastman School of Music.	
1921	56	Last visit to London (Jan), where he is reunited with Busoni (55). Composes *Suite mignonne* and *Suite champêtre*.	Saint-Saëns (86) dies 16 Dec.
1922	57	*Suite caractéristique* for orchestra and piano pieces, op. 99.	
1923	58	Concert tour of Norway and Sweden (Jan); conducts first perf. of Sixth Symphony (19 Feb). Visit to Rome, where he conducts at the Augusteo (11 Mar).	
1924	59	Completes Seventh Symphony (Mar).	Busoni (58) dies, 27 July; Fauré (79) dies, 4 Nov; Puccini (65) dies, 29 Nov.
1925	60	*Tapiola*.	First performance of Alban Berg's *Wozzeck*.
1926	61	Incidental Music to *The Tempest* written for production in Copenhagen.	Henze born, 1 July.
1927	62		Stenhammar (56) dies, 20 Nov.
1928	63		Janáček (74) dies, 12 Aug.
1929	64	Last published work with opus no.: *Three Pieces* for violin and piano, op. 116. Enters into retirement at Järvenpää.	
1930	65		
1931	66	Tells Olin Downes that the Eighth Symphony is finished. Death of Gallén-Kalela.	d'Indy (80) dies, 2 Dec; Nielsen (66) dies, 2 Oct; Ysaÿe (72) dies, 12 May.
1932	67		Attempted fascist coup in Finland.

1933	68	First movement of the Eighth Symphony sent to copyist.	
1934	69		Delius (72) dies, 10 June; Elgar (76) dies, 23 Feb; Holst (60) dies, 25 May; Schreker (55) dies, 21 Mar.
1935	70		Berg (50) dies, 24 Dec; Dukas (69) dies, 18 May; Halvorsen (71) dies, 4 Dec; Suk (61) dies, 29 May.
1936	71		Glazunov (70) dies, 21 Mar; Respighi (56) dies, 18 Apr.
1937	72		Ravel (62) dies, 28 Dec; Roussel (68) dies, 23 Aug; Szymanowski (54) dies, 29 Mar. Shostakovich's Fifth Symphony.
1938	73		Bartók's Violin Concerto (no. 2). Munich agreement.
1939	74	Declines offer of asylum in England.	Franz Schmidt (64) dies, 11 Feb. Hitler invades Poland, 1 Sep, and Britain and France declare war, 3 Sep. Stalin attacks Finland, 30 Nov.
1940	75		Finland sues for peace, Mar. Hitler invades Norway and Denmark, 9 Apr.
1941	76		Finland attacks USSR to regain territories lost in the first Winter War. Sinding dies (85), Dec. 3.
1942	77		
1943	78		Rakhmaninov (69) dies, 28 Mar.
1944	79		Finland forced to abandon struggle against USSR. Mannerheim assumes Presidency.
1945	80		Bartók (64) dies, 26 Sep; Webern (61) dies, 15 Sep. Britten's *Peter Grimes*. End of war in Europe, 6 May. Atomic bomb on Hiroshima, Aug, and end of war in the Far East.
1946	81		Bantock (78) dies, 16 Oct; Falla (69) dies, 14 Nov.
1947	82		Casella (63) dies, 15 May; Madetoja (60) dies, 6 Oct; Rangström (62) dies, 11 May.
1948	83		Treaty of co-operation signed between Finland and the USSR.
1949	84		Novák (78) dies, 18 July; Pfitzner (80) dies, 22 May; Strauss (85)

Sibelius

			dies, 8 Sep.
1950	85		Myaskovsky (69) dies, Aug; Moeran (55) dies, 1 Dec.
1951	86		Lambert (45) dies, 21 Aug; Palmgren (73) dies, 13 Dec; Schoenberg (76) dies, 13 July.
1952	87		Fartein Valen (65) dies, 14 Dec.
1953	88		Bax (69) dies, 3 Oct; Prokofiev (61) dies, 4 Mar. Shostakovich's Tenth Symphony. Death of Stalin.
1954	89		Ives (80) dies, 19 May.
1955	90		Enesco (74) dies, 14 May; Honegger (63) dies, 27 Nov; Ropartz (91) dies, 22 Nov.
1956	91		Glière (81) dies, 23 June.
1957	91	Sibelius dies of a cerebral haemorrhage in Järvenpää 20 Sep.	Alfvén 85, Barber 47, Niels Viggo Bentzon 38; Bloch 77, Britten 44, Copland 57, Dallapiccola 53, Dohnányi 80, Ginastera 41, Roy Harris 59, Hartman 52, Henze 32, Hindemith 62, Holmboe 48, Järnefelt 88, Yrjö Kilpinen 65, Klami 57, Kodály 75, Larsson 49, Malipiero 75, Martin 67, Martinů 67, Milhaud 65, Petrassi 53, Piston 63, Pizzetti 77, Poulenc 58, Rosenberg 65, Rubbra 56, Saeverud 60, Schmitt 87, Schoeck (81) dies, Schuman 47, Shostakovich 51, Stravinsky 75, Tippett 52, Varèse 72, Vaughan Williams 85, Villa Lobos 70, Walton 55, Wellesz 72, Dag Wirén 52.

Appendix B

List of works[1]

WORKS FOR ORCHESTRA

Op.

  6 *Cassazione* 1904, 1905

  7 *Kullervo.* Symphonic poem for soprano, baritone, male chorus and orchestra 1892
- 1. Introduction
- 2. Kullervo's youth
- 3. Kullervo and his sister
- 4. Kullervo goes to war
- 5. Kullervo's death

  9 *En Saga.* Tone-poem 1892, 1902

10 *Karelia* Overture 1893

11 *Karelia* Suite 1893
- 1. Intermezzo
- 2. Ballade
- 3. Alla marcia

14 *Rakastava* (The Lover), for strings, triangle and percussion 1911
- 1. The lover
- 2. The path of the beloved
- 3. Good night – Farewell!

15 *Skogsrået* (The Wood-Nymph), also known as *Ballade pour l'orchestre* ?1894.

16 *Vårsång* (Spring Song). Tone-poem 1894, 1895, 1903.

22 *Four Legends*
- 1. *Lemminkäinen and the Maidens of the Island* 1895, 1897, 1939
- 2. *The Swan of Tuonela* ?1893, 1897, 1900
- 3. *Lemminkäinen in Tuonela* 1895, 1897, 1939
- 4. *Lemminkäinen's Homeward Journey* 1895, 1897, 1900

25 *Scènes historiques I* 1899, 1911
- 1. *All'Overtura*
- 2. *Scena*
- 3. *Festivo*

26 *Finlandia.* Tone-poem 1899, 1900

39 Symphony No. 1 in E minor 1899, 1900

42 Romance in C major for strings 1904

43 Symphony no. 2 in D major 1902

45   1. *The Dryad.* Tone-poem 1910
    2. *Dance Intermezzo* 1904, 1907

49 *Pohjola's Daughter.* Symphonic fantasia 1906

52 Symphony no. 3 in C major 1904–7

53 *Pan and Echo (Dance Intermezzo III)* 1906

[1]The second (and in some cases third) date signifies the year of revision.

Sibelius

55 *Night Ride and Sunrise*. Tone-poem 1908
59 *In Memoriam*, Funeral march 1909, 1910
63 Symphony no. 4 in A minor 1909–11
64 *The Bard*, Tone-poem 1913, 1914
66 *Scènes historiques II* 1912
    1.The chase.
    2.Love-song.
    3.At the drawbridge.
73 *The Oceanides*. Tone-poem 1914
82 Symphony no. 5 in E flat 1915, 1916, 1919
96 Three Pieces
    1.*Valse lyrique* 1919
    2.*Autrefois, scène pastorale* 1919
    3.*Valse chevaleresque* 1921
98a *Suite mignonne*, for two flutes and strings 1921
    1.Petite scène
    2.Polka
    3.Epilogue
98b *Suite champêtre*, for strings 1921
    1.Pièce charactéristique
    2.Mélodie élégiaque
    3.Danse
100 *Suite charactéristique*, for harp and strings 1922
    1.Vivo
    2.Lento
    3.Commodo
104 Symphony no. 6 in D minor 1923
105 Symphony no. 7 in C major 1924
112 *Tapiola*. Tone-poem 1926
—Academic March (*Promootiomarssi*) 1919
—*Andante festivo*, for strings and percussion. ?1930 (for string quartet 1922)
—*Andante lirico*, for strings (arr. of Impromptu for piano, op. 5, no. 6) ?1893, ?1924
—*Björneborgarnas Marsch* ?1900
—Coronation March (arr. from Cantata for the coronation of Nicholas II) 1896
—*Cortège* 1901
—Impromptu for strings (arr. of Impromptu for piano, op. 5, no. 5) ?1893
—Menuetto (also known as *Menuett-Impromptu* and *Tempo di menuetto*) 1894
—*Morceau romantique sur un motif de M. Jacob de Julin* 1925
—Presto for strings (arr. of finale of Quartet in B flat, op. 4) 1889–90
—Overture in E major 1891
—Overture in A minor 1902
—*Scène de ballet* 1891

MUSIC FOR THE THEATRE

Op.
  8 *Ödlan* (The Lizard) (Lybeck), for violin and string quintet 1909
 27 *King Christian II* (Adolf Paul) 1898
    1.Élegie
    2.Musette
    3.Menuetto

210

4.*Sången om korsspindel* (Fool's song of the spider)
5.Nocturne
6.Serenade
7.Ballade
[44] *Kuolema* (Death) (Arvid Järnefelt). Six scenes, for strings and percussion 1903
  44 1.Scene 1 rev. as *Valse triste* 1904
     2.Scenes 3 & 4 rev. as *Scen med tranor* (Scene with cranes) 1906
  62a *Canzonetta* for strings (*Rondino der Liebenden*) 1911
  62b *Valse romantique* 1911
  46 *Pelléas et Mélisande* (Maeterlinck) 1905
     1.At the castle gate
     2.Mélisande
     3.By the seashore
     4.By a spring in the park
     5.The three blind sisters
     6.Pastorale
     7.Mélisande at the spinning-wheel
     8.Entr'acte
     9.The death of Mélisande
  51 *Belshazzar's Feast* (Hjalmar Procopé)[1] 1906
     1.Alla marcia
     2.Nocturne
     3.The Jewish's girl's song
     4.Allegretto
     5.Dance of life
     6.Dance of death
     7.Tempo sostenuto
     8.Allegro
  54 *Swanwhite* (Strindberg) 1908
     Suite (Original score: 14 scenes)
     1.The peacock
     2.The harp
     3.The maidens with roses
     4.Listen! The robin sings
     5.The prince alone
     6.Swanwhite and the prince
     7.Song of praise
  71 *Scaramouche* (Poul Knudsen), for piano and strings 1913
  83 *Jedermann* (Everyman) (Hofmannsthal), for mixed chorus, piano, organ and
     orchestra 1916
109 *The Tempest* (Shakespeare)[2] 1925
     (Original score in 34 sections)[3]
     1.Prelude
     2.Suite I
          1.The oak-tree
          2.Humoresque
          3.Caliban's song

[1]The concert suite comprises movements entitled 1. *Oriental Procession*, 2. *Night Music*, 3. *Solitude* and 4. *Khadra's Dance*.
[2]Translated into Danish by Edvard Lembcke.
[3]Sibelius added an additional number in 1927 for the Helsinki production.

        4.The harvesters
        5.Canon
        6.Scena
        7.Intrada-Berceuse
        8.Entr'acte
        9.Ariel's song
      10.The storm
   3.Suite II
        1.Chorus of the winds
        2.Intermezzo
        3.Dance of the nymphs
        4.Prospero
        5.Song I
        6.Song II
        7.Miranda
        8.The naiads
        9.Dance episode
—*The Language of the Birds* (Adolf Paul). Wedding March (Act III)   1911

SOLO INSTRUMENT AND ORCHESTRA

  47 Concerto in D minor for violin and orchestra   1903–4, 1905.
  69 Two Serenades for violin and orchestra
        1.in D major   1912
        2.in G minor   1913
  77 Two Pieces for violin (or cello) and orchestra.
        1.*Laetare anima mea. Cantique*   1914
        2.Devotion (*Ab imo pectore*)   1915
  87 Two Humoresques for violin and orchestra
        1.in D minor   1917, ?1939
        2.in D major   1917, 1923
  89 Four Humoresques for violin and orchestra (often numbered 3–6)
        1.in G minor (for strings)   1917, 1923
        2.in G minor (for strings)   1917, 1923
        3.in E flat major   1917, 1923
        4.in G minor   1918, 1922
 117 Suite for violin and string orchestra   1929
        1.Country-scenery, Allegretto
        2.Evening in spring, Andantino
        3.In the summer, Vivace

BRASS ENSEMBLE

  —Allegro in E flat minor, for brass septet and triangle   ?1889
  —Andantino (with Menuetto), for brass septet   1890–1
  —Overture in F minor for brass septet   1890–1
  —Preludium, for clarinet and brass sextet   1891
  —*Tiera*. Tone-poem for brass septet and percussion   ?1899

CHAMBER MUSIC WITH PIANO

  —Allegro in D major for piano trio   1886
  —Andante – allegro (in A major) for piano quintet   ?1888

—Andantino in G minor for piano trio   1887–8
—Menuetto in F major for two violins and piano   1883
—Quartet in C minor for two violins, cello and piano   1891
—Quartet in D minor for two violins, cello and piano   1884
—Quartet in G minor for violin, cello, harmonium and piano   ?1887
—Quintet in G minor for piano and strings   1890
—Scherzo for violin, cello and piano, four hands   ?1887
—Trio in A minor (three movements)   ?1884
—Trio in A minor (four movements)   1886
—Trio in C major ('Lovisa Trio')   1888
—Trio in D major ('Korpo Trio')   1887
—Trio in G major for two violins and piano   1883

CHAMBER MUSIC WITHOUT PIANO
  4   String Quartet in B flat   1890
 56   String Quartet in D minor (*Voces intimae*)   1909
  —String Quartet in A minor   1889
  —String Quartet in E flat major   1885
  —Suite (Trio) in A major for string trio   1889
  —Theme and variations in C sharp minor for string quartet   1888
  —Theme and variations in G minor for string quartet   1888–9
  —*Vattendroppar* (Water Drops) for violin and cello   1875–6

SOLO INSTRUMENT AND PIANO
  2   1.Romance in B minor, for violin and piano   1888, 1911
     2.Epilogue, for violin and piano   1888, 1911
 20   *Malinconia*, for cello and piano   1900
 71   *Scène d'amour* (*Scaramouche*) (1913), for violin and piano   1925
 77   Two Pieces, for violin (or cello) and piano (arr.)
     1.*Laetare anima mea. Cantique*   1914–15
     2.Devotion (*Ab imo pectore*)   1915
 78   Four Pieces, for violin (or cello) and piano
     1.Impromptu   1915
     2.Romance   1915
     3.Religioso   1917
     4.Rigaudon   1915
 79   Six Pieces for violin and piano
     1.Souvenir   ?1915
     2.Tempo di menuetto   1915
     3.Danse caractéristique   1916
     4.Sérénade   1916
     5.Dance Idyll   1917
     6.Berceuse   1917
 80   Sonatina in E major for violin and piano   1915
 81   Five Pieces for violin and piano
     1.Mazurka   1915
     2.Rondino   1917
     3.Valse   1917
     4.Aubade   1918
     5.Menuetto   1918
102   Novellette   1922

Sibelius

106 Five *Danses champêtres* for violin and piano   1925
115 Four Pieces for violin and piano 1929
     1.On the heath
     2.Ballade
     3.Humoresque
     4.The bells
116 Three Pieces for violin and piano   1929
     1.Scène de danse
     2.Danse caractéristique
     3.Rondeau romantique
—Allegretto (in C major), for violin and piano   ?1888
—Allegretto (in E flat major), for violin and piano   ?1888
—Allegro (in A minor), for violin and piano   1888–89
—Andante cantabile, for violin and piano   1887
—Andante grazioso, for violin and piano   1884–5
—Andante molto (in F minor), for cello and piano   ?1887
—Andantino (in C major), for cello and piano   ?1884
—Fantasia for cello and piano   ?1887
—Moderato maestoso for violin and piano   ?1888
—Rondo for viola and piano   1893
—Sonata in A minor for violin and piano   1884
—Sonata in F major for violin and piano   1889
—Suite (Sonata) in D minor for violin and piano   ?1888
—Suite in E major for violin and piano   1888–9
—*Tempo di valse*, in G minor for cello and piano   ?1887
—*Tempo di valse*, in F sharp minor for cello and piano ('Lulu Waltz')   1889
—Theme and variations in D minor for cello alone   ?1887

ORGAN MUSIC

Op.
111 Two Pieces
     1.Intrada   1925
     2.*Sorgmusik Surusoitto* (Funeral Music)   1931
—Postludium   ?1925
—Preludium   ?1925

PIANO MUSIC

Op.
  5 Six Impromptus   1890–3
 12 Sonata in F major   1893
 24 Ten Pieces
     1.Impromptu   ?1895
     2.Romance in A major   1895
     3.Caprice in E minor   1898–9
     4.Romance in D minor   1895
     5.Waltz in E major   ?1895
     6.Idyll   ?1898
     7.Andantino   1900
     8.Nocturne   1901
     9.Romance in D flat major   1901

10.Barcarola (also known as op. 38, no. 10)   1903
34 Ten Pieces
    1.Waltz in D flat major   1914–15
    2.Air de danse   ?1914
    3.Mazurka   1914–15
    4.Couplet   1914
    5.Boutade   1914
    6.Rêverie   1913
    7.Danse pastorale   1916
    8.Joueur de harpe   1916
    9.Reconnaissance   1916
    10.Souvenir   1916
40 *Pensées lyriques*
    1.Valsette   1912
    2.Chanson sans paroles   1913
    3.Humoresque   1913
    4.Menuetto   1913
    5.Berceuse   1913
    6.Pensée mélodique   1914
    7.Rondoletto   1914
    8.Scherzando   1915
    9.Petite sérénade   1915
    10.Polanaise   1916
41 *Kyllikki*. Three Lyric Pieces   1904
58 Ten Pieces   1909
    1.Rêverie
    2.Scherzino
    3.Air varié
    4.The shepherd
    5.The evening
    6.Dialogue
    7.Tempo di menuetto
    8.Fisher song
    9.Sérenade
    10.Summer Song
67 Three Sonatinas   1912
    1.in F sharp minor
    2.in E major
    3.in B flat minor
68 Two Rondinos   1911
    1.in G sharp minor
    2.in C sharp minor
74 Four Lyric Pieces   1914
    1.Eclogue
    2.Soft west wind
    3.At the dance
    4.In the old home
75 Five Pieces   1914
    1.When the rowan blossoms
    2.The lonely pine
    3.The aspen

4.The birch
5.The spruce
76 Thirteen Pieces
  1.Esquisse 1911
  2.Étude 1911
  3.Carillon ?1911
  4.Humoresque 1916
  5.Consolation 1919
  6.Romanezetta ?1914
  7.Affettuoso 1916
  8.Pièce enfantine 1916
  9.Arabesque 1916
  10.Elegiaco 1916
  11.Linnaea 1914
  12.Capriccietto 1913
  13.Harlequinade 1916
85 Five Pieces
  1.Bellis ?1917
  2.Oeillet 1916
  3.Iris 1916
  4.Aquileja 1917
  5.Campanula 1917
94 Six Pieces
  1.Danse 1919
  2.Nouvellette ?1914
  3.Sonnet 1919
  4.Berger et bergerette 1919
  5.Mélodie 1919
  6.Gavotte 1919
96 a.Valse lyrique 1919
  b.Autrefois 1919, 1920
  c.Valse chevaleresque 1921
97 Six Bagatelles 1920
  1.Humoresque I
  2.Song
  3.Little Waltz
  4.Humorous March
  5.Impromptu
  6.Humoresque II
99 Eight Pieces 1922
  1.Pièce humoristique
  2.Esquisse
  3.Souvenir
  4.Impromptu
  5.Couplet
  6.Animoso
  7.Moment de valse
  8.Petite marche
100 *Suite caractéristique* 1922 (see Works for Orchestra)
101 Five Romantic Pieces 1923
  1.Romance

216

    2.Chant du soir
    3.Scène lyrique
    4.Humoresque
    5.Scène romantique
103 Five Characteristic Impressions   1924
    1.The village church
    2.The fiddler
    3.The oarsman
    4.The storm
    5.In mournful mood
114 Five Esquisses   1929
    1.Landscape
    2.Winter scene
    3.Forest lake
    4.Song in the forest
    5.Spring vision
—À Betzy Lerche (Waltz)   1889
—Adagio (in D major)   ?1888
—Allegretto (in E major)   1889
—Allegretto (in F major)   1894–6
—Allegretto (in G minor)   ?1888
—Allegretto (in G minor)   1897
—Allegretto (in B flat minor)   ?1888
—Allegro (in E major)   ?1888
—Andante (in E flat major)   1887–8
—Andantino (in C major)   ?1887–8
—Andantino (in E major)   1888
—Au crépuscule   1887
—Caprizzio   1895
—Con moto, sempre una corda   1885
—*Florestan*. Suite in four movements   1889
—Finnish folksongs   1903
    1.*Minum kultani* (My beloved)
    2.*Sydämestäni rakastan* (I love you with all my heart)
    3.*Ilta tulee, ehtoo joutuu* (Evening comes)
    4.*Tuopa tyttö, kaunis tyttö* (That beautiful girl)
    5.*Velisurmaaja* (Fratricide)
    6.*Häämuistelma* (Wedding memories)
—*Kavaljern* (The cavalier)   1900
—Largo (in A major)   1888
—Lento (in E major)   1895–7
—*Mandolinato*   1917
—*Marche triste* (in E minor)   ?1901–3
—Menuetto (in F sharp minor)   ?1888
—Moderato – Presto   ?1887–8
—Molto andante (in F sharp minor)   ?1887
—*Morceau romantique*[1]   1925
—Più Lento – Tempo di valse (in E flat major)   ?1888
—Scherzo   ?1888

[1]An arrangement of the *Morceau romantique sur un motif de M. Jacob de Julin.*

Sibelius

—*Spagnuolo* 1913
—*Till trånaden* (To longing) 1913
—*Trånaden* (*Suckarnas mystär*) 1887
—To O. Parviainen ?1919
—Vivace (in D minor) 1888
—Vivace (in E flat major) ?1888

SONGS WITH ORCHESTRA

Op.
3 *Arioso* (Runeberg) 1911
13
    4.*Våren flyktar hastigt* (The Spring is flying) (1891) 1914
17
    1.*Se'n har jag ej frågat mera* (Runeberg) (And I questioned then no further)
    (?1894) 1903
Op.
27
    4.*Sången om korsspindeln* (Fool's song of the spider) (*King Christian II*) 1898
33 *Koskenlaskian morsiamet* (The rapid-shooter's or rapid-rider's brides), for baritone or mezzo-soprano 1897
36
    1.*Svarta rosor* (Black roses) (Josephson) (1899) ?1924–7
    6.*Demanten på Marssnön* (Wecksell) (The diamond on the March snow) 1900
37
    3.*Soluppgång* (Sunrise) (Hedberg) (1902) 1914
38
    1.*Höstkväll* (Autumn evening) (Rydberg) (1903) 1904
    2.*På verandan vid havet* (On a balcony by the sea) (Rydberg) (1903) 1903
    3.*I natten* (In the night) (Rydberg) (1903) 1903
60
    1.*Kom nu hit, död* (Come away, Death) (Shakespeare) (1909) 1957
70 *Luonnotar.* Tone-poem, for soprano 1913
—Serenade (Stagnelius), for baritone 1895

SONGS WITH PIANO

Op.
1 Five Christmas Songs
    1.*Nu står jul vid snöig port* (Now Christmas stands at the snowy porch)
    (Topelius) 1895, 1913
    2.*Nu så kommer jul* (Christmas is coming) (Topelius) 1895, 1913
    3.*Det mörknar ute* (Outside it is getting dark) (Topelius) ?1895
    4.*Giv mig ej glans, ej guld, ej prakt* (Give me no splendour, gold or pomp)[1]
    (Topelius)
    5.*Om hanget korkeat* (High are the snowdrifts) (Joukahainen) 1901
3 *Arioso* (Runeberg) ?1911

[1]Also known simply as *Julvisa* (Christmas song).

218

13 Seven Songs (Runeberg)
1.*Under strandens granar* (Under the fir-trees)   1892
2.*Kyssens hopp* (The kiss's hope)   1892
3.*Hjärtats morgon* (The heart's morning)   1890
4.*Våren flyktar hastigt* (The Spring is flying)   1891
5.*Drömmen* (The dream)   1891
6.*Till Frigga* (To Fricka)   1892
7.*Jägargossen* (The young huntsman)   1891
17 Seven Songs
1.*Se'n har jag ej frågat mera* (And I questioned then no further) (Runeberg)   ?1894
2.*Sov in!* (Sleep on!) (Tavaststjerna)   1892
3.*Fågellek* (Enticement) (Tavaststjerna)   1891
4.*Vilse* (Astray) (Tavaststjerna)   1902
5.*En slända* (A dragon-fly) (Levertin)   ?1904
6.*Illalle* (To evening) (Forsman-Koskimies)   1898
7.*Lastu lainehilla* (Driftwood) (Calamnius)   1902
35 Two Songs
1.*Jubal* (Josephson)   1907–8
2.*Teodora* (Gripenberg)   1908
36 Six Songs
1.*Svarta rosor* (Black roses) (Josephson)   1899
2.*Men min fågel märks dock icke* (But my bird is long in homing) (Runeberg)   1899
3.*Bollspelet vid Trianon* (Tennis at Trianon) (Fröding)   1899
4.*Säv, säv, susa* (Sigh, sedges, sigh) (Fröding)   1900
5.*Marssnön* (The March snow) (Wecksell)   1900
6.*Demanten på Marssnön* (The diamond on the March snow) (Wecksell)   1900
37
1.*Den första kyssen* (The first kiss) (Runeberg)   1900
2.*Lasse liten* (Little Lasse) (Topelius)   1902
3.*Soluppgång* (Sunrise) (Hedberg)   1902
4.*Var det en dröm?* (Was it a dream?) (Wecksell)   1902
5.*Flickan kom ifrån sin älsklings möte* (The girl returned from meeting her lover) (Runeberg)   1900–1
38
1.*Höstkväll* (Autumn evening) (Rydberg)   1903
2.*På verandan vid havet* (On a balcony by the sea) (Runeberg)   1903
3.*I natten* (In the night) (Rydberg)   1903
4.*Harpolekaren och hans son* (The harpist and his son) (Rydberg)   1904
5.*Jag ville jag vore i Indialand* (I would I were dwelling in India) (Fröding)
50 Six songs   1906
1.*Lenzegesang* (Spring song) (Fitger)
2.*Sehnsucht* (Longing) (Weiss)
3.*Im Feld ein Mädchen singt* (In the field a maiden sings) (Susman)
4.*Aus banger brust* (From anxious heart) (Dehmel)
5.*Die stille Stadt* (The silent town) (Dehmel)
6.*Rosenlied* (The song of the roses) (Ritter)
57 Eight Songs (Josephson)   1909
1.*Älven och snigeln* (The river and the snail)

Sibelius

2.*En blomma stod vid vägen* (A flower grew by the wayside)
3.*Kvarnhjulet* (The mill-wheel)
4.*Maj* (May)
5.*Jag är ett träd* (I am a tree)
6.*Hertig Magnus* (Duke Magnus)
7.*Vänskapens blomma* (The flower of friendship)
8.*Näcken* (The water-sprite)
60 Two Songs from Shakespeare's *Twelfth Night*[1] with piano or guitar 1909
1.*Kom nu hit, död* (Come away, Death)
2.*Och när som jag var en liten små dräng* (When that I was and a little tiny boy)
61 Eight Songs 1910
1.*Långsamt som kvällskyn* (Slowly as the evening sun) (Tavaststjerna)
2.*Vattenplask* (Lapping waters) (Rydberg)
3.*När jag drömmer* (When I dream) (Tavaststjerna)
4.*Romeo* (Tavaststjerna)
5.*Romans* (Romance) (Tavaststjerna)
6.*Dolce far niente* (Tavaststjerna)
7.*Fåfäng önskan* (Idle wishes) (Runeberg)
8.*Vårtagen* (Spring spell) (Gripenberg)
72 Six Songs
1.*Vi ses igen* (We will meet again)[2] (Rydberg) 1915
2.*Orions bälte* (Orion's girdle) (Topelius) 1915
3.*Kyssen* (The kiss) (Rydberg) 1915
4.*Kaiutar* (The echo-nymph) (Larin Kyösti) 1915
5.*Der Wanderer und der Bach* (The wayfarer and the stream) (Greif) 1915
6.*Hundra vägar* (A hundred ways) (Runeberg) ?1907
86 Six Songs
1.*Vårförnimmelser* (The coming of Spring) (Tavaststjerna) 1916
2.*Längtan heter min arvedel* (Longing is my heritage) (Karlfeldt) 1916
3.*Dold förening* (Hidden union) (Snoïlsky) 1916
4.*Och finns det en tanke?* (And is there a thought?) (Tavaststjerna) 1916
5.*Sångarlön* (The singer's reward) (Snoïlsky) 1916
6.*I systrar, I bröder* (Ye sisters, ye brothers) (Lybeck) 1917
88 Six Songs 1917
1.*Blåsippan* (The blue anemone) (Franzén)
2.*De bägge rosorna* (The two roses) (Franzén)
3.*Vitsippan* (The star-flower) (Franzén)
4.*Sippan* (The anemone) (Runeberg)
5.*Törnet* (The thorn) (Runeberg)
6.*Blommans öde* (The flower's destiny) (Runeberg)
90 Six Songs (Runeberg)
1.*Norden* (The north) 1917
2.*Hennes budskap* (Her message) 1917, 1918
3.*Morgonen* (The morning) 1917
4.*Fågelfångaren* (The bird-catcher) 1917
5.*Sommarnatten* (Summer night) 1917
6.*Vem styrde hit din väg?* (Who brought you here?) 1917–18

[1]Sibelius set the words in Hagberg's Swedish translation.
[2]Both *Vi ses igen* and *Orions bälte* are lost.

—*Den första kyssen* (The first kiss)[1] (Runeberg)   1891–2
—*En visa* (A Song) (Baeckman)   1888
—*Erloschen* (The fire has died out) (Busse Palmo)   1906
—*Hymn to Thaïs* (Borgström)   1909
—*Mummonsyntymäpäivänä* (Birthday song for Grandmother)   ?1919
—*Narciss* (Narcissus) (Gripenberg)   1925
—*Näcken* (The water-sprite) (Wennerberg) (with piano trio)   1888
—*Orgier* (Orgies) (Stenbäck)   1888–9
—*Segelfahrt* (Sailing) (Öhquist)   1899
—*Serenade* (Runeberg)   1888
—*Små flickorna* (The small girls) (Procopé)   1920
—*Souda, souda, sinisorsa* (Koskimies)   1899
—*Tanken* (The thought) (Runeberg) for two sopranos   1915
—*Vänskapens blomma* (The flower of friendship)[2] (Josephson)   1909

WORKS FOR CHOIR WITH ACCOMPANIMENT

7 *Kullervo* (see Works for Orchestra)
19 *Impromptu* for women's chorus and orchestra (Rydberg)[3]   1902, 1910
28 *Sandels*. Improvisation for male chorus and orchestra (Runeberg)   1898, 1915
29 *Snöfrid*. Improvisation for speaker, chorus and orchestra (Rydberg)   1900
30 *Islossningen i Uleå älv* (The breaking of the ice on the Oulu river). Improvisation for speaker, male voices and orchestra (Topelius)   1899[4]
31
    1.*Laulu Lemminkäiselle* (A song for Leimminkäinen) (Weijola), for male chorus and orchestra   1896
    2.*Har du mod?* (Have you courage?) (Wecksell), for male chorus and orchestra   1904, 1912
    3.*Atenarnes Sång* (Song of the Athenians or War song of Tyrtaeus) (Rydberg), for unison male voices, brass septet and percussion   1899
32 *Tulen synty* (The origin of fire or Ukko the firemaker) (*Kalevala*, *Runo* XLVII, 41–110), for baritone, male chorus and orchestra   1902, 1910
48 *Vapautettu kuningatar* (The captive queen) (Cajander), for mixed (or male) chorus and orchestra[5]   1906
91a *March of the Finnish Jaeger Battalion* (Nurmio), for male voices and piano (1917); arr. for orchestra   1918
91b *Scout-March* (*Partiolaisten marssi*) (Finne-Procopé), for mixed chorus and orchestra[6]   1921
92 *Oma maa* (Our native land) (Kallio), cantata for mixed chorus and orchestra   1918
93 *Jordens sång* (Song of the Earth) (Hemmer), cantata for mixed chorus and orchestra   1919

[1]Same poem but different setting from op. 37, no. 1.
[2]Same poem but completely different setting from op. 57, no. 7.
[3]Also known as *Livslust* and in its 1902 version as *Gossar och flickor* and in Rosa Newmarch's translation as *Thou, who guid'st the stars*.
[4]Sibelius later arranged this for female voices in about 1913–15.
[5]Composed to a German translation of Cajander and published as *Die gefangen Königin*; also known as *Siell'laulavi kuningatar* (There sings the queen) and *Snellmans Fest kantat*.
[6]In its arrangement for voices and piano of 1922 it is known as *De danske Spejderes March* (The Danish Scout March).

95 *Maan virsi* (Hymn of the Earth), cantata for mixed chorus and orchestra (Leino) 1920

110 *Väinön virsi* (Väinämöinens Song) (*Kalevala, Runo* XVIII 385–434), cantata for mixed chorus and orchestra 1926

—*Den höga himlen och den vida jorden*, for male voices and organ[1] 1926, ?1946–8

—Cantata for the Coronation of Nicholas II (Cajander), for mixed chorus and orchestra 1896

—Cantata for the University Ceremonies of 1894 (Lönnbohm-Leino), for soprano, baritone, mixed chorus and orchestra 1894

—Cantata for the University Ceremonies of 1897 (Forsman-Koskimies), for soprano, baritone, mixed chorus and orchestra 1897

—*Karjalan osa* (Karelia's fate) (Patriotic March) (Nurminen), for unison male voices and piano 1930

—Three Songs for American Schools 1913

    1.Autumn song (Dixon), duet with piano

    2.The sun upon the lake is low (Sir Walter Scott), for unaccompanied mixed voices

    3.A cavalry catch (Fiona Macleod), for unison male voices and piano

—*Upp genom luften* (Up through the air) (Atterbom), for mixed chorus and piano ?1888

—*Hvi kysser Du Fader min fästmö här?* (Why, father, do you kiss my sweetheart here?), for women's voices and piano 1890–1

WORKS FOR A CAPPELLA CHOIR

Op.

(14) *Rakastava* (The Lover), for baritone and male voices 1894

    1.*Miss'on kussa minum hyväni?* (Where is my beloved?) (*Kanteletar* I: 173)

    2.*Eilaa, eila* (My beloved's path) (*Kanteletar* I: 174)

    3.*Hyvää iltaa lintuseni* . . . (Good evening, my little bird) (*Kanteletar* I: 122)

    4.*Käsi kaulaan, lintuseni* . . . Put your hand on my shoulder (*Kanteletar* I: 122 contd)

  arr. with string orchestra 1894; arr. soprano, baritone and mixed chorus 1898

  See also Works for Orchestra

18

    1.*Sortunut ääni* (The broken voice) (*Kanteletar* I: 57) for male voices (also known as op. 18, no.7) 1899

    2.*Terve kuu* (Hail, O Moon) (Boruttau), for male voices (also known as op. 18, no. 8) 1901

    3.*Venematka* (The boat journey) (*Kalevala, Runo* XL: 1–16), for male voices (also known as op. 18, no. 9) 1893; arr. mixed choir 1914

    4.*Saarella palaa* (Fire on the island) (*Kanteletar* I: 186), for male voices (also known as op. 18, no. 3)[2] 1895

    5.*Metsämiehen laulu* (The woodman's song) (Kivi), for male voices 1899

    6.*Sydämeni laulu* (Song of my heart), for male voices 1898; arr. mixed choir 1904

    7.*Isänmalle* (To my country) (Cajander), for male voices 1899; rev. version for mixed choir 1900; arr. for male voices 1908

[1]Also known as *Suur' olet Herra* (You are mighty, O Lord).
[2]Also known as *Työnsa kumpasellaki* (Each had his work).

—*Veljeni vierailla mailla* (My brothers abroad), for male voices (also known as op. 18, no. 2)   1904

—*Min rastas raata* (The thrush's toiling) (*Kanteletar*: 219), for mixed voices (also known as op. 18, no. 4)   ?1898

21 Hymn (25.V.1896). Natus in curas (Gustafsson), for male voices (also known as op. 21, no. 2)   1896, ?1898

23 See Works for Choir with Accompaniment

    2.*Tuuli Tuudittele* (The wind rocks), for soprano, baritone and mixed chorus   ?1899

26 See Works for Orchestra

    7.*Finlandia-Hymn* (Koskenniemi), for male voices (almost indistinguishable from op. 113, no. 12)   1940 (also arr. mixed voices   1940)

84 Five Part-songs

    1.*Herr Lager och skön fager* (Mr Lager and the Fair One) (Fröding) for male voices   1914

    2.*På berget* (On the mountain) (Gripenberg), for male voices   1915

    3.*Ett drömackord* (A dream chord) (Fröding)   1915

    4.*Eviga Eros* (Eternal Eros) (Gripenberg), for baritone and male voices   1915

    5.*Till havs* (At sea) (Jonatan Reuter)   1917

108

    1.*Humoreski* (Humoresque) (Larin-Kyösti), for male voices   1925

    2.*Ne pitkän matkan kulkijat* (Wanderers on the long way) (Larin-Kyösti), for male voices   1925

113 Masonic Ritual Music, for male voices, piano and harmonium

    1.Opening hymn

    2.*Suloinen aate* (Thoughts be our comfort) (Schober trans. Leino)

    3.*Kulkue ja hymn* (Procession and hymn) (Chao trans. Tikkanen)

    4.*Kulkue Trio I – Trio II* (Processions and trios) (Goethe)

    5.*On kaunis maa* (sic) (How fair is the earth) (Sibelius)

    6.*Salem* (Onward ye brethren) (Rydberg)

    7.*Varje själ som längtan brinner* (Whosoever has a love) (Rydberg), all   1927

    8.*Veljessvirsi* (Ode to fraternity) (Sario)   1946, 1948

    9.*Ylistyshymni* (Song of praise) (Sario)   1946, 1948

    10.*Marche funèbre*   1927

    11.Ode   1926[1]

    12.*Finlandia-Hymn* (Wainö Sola) for male voices (almost indistinguishable from op. 26, no. 7)   1938

—*Aamusumussa*[2] (Morning mist) (J. H. Erkko) for children's choir   1896; arr. mixed choir   ?1898; arr. for male voices   1920

—*Ack, hör du Fröken Gyllenborg* (arr. of ballade) for mixed choir   1888–89

—*Brusande rusar en våg* (Surging the wave rushes forward) (Gösta Schybergson) for male voices   1918

—Cantata to words of Walter von Konow for female voices (*Härliga gåvor Herre Du oss giver*) (Great gifts has the Lord bestowed on us)   1911

—Carminalia (Latin songs 'from the 18th century'), for students, arr. for mixed choir, female voices with harmonium or piano   1898

    1.Ecce novum gaudium

    2.Angelus emittitur

---

[1]*Den höga himlen och den vita jorden* listed by Fabian Dahlström as possibly op. 107.
[2]Also known as *Päiv' ei pääse* (The day is not ended).

3.In stadio laboris
—*Den 25 oktober 1902.* Till Thérèse Hahl (Nils Wasastjerna). Two completely
    different settings,[1] both 1902
—*Drömmarna* (The Dreams) (Jonatan Reuter), for mixed choir   1917
—*Ej med klagan* (Till minnet av Albert Edelfelt 24.8.1905) (Not with lamenting
    shall your memory be celebrated) (Runeberg) for mixed choir   1905
—*Ensam i dunkla skogarnas famn* (Alone in the depths of the forest) for mixed
    choir ?1888
—*Fridolins dårskap* (Fridolin's folly) (Karlfelt), for male voices   1917
—*Hur blekt är allt . . .* (How pale it all is), for mixed choir ?1888
—*Isänmalle* (To my country) (Cajander), for male voices   1899, rev. version for
    mixed choir 1900, arr. for male voices   1908 (see also op. 18, no. 1)
—*Johdantovurolauluja* (Three Antiphons)   1925
—*Jone havsfärd* (Jonah's voyage) (Karlfelt), for male voices   1918
—*Kansakoululaisten marssi* (also known as *Uno Cygnaeuksen Muistolle*) (Primary
    schoolchildren's march) (Onnen Pekka, pseudonym)
—*Kotikaipaus* (Nostalgia) (von Konow), for female voices   1902
—*Koulutie* (The way to school) (Koskenniemi), for mixed voices   1916
—*Kuutamolla* (In the moonlight) (Suonio), for male voices   1916
—*Laulun mahti* (The power of the song) (*Kuurinmaata kunialla*; arr. of song by
    Jazeps Withol)   1895
—*Likhet* (Alikeness)[2] (Runeberg), for male voices   1922
—*Listen to the Water Mill*, for choir in unison and also arr. for mixed
    voices   1906–7
—*Min rastas raata* (The thrush's toiling) (*Kanteletar*: 219), for mixed voices (see
    also op. 18, no. 4) ?1898
—*När sig våren åter föder . . .* (When spring once more comes to life) ?1888
—*On Lapsonen syntynyt meille* (also known as *Nyt seimelle pienoisen Lapsen*)
    (Christmas song) (A. V. Jaakkola; alternative text by Forsman) for mixed
    choir 1928–9
—*Siltavahti* (The guard of the bridge) (Wainö Sola), for male voices   1928
—*Skolsång* (School song) (Nino Runeberg)
—*Syddskårsmarsch* (or *Syddskårssång*) (Song of the Defence Corps) (Nino
    Runeberg), for male voices with piano ad.lib.   1925–9
—*Tanke, se, hur fågeln svingar* (Imagine, see how the bird swoops) (Runeberg), for
    mixed choir ?1888
—*Työkansan marssi* (Workers' march) (J. H. Erkko), for mixed choir   1896
—*Ute hörs stormen* (Outside the storm is raging) (Gösta Schybergson) for male
    voices 1918
—*Uusmaalaisten laulu* (Song of the people of Uusimaa) (K. Terhi) for male
    voices 1912
—*Veljeni vierailla mailla* (My brothers abroad) (see also op. 18, no. 2)
—*Viipurin Laulu-Veikkojen kunniamarssi* (March of the singing brothers of
    Viipuri) (Eerola)   1920
—*Viipurin Laulu-Veikkojen kunniamarssi* (different setting)   1929

[1]Also known as *Sången klang i barnaåren* or *Lauloit piennä*.
[2]Sometimes translated as 'Resemblance'.

OPERAS

Op.

—*Veneen luominen* (The Building of the Boat). Sketches only (to a libretto of Sibelius himself). 1893

—*Jungfrun i tornet* (The Maiden in the Tower). Opera in one act (libretto Rafael Herzberg).

MELODRAMAS

Op.

15 *Skogsrået* (The Wood-Nymph), for piano, two horns and strings (to accompany verses of Rydberg) 1894. See also Works for Orchestra

29 *Snöfrid* 1900. See Works for Orchestra

—*Snöfrid* (to accompany verses of Rydberg) with accompaniment (Lost) 1893

—*O, Om du sett* (Oh! If you had seen) (Hackzell), for reciter and piano. Fragment ?1888–9

—*Ett ensamt skidspår* (A lonely ski trail). Recitation with piano to words of Gripenberg[1] 1925

—*Grefvinnans konterfej* (The Countess's portrait) (Topelius), for reciter and strings[2] 1906

—*Svartsjukans nätter* (Nights of jealousy) (Runeberg), for reciter, violin, cello and piano 1888

[1]Subsequently arranged for harp and string orchestra in 1948.
[2]Also known as *Porträtterna* (The portraits).

Appendix C
Personalia

Ackté, Aino (1876–1944), Finnish soprano who made her debut as Marguerite in *Faust* at the Opéra and sang frequently both in Paris and New York. She sang the role of Salome in Strauss's opera at Covent Garden under Beecham in 1908. In 1911 she and Fazer were instrumental in founding the Finnish Opera, whose director she later became. Some idea of her brilliance can be gained from *Luonnotar*, which Sibelius wrote for her.

Ahlqvist, August Engelbrekt (1826–89), Finnish poet and philologist. For many years professor of Finnish at Helsinki University, he published his poetry under the pseudonym Oksanen.

Becker, Albert Ernst Anton (1834–99), German composer and theorist. From 1881 until his death Becker taught composition at the Scharwenka Conservatoire, Berlin.

Beecham, Sir Thomas (1879–1961). The greatest British conductor of his day who founded no fewer than four orchestras during his long career, including the London Philharmonic and the Royal Philharmonic. A great Mozart interpreter, he was also a lifelong champion of Richard Strauss and Delius. He made the first recordings of many Sibelius works for the HMV Sibelius Society and frequently programmed Sibelius's work in the concert hall.

Bobrikov, Nikolai Ivanovich (1839–1904), Russian governor-general of Finland from 1898 until his death. His period of rule marked a distinct hardening of Russia's attitude to Finland, and these opppressive years, known as the *ofärdsåren*, are identified with Bobrikov's policies. He was assassinated in 1904 in the Finnish Senate.

Boult, Sir Adrian (1889–1983). One of the leading British conductors of his day and a formidable champion of such composers as Elgar, Holst and Vaughan Williams. He conducted the first performances of Berg's *Wozzeck*, Busoni's *Doktor Faust* and much contemporary music during his years as founder-conductor of the BBC Symphony Orchestra (1930–50). He made the first recordings of *Night Ride and Sunrise* and *The Oceanides* and recorded all the tone-poems with the London Philharmonic Orchestra in the 1950s. He consistently included Sibelius works in BBC programmes.

Cajander, Paul Emil (1846–1913), Finnish poet and translator. Lecturer in Finnish at Helsinki University from 1890 until 1912. His work as a translator overshadowed his original work and his poems were not collected until after his death. He is best known for his Finnish translation of Shakespeare, but he also translated Runeberg, Topelius and Wecksell from the Swedish.

Carpelan, Baron Axel (1858–1919). Although an aristocrat, Carpelan was not a man of means. He established a lifelong friendship with Sibelius and raised money to support him. He maintained a long correspondence with both Sibelius and the Swedish poet, Viktor Rydberg, and was the dedicatee of the Second Symphony. In 1985 his great nephew, the poet Bo Carpelan, published a fictional diary, *Axel*, which met with great acclaim.

Cohen, Harriet (1895–1967). British pianist who championed the music of Arnold Bax. Bartók composed the last book of his *Mikrokosmos* for her. She also maintained a long association and correspondence with Sibelius over the years.

Damrosch, Walter (1862–1950), German-born conductor and composer who settled in America. He conducted the New York Philharmonic and other American orchestras and was for some years musical adviser to the NBC. He included a number of Sibelius works in his programmes, and commissioned *Tapiola*.

Downes, Olin (1886–1955), American music critic, first of the *Boston Post* and subsequently the *New York Times*. An expert on Sibelius, he was awarded the Order of the White Rose of Finland, and when the composer's seventy-fifth birthday was celebrated in a broadcast, Downes was chosen as speaker and Toscanini as conductor. His writings include *The Lure of Music* (1918), *Symphonic Broadcasts* (1932) and *Symphonic Masterpieces* (1936).

Ekman, Ida (1875–1942), Finnish soprano. She studied at the Helsinki Music Institute and in Vienna and Paris, where she sang when the Finnish orchestra visited the French capital in 1900. After engagements at the Nuremberg opera she left the stage to devote herself to *Lieder*. She was the first Finnish singer to introduce Sibelius's songs to the Continent.

Ekman, Karl (1895–1961). Finnish writer on music, son of the above and the pianist, Karl Ekman (1869–1947), a pupil of Busoni and friend of Sibelius. He published the first Finnish biography to be translated into English.

Faltin, Friedrich Richard (1835–1918), Finnish musician of German origin who was for many years a dominant figure in Finnish musical life. After teaching at Viipuri (Viborg) he took up an appointment in Helsinki as conductor of the *Nya Teaterns Orkester* and organist of the Nicolai church. Together with Wegelius he took part in the foundation of the Helsinki Music Institute.

Flodin, Karl Theodore (1858–1918), Finnish critic and composer. A pupil of Faltin, he subsequently studied in Leipzig before acting as a critic in Helsinki during the latter part of the nineteenth century. He left the *Helsingfors Posten* in 1908, and spent the last years of his life in Buenos Aires.

Fougstedt, Nils-Erik (1910–1961), Finnish composer and conductor, from 1944 conductor of the Finnish Radio Orchestra. His works include three symphonies, a cello concerto, and chamber music.

Fröding, Gustaf (1860–1911), Swedish poet from Värmland in Central Sweden. After studying at Upsala, which he left without taking a degree, he returned to Värmland. His nervous health was precarious, and he spent over six years in Upsala hospital. In early years he was influenced by Goethe, Heine, Byron and Burns. One of his most important stylistic features is a skilful use of alliteration and assonance, as well as the mastery of rhythm which gives his poetry its distinct musical character. One of his most famous lyrics, *Ingalill*, was set by Sibelius and is known by its opening words, *Säv, säv, susa*.

Fuchs, Robert (1847–1927), Austrian composer and teacher. Fuchs studied in Vienna, where he taught composition from 1875 until 1912. His works include operas, *Die Königsbraut* (1889), *Die Teufelsglocken* (1892), choral works, three symphonies and a quantity of chamber music.

Furuhjelm, Erik Gustav (1883–1964), Finnish composer and critic. Furuhjelm studied with Wegelius and then with Robert Fuchs in Vienna. His work includes two symphonies and chamber music. He was for many years active as a critic for *Dagens Tidning*, and the author of *Jean Sibelius, hans tondiktning och drag ur hans liv* (1915), a pioneer study of the composer.

Gallén-Kallela, Axel (1865–1931), Finnish painter who, like Sibelius, was inspired by the legends recounted in the *Kalevala*.

Goldmark, Karl (1830–1915), Austro-Hungarian composer and teacher. Best known nowadays for his *Rustic Wedding* symphony, the overture *In Spring* and the first of his two violin concertos, he also wrote six operas, two on English subjects.

Gray, Cecil (1895–1951). Influential British writer and composer. He wrote an important monograph on Sibelius in 1931 and *The Symphonies of Sibelius* four years later.

Gripenberg, Bertel (1878–1947), Finnish poet. After the publication of some early erotic poems, he became one of the mouthpieces of Finnish nationalism in the early years of this century, and took part in the Finnish war of independence in 1918. He was also a vigorous supporter of the cause of the Swedish-speaking minority of Finland.

Heifetz, Jascha (1901–88). The greatest violinist of his age with an unmatched technical command and golden tone, who made the first recording of the Sibelius concerto in 1936 with Sir Thomas Beecham, and another with the Chicago Symphony Orchestra in 1961.

Järnefelt, Armas (1869–1958), Finnish composer and conductor. Sibelius's brother-in-law. After studies in Helsinki with Wegelius and Busoni, Järnefelt went to Berlin and then to Paris, where he studied with Massenet. From 1907 until 1932 he was conductor of the Royal Opera, Stockholm, after which he held conducting appointments in Helsinki. He was famous in the Scandinavian countries as a Beethoven conductor and for his readings of Mozart and Wagner operas. As a composer his larger works were overshadowed by the popularity of the *Berceuse* and *Praeludium*.

Järnefelt, Arvid (1861–1932), Finnish author, brother of above. He was much influenced by Tolstoy, whose theories he attempted to apply in Finland. His output includes several plays and novels, many of which are patriotic in character.

Järnefelt, Eero Nikolai (1863–1937). After studies in St Petersburg, Eero (Erik) developed into one of the most gifted talents of his generation. Although his art broke no new ground and his contribution to Finnish painting does not match that of Gallén-Kallela, he was a master of the idyllic Finnish landscape and an excellent portrait painter.

Josephson, Ernst Abraham (1851–1906), Swedish painter and poet. After studies in Stockholm he went to Paris, where he came under the influence of Manet. He spent most of his life in France, and made visits to Italy and Spain. His collections of verse include *Svarta rosor* (1888) and *Gula rosor* (1896).

Kajanus, Robert (1856–1933), Finnish conductor and composer. He began his studies at Helsinki with Talsin and Niemann, continuing in Leipzig under Hans Richter. After studies in Paris with Svendsen he returned in 1882 to found the Helsinki Philharmonic Society Orchestra, who gave regular concerts devoted to the standard classics. In 1900 he toured the principal European capitals with the orchestra. In 1919 he initiated the Nordic Music Festival, which since then has become a triennial event. He was the foremost Sibelius interpreter of his time, and made a number of historic recordings in the thirties subsidized by the Finnish Government. Sibelius dedicated *Pohjola's Daughter* to him. He wrote a modest quantity of music, including the *Aino* symphony, two Finnish rhapsodies and a sinfonietta.

Karajan, Herbert von (1908–1989). Of all the celebrated conductors of the day, none was a more consistent champion of Sibelius's music. The sheer range and refinement of sonority he produced have few parallels, and among the conductors of our time his achievement on record is prodigious. He first conducted the Sixth Symphony in Stockholm in the mid-1930s and went on to record no fewer than four versions of the Fifth and *Tapiola*, and three each of the Fourth and Sixth Symphonies.

Karlfeldt, Eric Axel (1864–1931), Swedish poet from Dalecarlia. Generally regarded as the leading poet of his day, and for many years secretary of the Swedish Academy. He was awarded the Nobel Prize for Literature posthumously in 1931.

Koussevitzky, Serge (1874–1951). One of the greatest twentieth-century conductors and one of Sibelius's greatest interpreters. Like Beecham, Kajanus and Karagan, he was closely identified in the public mind with Sibelius though unlike them he was a relatively late convert to his cause. Born in Vyzhni-Volochok about 200 miles to the north-west of Moscow, Koussevitzky learned to play the trumpet and studied the double-bass. He joined the Bolshoi Orchestra in 1894, later acquiring a formidable reputation as a virtuoso. After his marrage in 1905 to Nathalie Ushkov, a wealthy heiress, he embarked on a dual career as a soloist and conductor. In 1924 he became conductor of the Boston Symphony Orchestra and from the mid-1920s onwards championed Sibelius's music, much of which he recorded. His readings of the Seventh Symphony and *Tapiola* were particularly outstanding.

Lambert, Constant (1905–51), English composer, conductor and critic. His most outstanding works are *Summer's Last Will and Testament* and the popular *Horoscope* and *Rio Grande*. A brilliant ballet conductor, he directed the first performances of many new works and increased the appreciation of ballet in the thirties and forties. His book, *Music Ho!*, which deals appreciatively with Sibelius, was an influential factor in the 'cult' of Sibelius during the thirties.

Legge, Walter (1906–79), British record producer who founded the HMV Sibelius Society, the Hugo Wolf Society etc. during the 1930s. He was responsible for many Sibelius recordings after the war with Karajan and Kletzki and the Philharmonia Orchestra, which he founded in 1946.

Lönnrot, Elias (1802–84), Lönnrot collected a vast quantity of folk-literature during the first half of the nineteenth century, and published numerous key-works in Finnish literature, including *Kantele* (1829–31), poems and songs collected in the Finnish Karelia, the more celebrated *Kalevala* (1835–1836) and a collection of lyrics called *Kanteletar* (1840).

Lybeck, Mikael (1864–1925), Finnish poet, novelist and dramatist. One of the finest lyrical poets of the nineties in Finland, the *ofärdsåren*, when Russia increased her pressure on Finnish life; many of his poems express the anxieties of those years. His plays include a study of Schopenhauer and *Ödlan* (The Lizard), to which Sibelius provided music.

Mannerheim, Carl Gustav (1867–1951), Field Marshal of Finland. Commanded the Finnish forces in the Second World War (the defensive line across the Karelian isthmus was named after him). President in 1944–6.

Marx, Adolf Bernhard (1795–1866), German scholar, author and composer. His most important work is the four-volume *Lehre von der musikalischen Komposition* (Leipzig, 1837–47). He also published a study of Beethoven's keyboard music.

Neveu, Ginette (1919–49), French violinist, a grand-niece of Widor, who made a much admired recording of the Sibelius concerto in 1946, three years before her death in an air accident off the Azores.

Newman, Ernest (1868–1959). Distinguished British critic and author who was among the first to recognize Sibelius in the early years of the century and proved a consistent champion of his work.

Newmarch, Rosa (1857–1940), English writer on music. She visited Russia in 1897 and worked at the Imperial Public Library in St Petersburg under Vladimir Stassov. She was an energetic champion of Russian and Czech music, publishing studies of Tchaikovsky and Borodin and a translation of Hoffmeister's book on Dvořák. She was a prolific writer of programme notes and also the author of a history of Czech music. She corresponded with Sibelius for many years and did a great deal to popularize his music in England.

Oksanen. See *Ahlqvist*.

Ormandy, Eugene (1899–1985). During his long partnership with the Philadelphia Orchestra, which he brought to perfection, Ormandy regularly scheduled the Sibelius symphonies and made many recordings of them.

Pacius, Fredrik (1809–91), Finnish composer of German origin. A pupil of Spohr, an excellent violinist and a musician of considerable culture, Pacius was one of the dominating musical figures of nineteenth-century Finland.

Parmet (Pergament-Parmet), Simon (1897–1969), Finnish conductor. After studying in Petrograd, Helsinki and Berlin, he spent some years working in German opera houses. Later he went to America conducting in various parts of the country and remaining there until 1948, when he returned to Finland. His study of Sibelius's symphonies appeared in 1955.

Paul, Adolf (1863–1942), Finnish author. Born in Sweden, Paul moved to Finland as a child, though most of his adult life was spent in Germany. His novel *En bok om en människa* (1891) shows the influence of Strindberg, and includes a character alleged by some writers to portray some of Sibelius's traits. A second book, *The Ripper* (1892), was banned at the time on account of its supposedly erotic character. His plays include *King Christian II*, to which Sibelius provided a score; most of his dramatic works are in German. His output also includes a certain amount of poetry. During his later years he was an admirer of the Nazis.

Procopé, Hjalmar (1868–1927), Finnish poet and dramatist. Influenced by the poets of the nineties, Procopé was a writer of considerable intellectual distinction and, like Gripenberg, a spokesman of the Swedish-speaking minority. He was an outspoken champion of the independence movement. His works include collections of poems and plays, including *Belshazzars gästabud* (1905), *Fädrans anda* (1909) and *Inspektor på Siltala* (1915).

Ringbom, Nils-Eric (1907–1988), Finnish musicologist and composer. After studies at Åbo and in France he worked as a critic. He held the post of managing director of the Helsinki Orchestra. As a composer his work comprises three symphonies and a wind sextet, together with other chamber works. His critical writings include a history of Helsinki's orchestral life (1882–1932) and a study of Sibelius published in 1948.

Runeberg, Johan Ludvig (1804–77), Finnish poet. Generally regarded as one of the finest poets writing in the Swedish language during the nineteenth century. After studying at Åbo he was appointed lecturer in classical languages at Helsinki. His poetry is noted for its lyricism and dignity of feeling. His first original collection of lyrical verse was published in 1830, and his most important works include a number of epic poems like *Nadezhda* and *Kung Fjalar*, which followed during the forties. *Fänrik Ståls Sägner* (1848, 1860) is regarded as one of the classics of Swedish literature.

Rydberg, Abraham Viktor (1828–95), Swedish poet, philosopher and historian. His first lyrical poems date from the 1860s. His work includes a translation of *Faust*, a number of historical novels, several studies of German and Scandinavian mythology as well as a quantity of poetry. Among his most famous poems is the cantata written for the quatercentenary celebrations of Uppsala University in 1877. In his last years he was professor of the history of art and aesthetics at Stockholm University.

Schnéevoigt, Georg (1872–1947), Finnish conductor. Studied at Helsinki and Leipzig, becoming a pupil of Fuchs in Vienna. For some years he was a cellist in the Helsinki Orchestra, and taught that instrument at the conservatoire. In 1901 he conducted at Riga and succeeded Weingartner in a Munich appointment. From 1914 to 1924 he was conductor of the Stockholm *Konsertförenings Orkester*, and founded the Oslo Philharmonic. He conducted in Oslo and Los Angeles on numerous occasions before succeeding Kajanus in Helsinki. He conducted the Finnish National Orchestra (as it was then called) on a visit to this country in 1934, when he recorded the Sixth Symphony of Sibelius.

Sibelius, Christian (1869–1922), Sibelius's brother. A fine cellist, Christian took part in public concerts with some success as a youngster. He studied medicine in Helsinki as well as music, and completed his medical studies in 1897, when he gained a doctorate. He was in charge of Lappvikens Mental Hospital from 1904 until his death, and was professor of psychiatry there.

Snellman, Johan Vilhelm (1806–81), Finnish writer, statesman and philosopher, who played an important part in Finnish national life during the nineteenth century.

Stagnelius, Erik Johan (1793–1823), Swedish poet and author whose reputation soared after his early death. His works include an epic poem, *Vladimir den Store* (1817), and a collection of poems, *Liljor i Saron*, together with a tragedy, *Bacchanterna* (1823).

Stenhammar, Wilhelm (1871–1927), Swedish composer. A great admirer of both Sibelius and Nielsen, Stenhammar was undoubtedly the finest Swedish composer of his time. His output includes two symphonies, two piano concertos and six quartets. He was an enthusiastic conductor and directed performances of Sibelius's works in *Göteborgs Konsertförening*. The Sixth Symphony is dedicated to him.

Stokowski, Leopold (1882–1977). During his long career with the Philadelphia and other orchestras, Stokowski was a consistent Sibelian and made the very first recording of the Fourth Symphony.

Tavaststjerna, Karl August (1860–98), Finnish author and poet. His first collection of poetry appeared in 1883, *För morgonbris*, which already showed an independence of such models as Runeberg and Topelius. Tavaststjerna travelled widely and was cosmopolitan in outlook. Despite the cool reception of his work in Finland he was an outspoken patriot, and must be reckoned among the leading patriotic writers of the latter part of the century.

Topelius, Zacharias (1818–98), Finnish romantic poet. For many years he was editor of a Helsinki newspaper, and later became professor of history at Helsinki University. His most important prose work, *Fältskärns berätelser*, strove to foster a sense of national self-consciousness, and the novels of Walter Scott were the model on which he built. In later years he wrote mostly stories and poems for children.

Toscanini, Arturo (1867–1957). Legendary Italian conductor who made his début in Rio da Janeiro in 1886 conducting *Aida*, subsequently conducting the premières of *La Bohème* and *Pagliacci*. He first conducted *The Swan of Tuonela* in the first years of the century and was a noted champion of the Fourth Symphony. His Sibelius repertory was confined to *En Saga, Pohjola's Daughter, Lemminkäinen's Homeward Journey, Finlandia* and the Second Symphony.

Vecsey, Franz (1893–1935), Hungarian violinist. A pupil of Hubay and Joachim, Vecsey made his début internationally at the tender age of ten (1903) and was regarded as one of the greatest masters of his instrument during the early decades of the present century. Although the first performances of both the original and revised versions of the Sibelius concerto were given by lesser-known players, Viktor Nováček and Karl Halir respectively, the work is in fact dedicated to Vecsey.

Wecksell, Josef Julius (1838–1907), Finnish poet. He is noted for his lyrics, many of which reflect the influence of Heine, and for his play *Daniel Hjort*, one of the key dramatic works written in Swedish before Strindberg.

Wegelius, Martin (1846–1906), Finnish composer, pupil of Faltin. Wegelius was active in Helsinki both as conductor and critic. He founded the Helsinki Music Institute and became its first director. His work includes a choral piece, *Julnatten*, an overture to *Daniel Hjort* and a setting of Runeberg's cantata (1878). An influential teacher, he was also the author of a history of Western music.

Wennerberg, Gunnar (1817–1901), Swedish composer and poet associated largely with the *Gluntarne*, songs and poems of student life in Uppsala.

Wood, Sir Henry (1869–1944). Founder of London's *Promenade Concerts*, which he conducted until his death, Sir Henry Wood was a strong champion of new music and in particular was a consistent advocate of Sibelius, whose music he introduced to London as early as 1902.

Appendix D

Bibliography

Abraham, Gerald (ed.), *Sibelius: a Symposium* (London, 1947, 1952)
Aleksandrova, Vera & Brontin, Jelena, *Jan Sibelius* (Moscow, 1963)
Andersson, Otto, 'Jean Sibelius' (*Tidning för musik*, Helsinki, 1916)
—— *Jean Sibelius i Amerika* (Åbo, 1955)
—— *Jean Sibelius och Svenska teatern* (Åbo, 1956)
——, 'När Jean Sibelius erhöll statsstipendium' (*Hufvudstadsbladet*, Helsinki, 3 Jan 1957)
——, 'Sibelius och Kajanus som konkurrenter' (*Hufvudstadsbladet*, Helsinki, 8 Dec 1956)
Arnold, Elliot, *Finlandia: the Story of Sibelius* (New York, 1941, 1951)

Balogh, Pál, *Jean Sibelius* (Budapest, Gondolat 1961)
Bantock, Granville, 'Jean Sibelius', (*Monthly Musical Record*, London, Dec 1935)
Beecham, Thomas, 'Sibelius, the Craftsman', (*Living Age*, London, Feb 1939)
Berglund, Paavo, *A comparative study of the printed score and the manuscript of the Seventh Symphony of Sibelius* (Turku, 1970)
Blom, Eric, 'Sibelius' in Cobbett's *Cyclopedic Survey of Chamber Music*. (See also Abraham, 'The Piano Music')
Blum, Fred, *Jean Sibelius: an International Bibliography on the Occasion of the Centennial Celebrations 1965* (Detroit, 1965)
Brodin, Gereon, 'Jean Sibelius' livsverk', (*Vår Sång*, Stockholm, vol. xiii, 1940)
Brull, Erich, *Jean Sibelius* (Leipzig, 1986)

Cardus, Sir Neville, 'Sibelius', in *Ten Composers* (London, 1945)
Cherniavsky, David, 'The Use of Germ Motives by Sibelius' (*Music & Letters*, vol. xxiii, London, 1942)
——, 'Two Unpublished Tone-poems by Sibelius' (*Musical Times*, 1949, p. 272)
——, 'Sibelius's Tempo Corrections' (*Music & Letters*, vol. xxxi, 1950, p. 53)
——, 'Sibelius and Finland' (*Musical Times*, 1950) (See also Abraham.)
Coad, Philip, *Bruckner and Sibelius* (Diss., University of Cambridge, 1985)
—— 'Sibelius', in *Companion to the Symphony*, ed. Robert Layton (London, 1993)
Collins, M. S., *The Orchestral music of Sibelius* (Diss., University of Leeds, 1973)
Collins, Stuart, 'Germ Motives and Guff' (*Music Review*, vol. xxiii, 1962)

Dahlström, Fabian, *The works of Jean Sibelius* (Catalogue) (Helsinki, 1987)
Davie, Cedric Thrope, 'Sibelius's Piano Sonatinas' (*Tempo*, London, March 1945)
Dernoncourt, Sylvie, *Sibelius* (Madrid, 1985)
Desmond, Astra. See under Abraham, 'The Songs'
Diktonius, Elmer, *Opus 12, Musik* (Helsinki, 1933)
Downes, Olin, *Sibelius the Symphonist* (New York, 1956)

Sibelius

Dyson, George, 'Sibelius' (*Musical Times*, 1936, p. 987)

Ekman, Karl, *Jean, Sibelius: en konstnärs liv och personlighet* (Helsinki, 1935, 1936, 1956, 1959)
    Translated as *J.S.: his life and Personality* (London, 1936; New York, 1938, 1946)
Elliott, J. H., 'Jean Sibelius: a modern engima' (*The Chesterian*, London, vol. xii, no. 92)
——, 'The Sixth Symphony of Sibelius' (*Music & Letters*, London, vol. xvii, no. 3, July 1936)

Flodin, Karl, *Finska Musiker* (Helsinki, 1900)
Fougstedt, Nils-Erik, 'Sibelius' tonsättningar till Rydbergs texter' (*Musikvärlden*, Stockholm, vol. x, 1945, p. 16)
Friederich, J., 'Wegbereiter seiner Nation' (*Die Musik*, Berlin, vol. xxviii, 1935)
Frosterus, Sigurd, *Stålåldernas janusansikte och andra essäer* (Helsinki, 1935)
Funtek, L., 'Jean Sibelius' konstnärskap' (*Musikern*, Stockholm, vol. xviii, 1925)
Furuhjelm, Erik, *Jean Sibelius, hans tondiktning och drag ur hans liv* (Borgå, 1916)
    Translated into Finnish by Leevi Madetoja (Porvoo, 1916)
——, 'Jean Sibelius' (*Ord och Bild*, vol. xxiii, Stockholm, 1914)

Gerschefski, Peter Edwin, *The thematic, temporal and dynamic processes in the Symphonies of Jean Sibelius* (Diss., Florida State University, 1962)
Gilie, G., *Jean Sibelius som orkesterdirigent* (*Musikern*, Stockholm, 1925)
Goddard, Scott, 'Sibelius's Second Symphony' (*Music & Letters*, London, April 1931)
Göhler, G., 'Jean Sibeliuksen varhaisemmat orkesterisävellykset' ('The Earlier Orchestral Compositions of Sibelius') (*Kalevalaseuran vuosikirja*, Helsinki, 1926)
Gould, Glenn, 'The Piano Music of Jean Sibelius' in *The Glenn Gould Reader*, Tim Page, ed. (London 1984)
Gorohova, Ludmilla, *Jan Sibelius* (Moscow, 1973)
Gray, Cecil, *Sibelius* (London, 1931, 1934, 1945)
——, *Sibelius: the Symphonies* (London, 1935)
——, 'Sibelius, or Music and the Future' (*The Nation and Athenaeum*, 24 Dec, 1927)
——, *Musical Chairs.* (London, 1948, pp. 255–60)
Gripenberg, Bertel, *Till Jean Sibelius på 70-årsdagen* (Helsinki, 1935)

Haapanen, T., 'Den nationella betydelsen av Jean Sibelius' konst' (*Musikern*, Stockholm, 1925)
——, *Piirteitä Jean Sibeliuksen elämästä ja taiteesta* (Aspects of Sibelius's Life and Art) (Helsinki, 1925)
——, 'Jean Sibelius, elämä ja merkitys' ('Sibelius: his Life and Importance') (*Kulttuurin saavutuksia*, Helsinki, 1946)
Hannikainen, Ilmari, 'Hieman Sibeliuksen pianosävellyksistä' (*Suomen musik-kilehti*, Helsinki, 1935)
——, *Sibelius and the Development of Finnish Music* (London, 1948)
Hauch, Gunnar, *Jean Sibelius* (Copenhagen, 1915)
Helasvuo, Veikko 'Sibelius and the Music of Finland'. (Helsinki, 1952, 1957)

Hemming, Aare, *Jean Sibeliuksen Lemminkäis-sarjan kaksi osaa Lemminkäinen ja Saaren neidot sekä Lemminkäinen Tuonelassa: Muotoja teema-analyysiä* (Two Parts of Sibelius's *Lemminkäinen* Suite (Nos. 1 and 3): formal and thematic analysis) (Helsinki University, 1956)[1]

Herbage, Julian, 'Jean Sibelius', in *The Symphony*, Ralph Hill, ed. (London, 1949)

Hili, W. G., 'Some Aspects of Form in the Symphonies of Sibelius' (*Music Review*, vol. x, 1949)

Howell, Tim, *Jean Sibelius: Progress techniques in the symphonies and tone-poems* (New York, 1989)

Ingman, O., *Jean Sibelius: Voces Intimae* (Helsinki University, 1958)

Jacobs, R. L., 'Sibelius' Lemminkäinen and the Maidens of Saari' (*Music Review*, vol. xxiv, 1963)

Jalas, Jussi, 'Valse triste och musiken till "Kuolema"' (*Musikvärlden*, Stockholm, May 1948)

——, *Kirjoituksia Sibeliusken sinfonioista* (Helsinki, 1988)

Jalas, Margareta, *Jean Sibelius: kuvateos – in pictures* (Helsinki, 1952, 1958)

James, Burnett, *The music of Jean Sibelius* (London, 1983)

Jeanson, Gunner, 'Jean Sibelius och Carl Nielsen' (*Nordens kalendar*, Göteborg, 1934)

Johnson, Harold, *Jean Sibelius* (New York, 1959; London, 1960)

——, 'Jean Sibeliuksen "Andante lirico"' (*Helsingin Sanomat*, 15 June, 1958)

——, 'Sibelius fjärde symfoni – en stråkkvartett?' (Sibelius's Fourth Symphony – a string quartet?) (*Nya Pressen*, 7 June, 1958)

——, *Jean Sibelius: The Record Music* (Helsinki, 1958)

Kajanus, Robert, 'Sibelius – siaren' (*Musikern*, Stockholm, 1925)

Kilpeläinen, Kari, *The Jean Sibelius Musical Manuscripts at Helsinki University Library*. A complete catalogue (Wiesbaden, 1991)

Konow, Walter von, 'Muistoja Jean Sibeliuksen poikavuosilta' (*Aulos*, Helsinki, 1925)

——, 'Janne' (*Veckans Krönika*, 4 Dec, 1915)

Krohn, Ilmari, *Der Formenbau in den Symphonien von Jean Sibelius* (Helsinki, 1942)

——, *Der Stimmungsgehalt in den Symphonien von Jean Sibelius* (In two vols.) (Helsinki, 1945, 1946)

Kujawsky, Eric, *Double-perspective movements: formal ambiguity and conducting issues in orchestral works by Schoenberg, Sibelius and Carter* (Diss., Stanford University, 1985)

Lambert, Constant, *Music Ho! A study of music in decline* (Chapter entitled 'Sibelius and the Integration of Form') (London, 1934)

Lampilä, Hannu-Ilari, *Jean Sibelius: säveltäja ja ihminen* (Helsinki, 1982)

Layton, Robert, 'Sibelius: the early years' (*Proceedings of the Royal Musical Association*, 1964–5)

——, *Sibelius and his world* (London, 1970)

Leibowitz, René, *Jean Sibelius, le plus mauvais compositeur du monde* (Liège, 1955)

Levas, Santeri, *Jean Sibelius ja hänen Ainolansa* (Helsinki, 1945, 1955)

——, *Nuori Sibelius* (The Young Sibelius) (Porvoo, 1957)

——, *Sibelius, Muistelmia suuresta ihmisestä. Järvenpään mestari* (Porvoo, 1960)

——, *Jean Sibelius* (London, 1972)

[1]These are both licentiate theses in the library of Helsinki University.

Sibelius

Madetoja, Leevi, 'Jean Sibelius oppetajana' (*Aulos*, Helsinki, 1925)
Marvia, Einari, 'Jean Sibeliuksen musikaalinen sukuperintö' (*Uusi Musiikilehti*, no. 9, Helsinki, 1955, pp. 49–81)
Mellers, Wilfred, 'Sibelius and the Modern Mind' (*Music Survey*, vol. i, 1949, no. 6, pp. 177–183)
——, 'Sibelius at Ninety: A Revaluation' (*The Listener*, Dec. 1955)
Meyer, Alfred, 'Sibelius, Symphonist' (*Musical Quarterly*, New York, 1936)
Montgomery, Alan Gene, *An interpretative guide to Symphony No. 3 by Sibelius*, (Diss., Indiana University, Bloomington, 1976)

Newmarch, Rosa, *Jean Sibelius: A Finnish Composer* (Leipzig, 1906)
——, *Jean Sibelius: A Short History of a Long Friendship* (Boston, 1939; London, 1945)
Niemann, Walter, *Jean Sibelius* (Leipzig, 1917)
Nørgård, Per, 'Sibelius og Danmark' (*Suomen Musiikin Vuosirkirja*, 1964–65)
Normet, Leo, 'Ursi ja vanha Sibeliuksen Ensimmäisessä ja Toisessa sinfoniassa'. ('Old and new in the first two symphonies of Sibelius') (*Suomen Musiikin Vuosikirja*, 1964–65)
——, *Simfonii Sibeliusa* (Tallinn, Moscow, 1970)
Nyblom, C. G., *Jean Sibelius* (Stockholm, 1916)
Nyssönen, Juho & Fischer, Ivan, *Jean Sibelius* (Budapest, 1936)

Oramo, Ilkka, *Jean Sibelius – A biography in pictures* (Helsinki, 1967)
Ottelin, O., 'Sibelius Symfonier som personliga dokument och som nationell skatt' (*Studiekamraten*, vol. xxvii, Stockholm, 1945)
——, 'Sibelius och naturen'. (*Studiekamraten*, vol. xxii, Stockholm, 1940)
——, *Tolv nordiska porträtt* (Stockholm, 1945)

Pajanne, Martti, 'Muusikkojen muistelmia mestarista orkesterinjohtajana' (*Uusi Musikkilehti*, no. 9, Helsinki, 1955)
Parmet, Simon, *Sibelius Symfonier* (Helsinki, 1955) Translated as *The Symphonies of Sibelius* (London, 1959)
——, 'Ur en essä om interpretationen av Sibelius' musik' (*Nya Argus*, Helsinki, no. 10, 1949)
Paul, Adolf, 'Nar Sibelius dirigerade' (*Profiler*, Stockholm, 1937)
——, 'Mein Freund Sibelius' (*Volkischer Beobachter*, Berlin, 27 Jan, 1938)
Pfaler, S. von, 'Sånger av Sibelius till ord av Runeberg' (*Finsk tidskrift*, Åbo, 1945)
Pickenhayn, Jorge Oscar, *Sibelius* (Buenos Aires, 1960)
Pike, Lionel, Beethoven, Sibelius and 'the profound logic'. (London, 1978)
Pirsch, G., *Jean Sibelius* (Gilly-Charleroi, 1944)
Pyle, Virginia, *The song-style of Jean Sibelius* (Diss., Florida State University, 1972)

Ranta, J., 'Jean Sibeliuksen "Kullervo-symfonian" esitys v. 1892: vanhan miehen muistelmia' ('The Performance of Sibelius's Kullervo Symphony in 1892: A memoir') (*Musiikkitieto*, Helsinki, 1933, p. 140)
Ranta, Sulho, 'Jean Sibelius' (*Suomen säveltäjiä* (Finnish Composers), Porvoo, 1945)
——, 'Sibeliuksen musiikin esittelya' (*Kulttuurin saavutuksia*, Helsinki, 1946)
Ringbom, Nils-Eric, 'Litteraturen om Jean Sibelius' (*Svensk Tidskrift för Musikforskning*, Stockholm, 1942)
——, 'Sibelius och impressionismen' (*Finsk Tidskrift*, Åbo, 1948)

——, *Sibelius* (Stockholm, 1948) (Trans. Oklahoma, 1954)
——, 'Sibelius utvecklingsskeden' (*Musikrevy*, Stockholm, 1950)
——, 'De två versionerna av Sibelius' tondikt "En Saga"' (the two versions of Sibelius's tone-poem, *En Saga*) (Åbo, 1956)
Roiha, Eino, *Die Symphonien von Jean Sibelius: Eine formanalytische Studie* (Jyväskylä, 1941)
Rosas, John, 'Sibelius' musik till skådespelet Ödlan' ('Sibelius's incidental music to *The Lizard*) (*Suomen Musiikin Vuosikirja*, 1960–1)
——, '*Otryckta Kammarmusikverk av Jean Sibelius*' ('The unpublished chamber music of Jean Sibelius') (Åbo, 1961)
——, 'Bidrag till kännedom om tre Sibelius-verk'. (Notes towards an understanding of three Sibelius works'.) Suomen Musiikin Vuosikirja, 1964–5.
Rosenfeld, Paul, 'Sibelius' in *Musical Portraits* (London, 1922)

Salmenhaara, Erkki, 'Tapiola. Sinfoninen runo Tapiola Sibeliusken myöhäistyom edustajana', *Acta musicologica Fennica* (Helsinki, 1970)
——, *Sibeliusken Ainola* (Helsinki & Porvoo, 1976)
——, *Jean Sibelius* (Helsinki, 1984)
Sandberg, Börje, *Jean Sibelius* (Helsinki, 1940)
Sbarcea, George, Jean Sibelius. Viata si opera, (Bucharest, 1965)
Schouwman, H., *Sibelius* (Antwerp, 1949)
Similä, M., *Sibeliana* (Helsinki, 1945)
Simpson, Robert, *Sibelius and Nielsen* (London, 1965)
Solanterä, Lauri, *The Works of Jean Sibelius* (Helsinki, 1955)
——, *Sibelius* (Facsimiles of manuscripts: notes by Eino Roiha) (Helsinki, 1945)
Stupel, Aleksandr, *Jean Sibelius (1865–1957)* (Moscow, 1963)
Sugano, Hirokazu, *Jean Sibelius: shogai to sakuhin* (Tokyo, 1967)
Sundberg, Gunnar, *Der Klassizität in den Symphonien von Jean Sibelius* (Diss, University of Vienna, 1987)

Tammaro, Ferruccio, *Jean Sibelius* (Rome, 1984)
Tanzberger, E., *Jean Sibelius* (Wiesbaden, 1962)
——, *Die symphonischen Dichtungen von Jean Sibelius* (Würzburg, 1943)
——, 'Jean Sibelius als Symphoniker' (*Gesellschaft für Musikforschung, Kongressbericht*, Lüneberg, 1950)
Tarasti, Eero, *Myth and music: a semiotic approach to the aesthetics of myth in music especially that of Wagner, Sibelius and Stravinsky* (The Hague, Paris and New York, 1979)
Tawaststjerna, Erik, *The Pianoforte Compositions of Jean Sibelius* (Helsinki, 1957)
——, *Ton och Tolkning* (Swedish trans. with additional material) (Helsinki, 1957)
——, *Sibelius* vol. 1 (1865–1905) (Swedish orig.) Stockholm, 1968
——, *Sibelius* vol. 1 (1865–1892) (Finnish trans.) Helsinki, 1966
——, *Sibelius* vol. 2 (1892–1905) (Finnish trans.) Helsinki, 1967
——, *Sibelius* vol. 3 (1904–1914) (Finnish trans.) Helsinki, 1972
——, *Sibelius* vol. 1 (1865–1905) (English trans.) London, 1976
——, *Sibelius* vol. 4 (1914–1919) (Finnish trans.) Helsinki, 1978
——, *Sibelius* vol. 1 (1865–1905) (Russian trans.) Moscow, 1981
——, *Sibelius* vol. 2 (1904–1914) (English trans.) London, 1986
——, *Sibelius* vol. 5 (1919–1957) (Finnish trans.) Helsinki, 1988
——, *Sibelius* vol. 3 (1914–1957) (English trans. in preparation)

Sibelius

——, 'The Mystery of Sibelius's Eighth Symphony' *Finnish Musical Quarterly* (Helsinki, 1985)

Thomas, Guy, *The Symphonies of Jean Sibelius* (Indiana University, Bloomington, 1990)

Törnblom, Folke, 'Sibelius och Kalevala' (*Vår Sång*, Stockholm, 1942)

Törne, Bengt von, *Sibelius: A Close-Up* (London, Boston, 1937)

——, *Sibelius*, i närbild och samtal (Helsinki, 1945, 1955)

——, 'Sibelius som människa och konstnär' (*Nordisk Tidskrift*, Stockholm, 1946)

Tovey, Donald, Analyses of works by Sibelius in *Essays in Musical Analysis*, vols I–III (London 1935–9); (new edn, in 2 vols, Oxford, 1981)

Truscott, Harold, 'A Sibelian Fallacy' (*The Chesterian*, London, vol. xxxii, 1957)

——, 'The Greatness of Sibelius' (*The Listener*, 1963)

——, 'Sibelius' in *The Symphony*, Robert Simpson (ed.) (London, 1965)

Vacnadze, Margarita, *Jean Sibelius* (Moscow, 1963)

Vainio, A., 'Sibeliuksen kehitys orkesterisäveltäjäksi' ('Sibelius's Development as an orchestral composer') (*Suomalainen Suomi*, Helsinki, 1946)

Väisänen, A. O., 'Sibelius ja kansanmusiikki' ('Sibelius and Folk-Music') (*Kalevalaseuran vuosikirja*, Helsinki, vol. xvi, 1936)

——, 'Kalevala ja säveltaide' ('The Kalevala and Music') (*Kalevalaseuran vuosikirja*, Helsinki, vols. xxvii–xxviii, 1947–8)

——, 'Kanteletarta sävellettynä' ('Compositions to the Kantelar') (*Kalevalaseuran vuosikirja*, vol. xxxi, 1951)

——, 'Sibeliuksen Kullervo-sinfonian valta-aiheista' ('On the themes of Sibelius's Kullervo symphony') (*Kalevalaseuran vuosikirja*, vol. xxxiii, 1953)

——, 'Sibelius om sina Kalevala-kompositioner' (*Musikern*, Stockholm, 1925)

Vestdijk, Simon, *De symfonieën van Jean Sibelius* (Amsterdam, 1962)

Vignal, Marc, *Jean Sibelius* (Paris, 1965)

Vitt, B., Jean Sibelius. (*Allgemeine Musikzeitung*, Berlin, 1935)

Vuolijoki, S., *Hämettä ja hämäläisiä* ('Sibelius as a conductor') (Helsinki, 1945, pp. 43–7)

Wallner, Bo, 'Sibelius och den svenska tonkonsten' (Sibelius and Swedish music) (*Suomen Musiikin Vuosirkirja, 1964–65*)

Whittall, Arnold, 'Sibelius's Eighth Symphony' (*Music Review*, 1964)

Witeschnik, A., *Jean Sibelius, 'der getreue Eckart* (Vienna, 1940)

Wood, Ralph W., 'Sibelius's Use of Percussion' (*Music & Letters*, London, vol. xxxiii, 1942)

(See also Abraham, 'Orchestral and Theatre Music')

Index

Sibelius

244